MW00782458

ANXIOUS ANGELS

Also by George Pattison

AGNOSIS: Theology and the Void

ART, MODERNITY AND FAITH

KIERKEGAARD AND THE CRISIS OF FAITH

KIERKEGAARD ON ART AND COMMUNICATION (*editor*)

KIERKEGAARD: The Aesthetic and the Religious

KIERKEGAARD: The Self in Society (*co-editor with
Steven Shakespeare*)

PAINS OF GLASS (*with Wendy Beckett*)

POOR PARIS! Kierkegaard's Critique of the Spectacular City

SPIRIT AND TRADITION: An Essay on Change
(*with Stephen Platten*)

Anxious Angels

A Retrospective View of Religious Existentialism

George Pattison
Dean of Chapel
King's College
Cambridge

palgrave
macmillan

First published in Great Britain 1999 by

MACMILLAN PRESS LTD

Houndmills, Basingstoke, Hampshire RG21 6XS and London
Companies and representatives throughout the world

A catalogue record for this book is available from the British Library.

ISBN-13: 978-0-333-68738-3 (hardcover)
ISBN-13: 978-0-333-68739-0 (paperback)

First published in the United States of America 1999 by

ST. MARTIN'S PRESS, INC.,

Scholarly and Reference Division,
175 Fifth Avenue, New York, N.Y. 10010

ISBN 0–312–22011–1

Library of Congress Cataloging-in-Publication Data
Pattison, George, 1950–
Anxious angels : a retrospective view of religious existentialism
/ George Pattison.
p.   cm.
Includes bibliographical references and index.
ISBN 0–312–22011–1 (hardcover)
1. Christianity and existentialism—History.   I. Title.
BT84.P37   1999
230'.046—dc21   98–30657
                                                              CIP

This book is printed on paper suitable for recycling and made from fully managed
and sustained forest sources. Logging, pulping and manufacturing processes are
expected to conform to the environmental regulations of the country of origin.

10   9   8   7   6   5   4   3   2   1
08   07   06   05   04   03   02   01   00   99

For Ulrich, and for teachers and fellow students at
New College, Edinburgh, 1974–77

Contents

Blessed be the Lord God, the Mighty One, who dwells on high where no eye can reach, who alone is Holy, whose counsel is hidden in the darkness of the clouds wherewith He has girded Himself, and whose thoughts are as terrible lightnings, the course whereof no man knows.

In His mercy He looked down from His eternal throne and beheld the earth, and all that men did therein. And His heart grew heavy within Him, seeing their works, how they neglected righteousness, working wicked things, each according to their own liking. And behold, His mind grew dark, thinking thereon. And He reasoned thus with Himself, saying, Are these not creatures whom I created in my own likeness, that they might have dominion over the earth and no good thing be denied them? And have I ever ceased to show forth my steadfast love unto them? Did I not make my covenant with them, setting my bow in the sky as a sign to all generations? Did I not give the Law through my servant Moses, that they might do all that made for their peace? Did I not send unto them prophets and wise men, that all knowledge might be theirs, that they might repent and live? Have I not spoken unto them by angels, and have they not heard my very voice, speaking from the clouds of heaven? And yet they hearken not, continuing in their evil ways and doing all manner of abominable works.

And the Lord God, the Mighty One, Blessed be He!, summoned unto Him Gabriel, imparting unto him all that He pondered in His mind. To no other angel did He speak at that time, yet Cherubim and Seraphim and all orders of angels trembled at the thunder of His voice. They did not know whereof He spoke, yet were filled with dread lest some great ill might be the issue thereof. – But they mistook them, for all His purposes are for the healing of the nations, that the peoples of the earth might rejoice, that they might keep His Sabbaths and delight to do that which is right.

Of that day, and of the words of that counsel, none spoke thereafter. And from that time on the Lord God, the Mighty One, and Merciful, Blessed be He!, sent forth no new commandment, nor prophecy, nor vision. And His angels wondered greatly that He no longer sent them as of old, as unto Balaam and to Gideon, that they might direct the words and deeds of men.

Speaking to none, lest they might hear, nor opening the eyes of any, lest they might see, the angels yet go to and fro upon the earth, ever obeying the commandments of the Lord, who, in His mercy, is alone wise and whose thoughts are deeper than the ocean. And lo, *angels visit but are bound to keep silent*

as they pass among the children of men, keeping that silence
whereunto they are bound, their step betrays the trembling and the
dread that seized them in the day of the Lord God's counsel with
Gabriel. Though no man can speak of their visitation, and no sign
thereof is vouchsafed unto the children of men, yet the thoughts of
man fall silent and his heart grows deep within him when that
trembling and that dread are nigh. Then man ponders all that he
has wrought in the days of his life, and all that lies within the
power of his hand to do, and his spirit is anxious within him. For
who can tell if the thoughts of his heart and the works of his hand
are according to the knowledge and the will of the Lord God, the
Mighty One, who alone is Holy, who knows all our ways long
before, Blessed be He!

Hasidic legend

Acknowledgements

This book could not have been written without the contribution and support of many friends and colleagues over many years. Some of the original encounters with those discussed here took place so long ago that I cannot remember the circumstances. Certainly important foundations were laid during my years studying theology at New College, Edinburgh, and I would like generally to thank all those teachers and fellow students from that time who provided the context within which my own thought crystallized. Much of my academic study since then has been focused on Kierkegaard, and I have received so much help from so many fellow researchers that it is really impossible to single out individuals, but I am profoundly grateful to all who have assisted my attempts to come to terms with this most challenging of modern thinkers, including many who interpret him along quite different lines. My understanding of Dostoevsky has been greatly deepened by conversations with more specialist scholars, especially Diane Thompson; and Avril Pyman has been of particular help with regard to Berdyaev and Shestov. I owe an especial debt to the Divinity School in Cambridge University for allowing me to hold the lectures that became the basis for this book – and I am more than grateful to the small but committed band of students who sat through them all and whose presence and questions were a constant encouragement. Although I have received friendly advice on translations from non-English titles, I have to admit that all translations from non-English works are, unless otherwise indicated in the notes, my own and I alone am responsible for any errors or infelicities. I am grateful to the Oxford University Press for permission to quote from Karl Barth, *The Epistle to the Romans* (1993) and also to Karolina Larusdottir for permission to use her etching 'The Woman Who Didn't See the Angel' as the jacket illustration.

Abbreviations

For full publication details see Selective Bibliography.

KIERKEGAARD

JP   H. V. and E. H. Hong (trans. and eds.) *Søren Kierkegaard's Journals and Papers*

DOSTOEVSKY

I   *The Idiot*
BK   *The Brothers Karamazov*

DIALECTICAL THEOLOGY

BDT   J. M. Robinson (ed.), *The Beginnings of Dialectic Theology*
KB   Karl Barth, *The Epistle to the Romans*

BULTMANN

K&M   H.-W. Bartsch (ed.), *Kerygma and Myth*

TILLICH

BB   *The Boundaries of Being*
CB   *The Courage to Be*
ST   *Systematic Theology*

BERDYAEV

MCA   *The Meaning of the Creative Act*
SF   *Slavery and Freedom*
D   *Dostoevsky*

UNAMUNO

TSL   *Tragic Sense of Life*

MARCEL

MJ   *A Metaphysical Journal*
MB   *The Mystery of Being*
BH   *Being and Having*

BUBER

Dan   *Daniel. Dialogues on Realization*
BMM   *Between Man and Man*
I&T   *I and Thou*

ROSENZWEIG

Star   *The Star of Redemption*
USH   *Understanding the Sick and the Healthy*

Foreword

This book is primarily intended to introduce readers to the authors and works dealt with in its pages and does not presume on any prior knowledge of the field. Although those I am calling the anxious angels dominated much of the debate about religion in the middle years of the twentieth century, many of them are now little read, their books are out of print and many students lack the context in which to make sense of what they are saying. Because of the nature of the work, I have avoided excessive footnotes, although interested students will be able to use the Selective Bibliography for the next stage of their reading. However, entering into the morass of secondary literature is no substitute for engagement with the primary texts and the purpose of this study will have been achieved if it encourages readers to do just that.

Although this is not a work for specialists, I do believe that the story of the anxious angels, and the exercise of considering them as a group, particularly at this juncture in intellectual history, does constitute an argument for reconsidering a number of prejudices regarding our recent intellectual past that are in danger of taking permanent root in the academy. Vigilance with regard to prejudice should be a primary concern of any philosophical enterprise. However, it has to be admitted that fashion is usually more seductive, and sometimes all one can hope to achieve is to register a protest. Those against whom this protest is made will doubtless dismiss this study as a return to old-fashioned and discredited positions. In reply I can only plead for further reflection on the nature of the history of ideas, and for the image of 'a retrospective view' to be taken with complete seriousness. The debate cannot be said to be over when it has scarcely begun.

1
Introduction

There was a time, about the middle of the twentieth century, when it was widely assumed that existentialism was destined to determine the presuppositions and concerns of any future philosophy. Such claims now appear so absurdly and so obviously overstated that it is hard to imagine they could have been stated so seriously by so many weighty pundits. None the less, it would be no less short-sighted of us to swing to the opposite extreme and to dismiss existentialism as a mere fashion of the 1940s and 1950s, something that went with a taste for Gauloises and black roll-neck jumpers.

In considering the vicissitudes of this or any movement of ideas we need to be wary of applying a specious model of intellectual progress drawn from the history of science. Because of the high profile and quite extraordinary success of modern science, we are tempted to think that the problems of past thinkers have been made redundant by subsequent research. We would not expect students of physics to have to grapple with Aristotelian notions of possibility and actuality or the intricacies of phlogiston, so why should students of philosophy have to attend to positions the shortcomings of which are now generally apparent? But what if the history of ideas is not like science? In the world of ideas, perhaps, no significant movement completely vanishes without trace, but each generation's reworking, revitalizing and reinvention of certain fundamental problems enter into the landscape of their successors. It is not merely 'overcome' and left behind for, as Kant remarked, if we are far-seeing, it is probably not because of our own stature, but because we stand on giants' shoulders. It would therefore seem not a bad idea to look down from time to time at the shoulders we are standing on, if only to reach a more just appraisal of our own achievements and our own possibilities. That is why philosophy, at least since Hegel, requires engagement with the history of philosophy.

In this respect, then, art might offer a better model than science. For art remains constitutionally respectful and concerned with its history in a way that, for the most part, science does not. Attention

1

to the tradition, whether respectful or iconoclastic, is a part of the discipline of working artists. A major retrospective is not just an event for cultural tourists but can also be a catalyst for artists engaged in the continuing process of re-examining and developing their own work. Manet's discovery of the Spanish tradition or the modernists' discovery of so-called 'primitive art' are well-known examples of how this encounter with an artist's predecessors can inspire new initiatives and breakthroughs. This book is offered in the hope that the religious existentialists have a comparable power to provoke us to an invigorating and renewing confrontation with the fundamental questions concerning the self-understanding of religious faith in the situation of modernity and postmodernity (or, as I would prefer to think of it, radical modernity). That is why I have referred to it in the sub-title as 'A Retrospective View'.

One problem that we are immediately confronted with is the problem of the relationship between religious and philosophical existentialism. It is not my task here to see how far religious questions and religious writings determined the agenda of the more purely philosophical existentialism of a Heidegger or a Sartre, although it is clear that there was a significant presence of such religious writers as Kierkegaard, Luther and Meister Eckhart in Heidegger's early thought. On the other hand, even when religious existentialism passionately repudiated the aims and methods of philosophy, as it did in Kierkegaard, it did so in such a way as to have profound and far-reaching implications for our understanding of the relationship between faith and knowledge, and is therefore itself philosophically interesting. There can therefore be no single, simple answer to the question as to the relationship between religious and philosophical existentialism: the issue is complex and takes a variety of forms to which we shall need to be attentive in the context of each figure to be studied.

With that qualification, I shall none the less be arguing that religious existentialism is a phenomenon *sui generis* and not a mere derivative of secular existentialism. The major figures of religious existentialism were pursuing a set of questions and concerns that arose almost inevitably out of the confrontation between religion and modernity – and I hope that chapter after chapter that follows will vindicate this assertion. It will, I hope, also prove to be quite clear that few if any of them can be charged with the kind of solipsism often levelled at the existentialists of the Left Bank. Indeed, whilst taking seriously the extent to which modern culture

my were in fact concerned w/ Social whole

spawned such solipsistic offspring by virtue of its own inner dynamics, many of their efforts were devoted to finding a way out of the situation of extreme individualism and to healing the fragmentation of the social whole. At the same time they were, for the most part, realistic enough to recognize that there was no utopia just round the corner. For the foreseeable future the labour of healing could not be separated from a thorough-going acceptance of the limitations of the human situation and an acknowledgement of the possibility of tragedy. Their concern was with the integrity of the human person in times and situations that, as Gabriel Marcel was to say, vilified the personal life. As we enter a new millennium and a new phase of the globalization of human culture, coupled with the extraordinary possibilities for the virtual mutation of the human species offered by genetic engineering and information technology, can we say that questions concerning that integrity have become less urgent?

As we proceed through the rooms of this intellectual gallery it will become clear – as it would in any exhibition of Impressionists, Expressionists or Abstractionists – that each of the figures we are examining has a characteristic and highly singular style. They cannot be pressed into the constraints of any single creed or programme, representing as they do each of the main branches of Christianity – Protestant, Catholic and Orthodox – and, no less importantly, Judaism. Nor can we rule out the possibility that other major religious traditions have produced their own 'anxious angels' – certainly there are strong affinities with tendencies in modern Buddhism, especially in Japan.

And yet the thinkers represented here are also linked together, although it is not easy to define those links in any simple formula. We would perhaps do better to think in terms of family resemblances, of overlapping and interacting sources, themes, interests and motifs. Each of the thinkers concerned may only show a selection of these resemblances and maybe none shows them all, but from a certain distance they constitute a distinctive group. Let us therefore seek to identify some of their distinguishing marks.

In the first instance we might notice a shared rejection, with varying degrees of hostility, of the ambition of formulating a unitary world-view. Hegelian idealism is often the target chosen for their polemics, but the pursuit of totality is no less suspect when it appears in a materialistic transformation in Marx or in a more aesthetic mode as in Goethe and in Romanticism. Moreover, Hegel's claims concerning knowledge imply an optimism concerning the realization of human possibilities in history that is, once more, reformulated by his Marxist heirs and that is also, once more, rejected by his existentialist critics. Optimism, in the form of belief in progress, was to be characteristic of many currents of nineteenth-century thought, including the late nineteenth-century theological liberalism that, if lacking the kind of claims to totality made by Hegel, still believed both that history had an attainable goal. All such optimism was suspect to the existentialists – and if the First World War was to put an end to the era of optimism, Kierkegaard and Dostoevsky remind us that the critique of such assumptions about progress did not begin in 1918. Even when Marcel makes 'hope' into one of the basic categories of his philosophy, he means something very different from nineteenth-century optimism.

But it was not only the optimism of the nineteenth century that the religious existentialists rejected. They also refused many of the models of human good associated with the belief in progress. In particular, they questioned the view that the satisfaction of material needs and comforts and the fulfilment of political hopes, whether nationalistic or class-based, could satisfy the human quest for meaning. They were similarly sceptical of doctrines of human happiness that privileged sexual, aesthetic or moral fulfilment. Repeatedly we hear the warning that although each of these things may be a partial good, none of them singly, nor all of them together, can constitute an absolute measure of human worth and value.

What of the will? Especially what of the dark, irrational will that is deeper and more forceful than the rational and moral will of Kantian ethics? Can this perhaps do the task that reason, progress, material fulfilment and the rest cannot achieve? But here too the answer is, for the most part, 'no': 'no' because although the religious existentialists recognized the lure of the will (and, as a consequence, can veer towards the fideistic), they had also learned from the Augustinian tradition about the 'bondage of the will' and the insufficiency of any single faculty to be the bearer of meaning and value. The 'subjectivity' associated with existentialism was never equated with the will, but with a kind of passion for meaning that incorporated an insight into the inability of willpower alone to sustain the project of giving value and purpose to existence.

One feature shared by many of those to be discussed here is the often discomforting penetration with which they critiqued prevailing constructions of selfhood. They were indeed masters of the hermeneutics of suspicion, exposing the deceptions and self-deceptions of the various ideologies – idealistic, materialistic, nationalistic or individualistic – that they encountered amongst their contemporaries. If today we tend to think of the hermeneutics of suspicion in connection with thinkers such as Marx, Nietzsche and Freud, whose diagnostic gaze was chiefly directed towards religion, we would be doing a disservice to the Christian tradition if we forgot that it was well schooled in critically appraising the self-deceiving self-justifications of the worldly mind long before the advent of secularism. Already in the early modern period a succession of spiritual writers, confessors and polemicists had bequeathed to European intellectual life a thorough training in the art of distinguishing between consciously held aims, opinions and values and the frequently less commendable motives and passions stirring beneath the surface – let us call it 'the habit of suspicion'. The anxious angels were heirs to this tradition, and if they could also give expression to positive enthusiasms, they rarely let those enthusiasms overwhelm their self-critical intellectual conscience. Even today, after over a century of secular suspicion, their psychological acuity can still disturb the assumptions that enable us to jog along in a kind of peace with ourselves, a peace that leaves many of the most difficult questions unanswered, too easily answered or simply unasked.

In rejecting many of the current self-interpretations of 'nineteenth-century rational man', the religious existentialists may seem to have entered on a path of negation, a modern *via negativa* – and there may be some connections with this ancient tradition of theology. Certainly the spirit of the great refusal is essential to most of those thinkers we shall be examining here. Theirs is a choice deliberately to steer away from the mainstream of their contemporary world. In doing so they realize to the full how demanding, how comfortless and how infinitely exposed to misunderstanding they must become. Deprived – or depriving themselves – of the classic theological resources of dogma, reason, will and experience they enter into a new and undefined cultural space. From one side – from the side of those who believe it is still possible to inhabit a world of unbroken traditions – this space may seem empty, drear and void, but it would be premature to judge it in exclusively negative terms. For the end of an old world is here, as elsewhere, the opportunity for the beginning of a new *even if it is realized that this new world can never be expressed or explained in a simple, direct way.*

At this point we touch on what is one of the most significant aspects of the anxious angels' inheritance from Kierkegaard: a concern with the media and manner of communication. Kierkegaard's own indirect communication, Dostoevsky's dialogical art, Bultmann's concern for a demythologized *kerygma*, Tillich's doctrine of symbolism and his promotion of the visual arts, Berdyaev's insistence on the aphoristic nature of philosophy, Buber's re-telling of Hasidic tales, Unamuno's paradoxical prose and Marcel's plays: all of these are examples of individual creative responses to the perception that if religion is to become a live option for post-Enlightenment humanity, it cannot be presented in the direct form of traditional teaching. For whenever the truths of religion are made the matter of direct statement, they must succumb to the critique of Enlightenment arguments and objections. On its own ground, the ground of reason and of fact, the Enlightenment will always prevail, but the exploration of new understandings and new methods of communication rescues the religious existentialists' endeavour from mere negativity, opening a realm of possibilities that is far from exhausted.

There is a similar ambiguity with regard to their attitude to politics and society. There can be no doubting the vehemence of their refusal of prevailing models and ideals of social and political change. Yet it would be mistaken to categorize them as indifferent to or aloof from politics. Buber, Marcel, Tillich, Berdyaev, Unamuno and Dostoevsky were all in their various ways intensely political thinkers and, in varying degrees, strongly attracted to the programme of the left, even when critical of the totalitarian turn in socialist politics. Even the politically conservative Kierkegaard was by no means indifferent, but followed the political situation of his time with intense interest, especially the internal politics of Denmark, and, in his own way, contributed to the processes of change that he simultaneously critiqued. Indeed, although it would be going too far to press all of those represented here into a single political mould, it can be said that one feature widely shared amongst them is a concern to spiritualize the thrust of the socialist critique of bourgeois society, whilst warning against the socialist tendency to make an idol of history itself. Tillich's response to Ernst Bloch – 'Utopia: No; the Spirit of Utopia: Yes' – is characteristic for a number of our anxious angels.

Critics of closure, masters of suspicion, experimenters in new modes of communication and utopists who cannot believe in utopia, these anxious angels emerge as believers who have internalized the disbelief of their age, defenders of the value and integrity of the personal life even when that life is pushed back beyond its last line of defence to leave only the cry of Job and the faith that in the midst of suffering and loss of meaning somewhere and somehow there is a meaning to be found. Yet none of this defines a position or a school in any narrow sense. If we wish to judge who's in and who's out of their company we must avail ourselves of complex criteria and be ready to revise our terms of membership. None the less, I believe that those selected for inclusion in this 'retrospective view' do constitute the key representatives of a distinctive body of reli-gious writers and thinkers, whose work not only helped shape the intellectual profile of religious belief in the situation of high mod-ernism but also, I am convinced, remain an invaluable resource for understanding our present religious situation. Consideration of what we might still learn from them, however, must await the exposition of the works and authors themselves.

2

Forerunners

Although existentialist themes can arguably be found in religious writers of many ages, it is only in the nineteenth century that these themes begin to be worked together into a coherent discourse to produce a family of diverse but related thinkers who can be identified as religious existentialists in an eminent sense. We shall return to the question as to how this specific form of religious existentialism relates to figures such as Augustine, Luther and Pascal (who are often cited as examples of existentialism *avant la lettre*), but we begin with the development of religious existentialism in the modern sense, a development that is inseparable from the crisis of German Idealism.

Each of the major figures of the German Idealist movement between the 1790s and early 1800s has some point of contact with later existentialism. Kant's insistence on the limitations of knowledge, his linking of belief in God to the exigencies of ethical existence and his sense of radical evil as a permanent possibility for human existence are all features of subsequent existentialist discourse. Fichte, although convinced of the feasibility of a self-authenticating system of knowledge, also showed a passionate ethical concern and, in a popular book such as *The Destiny of Man*, demonstrated how philosophical problems are connected to existential questions concerning the meaning of life.[1]

Of particular importance, however, is Hegel. Although generally appearing in existentialist literature as 'the one they love to hate' because of his claims on behalf of a totalizing system of knowledge and his privileging of the universal over the individual and particular, Hegel was in fact committed to showing how the Absolute cannot be understood as mere abstract Being-in-Itself, separate from the world, but must appear in, with and under the conditions and contingencies of historical life. Occasionally his own language seems to catch something of the existentialist passion, as when he speaks of the need for Spirit to look Death in the face, to find itself in the encounter with despair, or to admit dimensions of otherness and nothingness into its self-understanding.

8

Moreover, whereas Hegel is often represented as having produced an artificial interpretation of history in which every event is forced onto the Procrustean bed of a triadic logic of thesis–antithesis–synthesis, he himself warns against applying this triadic pattern as if it were 'a lifeless schema' that can be applied to the concreteness of existence in a purely formalistic way, without regard to the specificity of the content concerned.[3] More important than the triadic formula itself is the active and dynamic role of negation which Hegel sees as the moving power of history. Change happens in history, Hegel argues, because of the way in which each particular historical form (and this can be a political order, a school of philosophy or religion or a movement in the world of art and culture) only ever expresses one side or aspect of the truth; this one-sidedness elicits a corresponding negation in which the content of the foregoing form is negated in such a way as to generate a new form. Thus Aristotle's critique of the idealism of Plato generates a more empirically oriented form of philosophy or (to take an example that was also very important for Hegel) the externality of medieval Christendom calls forth the Protestant emphasis on inward faith. The motor-force of history is thus the power of the negative, a negative that is not merely logical, but expresses itself in great historical and cultural revolutions and movements. The logical schematization only comes after the event. In one of his best-known sayings Hegel summoned the image of the Owl of Minerva (the sacred bird of the goddess of wisdom): the Owl of Minerva, he remarked, 'spread its wings only with the falling of the dusk', meaning that 'When philosophy paints its grey in grey, then has a shape of life grown old. By philosophy's grey in grey it cannot be rejuvenated but only understood.'[4] Philosophy does not crudely dictate how the world should be, but finds meaning, order and coherence in what otherwise seems to be only a random and chaotic sequence of events.

None the less, it is true that Hegel exudes a kind of confidence in the final triumph of reason and in the value of systematization, which, taken together with his prejudice against whatever is 'merely individual', makes him the natural butt of many existentialist sallies. His legacy to the existentialist tradition is therefore highly paradoxical: by requiring philosophy to engage with the concreteness of historical existence, Hegel himself established the criterion by which so many of his successors were to find his own philosophy wanting and he thus sowed the seeds of his own destruction.

If any one of the German Idealists is to be counted as the immediate ancestor of religious existentialism, this has generally been
taken to be Schelling. F. W. J. Schelling, born in 1775 and a slightly
younger student friend of Hegel (and also of the poet Hölderlin),
is one of history's very rare philosophical prodigies, having several
works published in his teens and attaining the Chair of Philosophy
at Jena University in his early twenties. His early works belong
very much to the philosophy of Romanticism, with a strong emphasis on the manifestation of the Idea in nature, in imagination and
in art. Whereas Fichte looked to an 'intellectual intuition' to serve
as the basis for a system of knowledge, Schelling looked to an
'aesthetic intuition' and to art as the organ of knowledge of the
absolute. Despite his early success, however, Schelling's reputation
was eclipsed by that of Hegel – a case, perhaps, of the tortoise
and the hare, as the youthful high-flyer was gradually overtaken by
the duller but more methodical plodder. Hegel's systematic
approach to philosophy offered itself as an advance on the vacuous
enthusiasm of Romanticism, as Hegel proclaimed Schellingian
philosophy to be 'merely immediate' and declared that 'the poetry
of imagination' must yield to 'the prose of thought'.[5] Although
Hegel's own ideas soon came to be regarded as too limited by the
more radical thinkers who called themselves 'Young Germany',
many of them recognized a debt to Hegel, who was regarded by
some in the establishment as the intellectual progenitor of militant
atheism and political subversion.

Hegel died in 1831, and when Schelling was called to the Chair of
Philosophy at Berlin University in 1841, his advertised intention of
delivering a new kind of philosophy attracted immediate interest.
After all, here was a philosopher belonging to an almost legendary
era of literary, intellectual and political ferment returning to refute a
philosophy that was at the centre of many of the most exciting contemporary movements of ideas.[6]

Schelling's audience included many of the most brilliant students
of the day – students as diverse as Friedrich Engels, Søren
Kierkegaard and Jakob Burckhardt – and the sense of excitement
was almost palpable. Writing back to Copenhagen, Kierkegaard
commented that 'during the first lectures it was almost a matter of
risking one's life to hear him [Schelling]'.[7] To another friend he
wrote that 'Schelling has commenced, but amidst so much noise
and bustle, whistling, and knocking on windows by those who cannot get in the door, in such an overcrowded lecture hall, that one is

almost tempted to give up listening to him if this is to continue.' But, he adds, 'I have put my trust in Schelling and at the risk of my life I have the courage to hear him once more.'[8] A similar testimony is offered by Engels:

> Ask anybody in Berlin today on what field the battle for domin-
> ion over German public opinion in politics and religion, that is,
> over Germany itself, is being fought, and if he has any idea of the
> power of the mind over the world he will reply that the battle-
> field is the University, in public Lecture-hall number 6, where
> Schelling is giving his lectures on the philosophy of revelation.[9]

Both Kierkegaard and Engels understood these lectures as a direct assault on Hegelianism. Kierkegaard mused whether Hegel might not turn out after all to have been merely a parenthesis in the history of philosophy, flanked on either side by the philosophy of Schelling. Engels put it more caustically:

> Two old friends of younger days, room mates in the Tübingen
> Theological Seminary, are after forty years meeting each other
> face to face as opponents; one of them ten years dead but
> more alive than ever in his pupils; the other, as the latter say,
> intellectually dead for three decades, but now suddenly claiming
> for himself the full power and authority of life.[10]

The high hopes of many of Schelling's audience were soon to be dashed. At first the omens looked good. Kierkegaard, for example, wrote in his notebook:

> I am so happy to have heard Schelling's second lecture – inde-
> scribably. I have been pining and thinking mournful thoughts
> long enough. The embryonic child of thought leapt for joy within
> me as in Elizabeth, when he mentioned the word 'actuality' in
> connection with the relation of philosophy to actuality. I remem-
> ber almost every word he said after that. Here, perhaps, clarity
> can be achieved.[11]

However, shortly afterwards his letters begin to sound an ironic note when mentioning Schelling; by January (the lectures had begun in mid-November) he is writing, 'Schelling's most recent lectures have not been of much significance' (letter 62) and by

February (to his friend Emil Boesen): 'Schelling talks endless non-sense both in an extensive and an intensive sense' (Letter 69) and (to his brother Peter): 'Schelling talks the most insufferable non-sense' (Letter 70). To which he adds: 'I have never in my life felt like travelling as much as I do now. I owe that to Schelling. Had Schelling not lectured in Berlin, I would not have gone, and had Schelling not been so nonsensical, I would probably never have travelled again.'[12] Although Engels had been less sympathetic at the outset, his judgement was increasingly damning, as he accused Schelling of smuggling 'belief in dogma, sentimental mysticism, gnostic fantasy into the free science of thinking'.[13] He also published a satirical account of Schelling's ideas in a pamphlet entitled *Schelling: The Philosopher of Christianity or The Transfiguration of Worldly Wisdom and Divine Wisdom (for faithful Christians who do not have the philosophical manner of speaking).*[14]

What was it, then, that stirred the expectations of Schelling's audience and what was it that made Kierkegaard 'indescribably happy' when he heard Schelling mention the word actuality – and, no less importantly, why were so many of Schelling's auditors disappointed in the outcome of the lectures?

To answer these questions fully and to see something of those areas in which Schelling was to be an important source for several later religious existentialists (such as Tillich, Berdyaev and Marcel) we need to go back a number of years in Schelling's intellectual development, for these lectures were the culmination of a long sequence of works. It should be noted, however, that we are not seeking a thorough-going exposition of Schelling's thought, but only to highlight those points at which he importantly anticipated existentialist themes.

Schelling's earliest philosophy has been called the philosophy of identity. What does this mean? In an intellectual situation in which philosophers understood the field of possible knowledge as divisible in terms of a sequence of polarized concepts (subject/object, ideal/real, being/non-being, etc.), a philosophy of identity involves regarding these polarities as being ultimately identical when seen from the perspective of 'the Absolute'. But how to attain such a perspective? For the young Schelling (and here we see the 'Romantic' element in his thought) we gain knowledge of the Absolute through art or through the aesthetic intuition art. This claim found expression in the poetry of Romantic writers such as Coleridge – widely accused of plagiarizing Schelling in his own theoretical writings.

Take, for example, Coleridge's poem *The Eolian Harp*. Here Coleridge uses the analogy of a wind-harp to express a Schellingian vision of nature:

> And what if all of animated nature
> Be but organic Harps diversely fram'd,
> That tremble into thought, as o'er them sweeps
> Plastic and vast, one intellectual breeze,
> At once the Soul of each, and God of all?

Poetic intuitions of the Absolute, of the many in the One and the One in the many, were taken as true visions of the nature of things, securing philosophy's confidence in the capacity of human thought to give an account of how things really are.

From the early 1800s, however, Schelling began to find this philosophy of identity inadequate and his thought began to acquire a more decidedly Christian character. This shift can be seen in a work such as *The Gods of Samothrace*, where Schelling argues against the view that the origins of Greek mythology (and therefore the basic ideas of Greek philosophy) are to be sought in the East. Instead, he claims, they are of Semitic origin. The point may seem obscure, but it has immense ideological ramifications, for if the basic agenda of Greek philosophy is derived from Semitic culture, then it is easier for Schelling to go on to argue that it is the biblical – and ultimately Christian – revelation that contains the key to philosophy's mysteries. This is a direct answer to the early Romantic search for a wisdom (such as the wisdom of India) that is independent of and supposedly superior to that provided by biblical revelation. In turning away from the philosophy of identity, Schelling thus moves closer to Christian claims that truth depends on divine revelation and cannot be found by immediate intuition, since, as Christian doctrine claimed, our capacity for knowing the truth was marred or even destroyed by the Fall and is only restored in the saving revelation of Christ.

Under the influence of the late sixteenth-/early seventeenth-century German mystical writer Jacob Boehme, Schelling maps these questions onto an all-embracing vision of cosmic and human history. How this works out can be seen in a work such as *On the Nature of Human Freedom* (1809), where Schelling seeks to harmonize the principles of freedom and necessity. The former issues in the belief that human beings are free and therefore ultimately

responsible for their own destiny. The latter is reflected in the conviction of philosophers that the world can be understood as a
whole and comprehended in 'a total world-view', within which
human freedom appears as one subordinate element, determined
by its relation to other elements and therefore 'free' only in a very
limited sense. When the problem is stated in these terms it is hard
to see how the principle of freedom can make any concessions to
the principle of necessity without undermining itself and leading to
fatalism, to the view that the individual 'free' will is no more than
one manifestation amongst others of a causal nexus over which it
has no control, a mere wave in the ocean of cosmic becoming. And,
orthodox theists argued, this leads to pantheism, since it excludes
any significant role for the divine will or for any principle external
to the causally interconnected whole that is the world. Schelling's
question therefore comes to be a question about the relationship
between Christianity and philosophy: Is philosophy's aspiration
towards a completely exhaustive understanding of the rational
interconnectedness of reality inherently opposed to Christianity's
insistence on human freedom and divine creativity?

Schelling's aim in *On the Nature of Human Freedom* is none the less
to seek to reconcile the two principles, taking the belief in human
freedom as his starting-point. The relationship between God and the
world, he says, is like the relationship between antecedent ground
and consequent conclusion in logic: nothing can be adduced in the
consequent term that is not already in its antecedent. Therefore,
since man (= consequent) is free it follows that God (= antecedent) is
also free. 'The procession of things from God is a self-revelation of
God,' he states. 'But God can only reveal himself in what is kin to
him, in a free, self-activating essence [Ger: *Wesen*] for whose being
[Ger: *Sein*] there is no ground but God, but who exists, as God
exists.'[15] Human freedom thus provides an analogue by which we
can infer the prior freedom of God.

This, however, rapidly leads Schelling into what, from the standpoint of Christian theology, seem to be highly unorthodox reflections. For, he goes on to say, freedom as we know it in human
beings is essentially the possibility of choosing good or evil: unless
we are faced with the real possibility of such a choice, we cannot
properly talk of freedom at all. Human freedom exists, therefore,
only in a state of continual strife, as we seek to overcome evil and to
subordinate the darkness in us to the light. Schelling's faithfulness
to what he regards as logical consistency leads him to claim that

even here, where traditional Christian theology would insist on the *dissimilarity* between the divine and the human, we can speak of a likeness, and he speculates that even in God there is something like 'an eternally dark ground'[16] and that God exists as good only as the continual overcoming of this dark ground in himself, defined as 'what in God is not God himself'.[17] Even God's own life is subject to the law that 'All birth is birth out of darkness into light; [that] the seed must be buried in the earth and die if the more beautiful luminous form is to arise and unfold in the light of the sun.'[18]

From the interaction between darkness and light within the life of God the whole process of cosmic evolution is set in motion as the manifestation of a drama that is already concealed in the mystery of God's own life. Against the claims of his own earlier philosophy of identity, Schelling now argues that what is eternally *identical* in God (in God, good has always already overcome the evil possibility) experiences *separation* (since the conflict between good and evil, if it is to be *real* or *actual*, requires the two sides to be really opposed). The human subject, by living out the struggle between good and evil in the light of its own freedom and responsibility, thus complements and, in an important sense, completes the conflict within God Himself by giving it external form and actuality. The drama thus unfolds on two different levels simultaneously. On the one hand, it occurs eternally, as the eternal overcoming by God of his own evil in such a way that evil is always already conquered. On the other hand, the same conflict is worked out temporally in the course of world history in such a way that this history is also the history of God himself, seeking to manifest in time and history the goodness that he already, in Himself, is. In this history, then, God himself lives, suffers and dies: 'Without the concept of a humanly suffering God,' writes Schelling, '…history remains altogether incomprehensible.'[19]

With this underlying thought, Schelling interprets history by means of a sequence of contrary but interactive principles, such as the conflicts between Nature and Humanity, between Old Testament and New, between the religion of the Father and the religion of the Son, between Law and Gospel (or freedom), between Petrine and Pauline Christianity. The pattern that emerges is therefore the temporal projection of the inner life of the Trinitarian God. His theological perspective, however, enables Schelling to argue that history is not jut a saga of never-ending conflict, since a final resolution is found in the manifestation of the Spirit, in which Father and Son are finally reconciled. The scriptural testimony to this reconciliation is to be found above all in the Johannine gospel, in which Petrine and Pauline Christianity are reconciled, and it is consummated in the rule of love, reconciling Law and Freedom.

In a subsequent work, *The Ages of the World*, Schelling traces at greater length the necessary emergence of the material world on the basis of the inner conflicts within the life of God and of the development of freedom out of the determinate being of inorganic life. Here the polarities of activity and passivity, and of expansion and contraction play a leading role in shaping the paradoxical logic of freedom. As Schelling describes it, the emergence of freedom in history is the result of a titanic struggle of conflicting powers, a struggle that becomes more and more intense until the moment of breakthrough. Whereas in traditional theologies God had been characterized as impassible and immune from suffering, Schelling's God only comes to be the freedom that he is in and through a process involving extremes of pain and anguish:

> Pain is something universal and necessary in all life, the inevitable point of transition to freedom ... Suffering is generally the way to glory, not only with regard to man, but also in respect to the creator. God leads human nature through no other course than that through which his own nature must pass. Participation in everything blind, dark, and suffering of God's nature is necessary in order to raise him to highest consciousness. Each being must learn to know its own depths; this is impossible without suffering. Pain comes only from being ...[20]

Schelling goes on to speak of how, as nature approaches the point at which human self-consciousness and the life of freedom emerge into the light of day, it is convulsed by an extraordinary turbulence:

> the nature existing in this conflict struggles as in heavy dreams ... With growing conflict, those nocturnal births soon pass like wild phantasies through that nature's interior, and in them for the first time it experiences all the horrors of its own nature. The predominant feeling that expresses the conflict of tendencies in being, when there is no knowing which way to turn, is that of dread ['Angst']. Meanwhile the orgasm of powers increases more and more, and lets the integrating power fear total dissociation,

complete dissolution … [until] … the quiet purity of the spirit arises before it as in a flash.[21]

The transition to freedom is thus only possible in the face of 'a continual solicitation to madness'.[22] At each and every moment of its emergence freedom is at risk and only becomes what it is through the distortions and excesses of Dionysian ecstasy and suffering.

It is, of course, difficult to determine exactly what kind of status Schelling means these descriptions to have. He is clearly not offering something that we would regard as a proper scientific account of evolution. On the other hand, he does seems to think that this is more than a merely subjective account of the nature of freedom. The mythological aspect is not just illustration or colouring, but reveals what Schelling believes are the real processes that have culminated in human history and that will be brought to a conclusion when that history resolves itself in a community of love, established on the basis of the free choice of its members.

It is also important to note that whereas Hegel also spoke of the necessity of Spirit submitting itself to suffering and the travail of history, Schelling insists that the moment of transition cannot be grasped logically or rationally: that it is only in the language of mythology and religion that the real nature of this transition reveals itself and that it will always elude the attempt of reason to grasp and fix it. Connected with this is the distinction in Schelling's later philosophy between what he called a merely 'negative' philosophy (= Hegel) and 'positive' philosophy (his own). The point of this distinction is that whereas, according to Schelling, Hegel proceeded by way of logical negation, he (Schelling) based himself on what was *given* to thought, what is presupposed by thought and which thought itself can never deduce. In the light of this claim Schelling believed himself to be proceeding on the basis of *a posteriori* thinking, practising 'an empiricism that is supra-sensible and nevertheless is empiricism, a metaphysical [empiricism]' because it takes account of 'the absolute transcendence that comes before thought', the 'absolute prius' – '*unvordenkliche Seyn*', being behind which thought cannot go.[23] This being-which-cannot-be-conceived-in-advance-by-thought, and the key role of the will limit the scope of any purely rationalistic philosophy and, for Schelling, demonstrate the impossibility of carrying through the project of philsophy as conceived by Hegel. As Engels understood him, Schelling's implication is that proofs do not work by virtue of their logical content alone, but only if that content is willed or chosen by the thinker. None the less, even though its basis is will and not reason, the world-process *is* explicable and Schelling is confident that his 'system' is philosophy and not 'merely' poetry, devoid of cognitive import.

It is perhaps unfortunate that this account of the anxious angels should have to begin with Schelling, whose work poses interpretative problems of unique complexity, and which critics from Engels and Kierkegaard on have found frankly incomprehensible. For all its suggestiveness and flashes of imaginative brilliance, we can understand the frustration and disappointment of his auditors in 1841–2. His philosophy promised so much but, ultimately, it was far from clear what it had actually delivered. Yet even if Kierkegaard was to move in a quite different direction and would take issue with some of Schelling's basic claims, it remains true that there are significant adumbrations of later existentialist themes in Schelling's work: the agonistic character of freedom and its association with suffering and anxiety, the priority of the unthinkable over the thinkable, an emphasis on the crucial element of will and of the continuing role of the irrational in the economy of consciousness – all are topics we shall be revisiting in a variety of contexts. Moreover, although thinkers such as Kierkegaard completely dissociated themselves from the kind of mythological cosmology found in Schelling's later thought, Tillich and Berdyaev, who were especially influenced by Schelling, seem reluctant to surrender the cosmological context within which the drama of human existence is played out. Indeed, even if Schelling's vision is too much in the grand style for twentieth-century tastes, the impulse to understand the drama of freedom played out in human affairs as revealing a more-than-human truth is one that religious thinkers must find understandable, for even the most radical of modern humanistic theologies has found it difficult to restrict itself to a *purely* human framework of understanding. To do that, it would seem, is to forgo the possibility of any truly *theo*logical discourse. Theology seems committed by its very nature to see in the human story also the divine story, but whether this is a legitimate topic for philosophy is another story. Engels' complaint about Schelling was, of course, precisely this: that he confused the tasks of theology and philosophy and, whilst claiming to practise the latter, actually practised the former. Kierkegaard too – though from a different perspective – was to make a similar complaint.

The other immediate ancestor of religious existentialism, Ludwig Feuerbach, represents a style of philosophizing very different from that of Schelling. Yet, although Feuerbach put himself forward as a critic of idealism and appealed to the immediate sensuousness of existence as, ultimately, the sole ground of meaning, he too (especially in his earlier work) had been influenced by Hegel's theory of consciousness. Born in 1804 in Bavaria, Feuerbach initially studied theology at Heidelberg before switching to philosophy and, after a period in Berlin where he heard both Hegel and the Romantic theologian F. D. E. Schleiermacher, gained a doctorate from the University of Erlangen for his dissertation on *Reason: Its Unity, Universality and Infinity* (1828). Shortly after beginning his career as a docent, however, he published an anonymous work, *Thoughts on Death and Immortality* (1830), which criticized the political role of theology and led to his being barred from appointments to university posts. Supported by his wife's income, Feuerbach persisted in his philosophical writing. In 1841 his critical work, *The Essence of Christianity*, established his position as one of the leaders of the left-wing intelligentsia. In this work Feuerbach famously argued that the secret of all theology was anthropology and that religious beliefs were nothing but the projections of human qualities and human values onto a (non-existent) deity. As humanity gradually overcame its self-estrangement it would come to reclaim these qualities and values, whose real function was to engage the individual for the common tasks of the species-being. Thus, the history of Christianity shows that religion itself approximates ever more closely to the insight of the real unity between the divine and the human and that, in a theologian like Schleiermacher, it is made clear that human feeling is the real measure of religious truth. God is not 'out there': God is nothing but the universal aspect of our own human being. Moreover, the human essence is not to be conceived (as, Feuerbach thinks, Hegel had thought) as primarily rational but as fundamentally material. It is therefore in the materiality of a common human life that the 'secret' of religion is to be found. *The Essence of Christianity* gives many examples of how this works out. Baptism, for instance, has a 'real' human and material meaning in the value of water for bodily health:

To purify oneself, to bathe, is the first, though the lowest of the virtues. In the stream of water the fever of selfishness is allayed. Water is the readiest means of making friends with nature ... Baptism, as a single act, is either an altogether useless and unmeaning institution, or, if real effects are attributed to it, a superstitious one. But it is a rational, a venerable institution, if it is understood to typify and celebrate the moral and physical curative virtues of water.[24]

The reductive analysis of religious beliefs in *The Essence of Christianity* had an epochal significance in the history of thinking about religion. However, Feuerbach's significance for the development of religious existentialism is better represented in a smaller work, *Principles of the Philosophy of the Future* (1844).

Here Feuerbach sloughs off some of the residual Hegelianism which still clung to his form of argumentation in *The Essence of Christianity*. He argues that speculative philosophy itself (i.e. German Idealism) had already taken the step of identifying the divine and the human and had, in effect, already reduced the divine to the human. Hegel's 'Spirit' was no longer the God of theism, a being existing independently apart from and prior to the world, but was merely 'Man' writ large. However, idealism itself had conceived of humanity much too one-sidedly, focusing on its rationality. Hegel's absolute being is simply 'absolute thought'. Consequently, Hegelianism is vitiated by the same fault as traditional theism. 'By the same token that abstraction from all that is sensuous and material was once the necessary condition of theology, so was it also the necessary condition of speculative philosophy ...'[25] It thus turns out that Hegelianism only negates theology by means of philosophy in order to negate philosophy by means of theology: 'Theology constitutes the beginning and the end ... At first everything is overthrown, but then everything is put again in its former place ... The Hegelian philosophy is the last magnificent attempt to restore Christianity ...'[26] Really, however, it is nothing but the apotheosis of reason and thought. Hegelianism speaks in abstract terms of 'being' but does not recognize that the only things that can have 'being' are things that exist by virtue of their sensuousness, for it is only sensuous objects that have real existence, accessible to others. 'The heart does not want abstract, metaphysical or theological objects; it wants real and sensuous objects and beings.'[27]

Philosophers have thought to provide a theoretical understanding of the essential unity of being and thought but this unity, Feuerbach insists, can only be grasped when humanity itself is

understood in its concreteness and sensuousness. This leads him to
what is perhaps the key thought of the *Principles*:

> Desire not to be a philosopher, as distinct from a man; be nothing
> else than a thinking man. Do not think as a thinker, that is, with a
> faculty torn from the totality of the real human being and iso-
> lated for itself; think as a real and living being, as one exposed to
> the vivifying and refreshing waves of the world's oceans. Think
> in existence, in the world as a member of it, not in the vacuum of
> abstraction as a solitary monad ...[28] *don't abstract*

This summons – apart from its materialistic edge – could almost
be taken from the pages of Kierkegaard and, more surely than anything to be found in Schelling, it points to a fundamental imperative shared by both religious and atheistic existentialists: that even
if God exists, the only resources we have for thinking of God are
those which we have as existent, finite, material beings; we have no
faculty of intuition or speculation by which to see over the horizons
of our creaturely limitations. Of course, neither religious nor anti-
religious existentialists generally share Feuerbach's implied programme of explaining human freedom reductively in terms of
material processes. Indeed, as regards his materialism (i.e. precisely
that aspect of his thought that has led to his being claimed as an
immediate ancestor of Marxism), Feuerbach was to be seen by
thinkers such as Kierkegaard and Dostoevsky as representative of
the same kind of denial of freedom that they saw in Hegel. In each
case what is on offer appears to be an all-embracing explanatory
system. But even if this crucial difference is taken into account,
what Feuerbach bequeaths to existentialism (including religious
existentialism) is an insight into the situatedness of our self-
understanding. What we know, we can know only on this basis.
Thus, even those in whom the influence of Schelling is most
marked – Berdyaev, Tillich and Marcel – insist that the symbols of
theological reality cannot be construed as constituting objective
knowledge and cannot be taken as the grounds for explaining the
objective structures of the material world (as it seems Schelling
tried to do). Their truth is a truth only for those prepared to stake
on what is disclosed, in freedom, to the passional heart.

But this is already to be speaking the language of later thinkers.
Indeed, it is pertinent to remind ourselves that neither Schelling nor
Feuerbach can themselves be regarded as unqualifiedly 'existential'

[handwritten: rejection of systematizing and totalizing idealism of Hegel]

thinkers. Both share with later existentialists the negative reaction against the systematizing and totalizing idealism of Hegel. Schelling's protest is made in the name of the radical, abyssal quality of <u>human</u> <u>freedom</u>, freedom that exists as the unceasing conflict <u>between</u> <u>good</u> and evil and that, as such, is the [revelation on the plane of history of the eternal triumph of good over evil in the inner life of God.] Feuerbach's objections, on the other hand, focus on the [material, sensuous finitude of the human subject,] on the conviction that who I am is inseparable from my being here in the concrete reality of my [embodied, social life.] It is perhaps typical of many of those we shall go on to study that they seek to embrace both emphases: both the emphasis on the radical, abyssal freedom of the human subject *and* its situatedness as a finite, material and (perhaps above all) mortal being, whose life in the world neither metaphysics nor mysticism are able to explain.

[handwritten: we will see people who emphasize both radical freedom and situatedness]

NOTES

1. Cf. J. G. Fichte, *The Vocation of Man* (New York: Bobbs Merrill, 1956).
2. On the question as to how far the popular image of Hegel is really fair to the facts, see Jon Stewart (ed.), *The Hegel Myths and Legends* (Evanston: Northwestern University Press).
3. See G. W. F. Hegel, *Phenomenology of Spirit*, trans. Miller (Oxford: Clarendon, 1977), p. 29.
4. Idem., *Philosophy of Right*, trans. Knox (Oxford: Clarendon, 1952), p. 13.
5. Idem., *Aesthetics. Lectures on Fine Art*, trans. Knox (Oxford: Oxford University Press, 1975), p. 89.
6. It is important to realize that 'philosophy' in this context was not simply the exchange of erudite opinions but concerned the way in which knowledge could be legitimated in the public institution of a state-sponsored university. This meant that philosophy could never be anything but intensely political in so far as it claimed to regulate for the public sphere what could or could not count as 'right opinion'.
7. S. Kierkegaard, *Letters and Documents*, trans. Rosenmeier (Princeton: Princeton University Press, 1978), Letter 55.
8. Ibid., Letter 51.
9. F. Engels, 'Schelling on Hegel', in Karl Marx and Frederick Engels, *Collected Works* (Moscow: Progess, 1975), Vol. 2, p. 181.
10. Ibid.
11. S. Kierkegaard, *Journals and Papers* (Bloomington: Indiana University Press, 1967–78),Vol. 5, pp. 181–2.
12. Idem., *Letters and Documents*, letters 62, 69 and 70.

13. Engels, 'Schelling and Revelation' in Works, Vol. 2, p. 201.
14. Ibid., pp. 241–64.
15. F. W. J. Schelling, *Philosophische Untersuchungen über das Wesen der menschlichen Freiheit und die damit zusammenhängenden Gegenstände* (Frankfurt a.M.: Suhrkamp, 1975), p. 42.
16. Ibid., p. 53.
17. Ibid., p. 54.
18. Ibid., p. 55.
19. Ibid., p. 95.
20. F. W. J. Schelling, *The Ages of the World* (New York: Columbia University Press, 1942), p. 225.
21. Ibid., p. 226.
22. Ibid., p. 228.
23. S. Kierkegaard, *The Concept of Irony* together with *Notes on Schelling's Berlin Lectures* (Princeton: Princeton University Press, 1989), pp. 360ff. See also Paul Tillich, *Theology of Culture* (New York: Oxford University Press, 1959), pp. 86–8, for a summary of Schelling's 'higher empiricism'.
24. L. Feuerbach, *The Essence of Christianity* (New York: Harper and Row, 1957), pp. 275–6.
25. Idem., *Principles of the Philosophy of the Future* (Indianapolis: Hackett, 1986), p. 13.
26. Ibid., pp. 33–4.
27. Ibid., p. 54.
28. Ibid., p. 67. For an interesting comment on the significance of the *Principles* for theology, see 'An Introductory Essay' by Karl Barth, in Feuerbach, *The Essence of Christianity* (1957).

3

The Storm Bird

I

In his journals for 1845 Kierkegaard wrote of himself: 'There is a
bird called the stormy-petrel, and that is what I am, when in a
generation storms begin to gather, individuals of my type appear.'[1]
Certainly, Søren Kierkegaard (1813–55) has often been described as
a prophet, one whose life and writings anticipated many of the fundamental features of twentieth-century existentialism. It is indeed
true that many of the key terms and concepts of later existentialism
are foreshadowed in his work: anxiety, subjectivity, guilt, repetition
and the absurd are only some especially striking examples. Yet
Kierkegaard was himself very much a man of his own time, passionately engaged with the intellectual landscape shaped by
Romanticism, Hegelianism and the kind of left-wing materialism represented by Feuerbach – as well as with the ecclesiastical and political
constitution of his native Denmark.

The Denmark of Kierkegaard's day was a country which, although
it could easily be regarded as provincial in relation to the European
mainstream, was undergoing a rapid and traumatic encounter with
the experience of modernity – and the experience and the expression
of a profound ambivalence towards modernity is a characteristic of
the anxious angels that we shall encounter many times. Modernity
is, in fact, a crucial element in any account of existentialism. On the
one hand, existentialism itself is a profoundly modernist movement,
embracing the modernist protest against submission to the authority
of the social, religious and intellectual status quo. On the other hand,
the existentialists (and the religious existentialists in particular) cast
suspicious eyes on the modernists' intellectual faith in scientific
rationality, their moral faith in the principle of autonomy and their
political faith in the pursuit of utopia. Existentialism is thus neither
simply 'modernist' nor simply 'anti-modernist'. Rather, it is a movement from within modernity against modernity and involves a peculiar heightening of the self-critical tendency in modernity itself.[2] All
of this is pre-eminently true of Kierkegaard himself.

24

Although the main events of Kierkegaard's life have often been rehearsed, it is important to recall them here because Kierkegaard is one of those thinkers whose life has contributed in large measure (some might say too large a measure) to the interpretation of his work. Not that it was an extraordinarily eventful life. To a very considerable extent he realized his vocation in and through his writing: whatever he did for Christianity, he did as a writer. But this writing is virtually unintelligible without reference to two crucial relationships and two public controversies. The relationships are those involving his father, Michael Pedersen Kierkegaard, and the fiancée, Regine Olsen, to whom he was only briefly engaged yet whom, at some level, he never ceased to love. The controversies were with the satirical newspaper, *The Corsair*, and, in the very last year of his short life, with the state establishment of the Lutheran Church in Denmark.

The Kierkegaard family home was in many respects a sombre place. The atmosphere was determined by the dour, stern and even depressive religiosity of the father and coloured by the religious outlook of pietism. Although not unparalleled in those times, the deaths of M. P. Kierkegaard's two wives and of many of Søren's siblings undoubtedly fuelled the old man's conviction that he deserved divine retribution for some crime that has never been entirely or satisfactorily clarified. His own rise from humble origins to a very comfortable position amongst the Copenhagen bourgeoisie, did nothing to alleviate this interpretation of things. As Kierkegaard himself described the situation in a passage from his journals to which he gave the title 'The Great Earthquake':

> Then I surmised that my father's old-age was not a divine blessing, but rather a curse, that our family's exceptional intellectual capacities were only for mutually harrowing one another; then I felt the stillness of death deepen around me, when I saw in my father an unhappy man who would survive us all, a memorial cross on the grave of all his personal hopes. A guilt must rest upon the entire family, a punishment of God must be upon it: it was supposed to disappear, obliterated by the mighty hand of God, erased like a mistake ... (*JP* 5430)

This dour upbringing was, almost inevitably, succeeded by a period of extravagance in Søren's very protracted student years. There is little evidence of serious debauchery, but bills were run up with tailors, dinners were enjoyed and wine and cigars were consumed. Intellectually, the study of theology was only one ingredient in a diet of voracious reading. In Kierkegaard's early journals we find entries on the most diverse literary, philosophical and religious works and topics. In these journals Kierkegaard explores and comments on (amongst other things) the meanings of Romanticism, Classicism, art, the Middle Ages, folk literature, Faust, Don Juan, the Wandering Jew, irony, humour and Christianity, as well as notes for at least one uncompleted novel and fragments of autobiography.

It is little wonder that, in relation to his home background, Kierkegaard experienced this (newfound freedom) as quite vertiginous and the terrible tension between what he called his religious presuppositions and the life he was now leading find an echo in many entries, perhaps most famously in the description of a party, where, he said, he was the life and soul:

> ... witticisms flowed out of my mouth; everybody laughed, admired me – but I left, yes, the dash ought to be as long as the radii of the earth's orbit
>
> ————————————————————————
> ————————————————————————
> ————————————————————————
>
> and wanted to shoot myself. (*JP* 5141)

The seriousness inculcated by his upbringing and the range of possibilities opened to him by his academic brilliance made for a volatile situation that caused Kierkegaard to be more than usually susceptible to the kinds of anxiety that most adolescents feel when on the verge of stepping out into the world. In a series of more or less fictionalized journal entries that evoke a summer visit to the north coast of Sjælland, Kierkegaard describes how the question of the meaning of life is forced on him during long walks on the cliff tops. Out here, away from the city with all its bustle and confusion, his essential solitude is brought home to him:

> One quiet evening as I stood there listening to the deep but quietly earnest song of the sea, seeing not a sail on the enormous expanse of water but only the sea enclosing the sky and the sky the sea, while on the other side the busy hum of life became

silent and the birds sang their evening prayers – then the few dear departed ones rose from the grave before me … and I felt as if transported out of my body and floating about with them in a higher ether – but then (the seagull's harsh screech) reminded me that I stood alone … and I turned back with a heavy heart to mingle with the world's crowds … (*JP* 5099)

Caught between his existential solitude and the demands of the crowd of possibilities that life holds before him (Søren knows that he must choose) and choose rightly – for what he chooses will be his life:

What I really need is to get clear about *what I must do*, not what I must know, except in so far as knowledge must precede every act. What matters is to find a purpose, to see what it really is that God wills that I shall do; the crucial thing is to find a truth which is truth *for me*, to find *the idea for which I am willing to live and die.* Of what use would it be to me to discover a so-called objective truth … constructing a world I did not live in but merely held up for others to see … – if it had no deeper meaning *for me and for my life?* (*JP* 5100)

Such were the meditations of the 23-year-old, yet it was to be many years yet before it did become clear to him what he should do – indeed, it is arguable that (he never ceased to experience the tension between his religious seriousness and his intellectual and aesthetic virtuosity.)

Although Kierkegaard was often critical of the intellectual authorities of his day, moving from admiration to scorn with sometimes indecent haste, there was one of his university teachers whom he held in singular esteem: Poul Martin Møller. Møller was renowned both as a poet and as an academic. Like a number of his Danish contemporaries, he had been strongly touched by Romanticism and regarded Hegelianism as too rationalistic. He judged the critical temper of the age to be one-sided, and needing to be rooted in the ground of empirical experience and natural feeling as well as to be nurtured by a supporting social framework. He sensed that such balance was, however, increasingly lacking and he foresaw a time – perhaps quite imminent – in which all the values sustaining an integrated life would be overturned and humanity led into a wilderness of nihilism. As he put it in one of his poems:

> In melancholy hours I often bewail
> You, you nineteenth-century rational man.
> Poetry's flower has withered in your fields,
> You seek the promised land in a wilderness.
> Your child is an old man who never jokes,
> His music, the ringing of the chimes of rebellion.[3]

Sharing with his pupil a fascination for the fashionable legend of Ahasverus, the Wandering Jew, Møller saw in this figure a symbol of the tendency of contemporary thought to relativize all values and to regard itself as beyond good and evil. Despite his own aversion to the radical left, Møller was sceptical of the firmness of the resolve of the establishment in the face of modernity. It therefore seemed to him that it would be necessary for nihilism to run its course in order for its essential destructiveness to be revealed before there could be any hope of a return to a more balanced world-view. In the meantime the best that could be done was for 'those who do not share the peculiar passion for destruction ... to build themselves an ark in which they can establish themselves in the hope of better times.'[4]

Møller died in 1838, the same year as Kierkegaard's father and at a time when Kierkegaard himself was still far from finished with his long drawn-out studentship. In 1840, however, he did complete his degree and in September of that year set in motion what was to be the defining crisis of his life by proposing to a young woman, Regine Olsen. Almost immediately he came to believe that this had been a terrible mistake and that it would be impossible for him to go through with the marriage. It is perhaps hard for us now to appreciate the seriousness of his predicament and we must remember that an engagement in the upper middle classes of Copenhagen in the 1840s was probably taken at least as seriously as many marriage ceremonies today. It was a very public and very binding affair and to break it off could be taken as implying some dishonour on the part of the rejected party.

Despite the power of his feelings for Regine – and the strength of their mutual attraction shines through every word that either of them ever wrote or spoke on the subject – he spent much of the next year in an agony of indecision. The reasons for his conviction

regarding the impossibility of marriage have never been satisfactorily established and the secondary literature is littered with uncon-
vincing hypotheses. Amongst the most commonly mentioned are:
that it was connected with his secret knowledge of a moral lapse
(perhaps with <u>congenital consequences</u>) on the part of his father,
which marriage would require him to reveal – a possibility not
unconnected with the brooding question of hereditary guilt
explored in 'The Great Earthquake'; that Søren himself had paid a
visit to a brothel and feared bringing the physical as well as the
moral consequences into a marriage; that he was latently homosex-
ual – or impotent; or, simply that God called him to a higher task.
Interpreting these events is made more difficult by the fact that
Kierkegaard deliberately inserted into his writings passages that
might be taken as implying any of these possibilities – as well as the
totally fictitious ploy that he really wanted to break the engagement
in order to sow a few more wild oats before settling down. All we
can safely say is that no hypothesis has been proved beyond doubt
and that, in any case, the precise cause of his anxieties is not the
main issue. What matters is simply that he experienced the impossibility of marriage as an event that brought into the sharpest focus
the religious requirement to take complete responbsibility for his
life } to 'become guilty' in the sense of accepting full answerability
for his decision, even when that meant flying in the face of conventional morality and bringing pain to the one person he believed he
loved and to whom, together with his father, he would dedicate his
authorship, to whom also (against all rules of propriety) he would
leave all his wordly goods. She herself remembered all her life his
words to her: 'Look, Regine, there is no such thing as marriage in
eternity; there both Schlegel [the man whom she subsequently mar-
ried] and I will be able to rejoice in being together with you.'[5]

After the breaking of the engagement Kierkegaard presented his
dissertation *On the Concept of Irony* and began work on the series
of pseudonymous books for which he is best known. Between
February 1843 and February 1846 he published *Either/Or*, *Repetition*,
Fear and Trembling, *Philosophical Fragments*, *The Concept of Anxiety*,
Prefaces, *Stages on Life's Way* and *Concluding Unscientific Postscript*, as
well as a sequence of substantial religious meditations. We shall
return to the contents of these works, but we now move immediately to the first major public crisis of Kierkegaard's career – the
attacks made on him in the satirical publication *The Corsair*.[6]
Although Kierkegaard himself provoked these attacks and although

many of the cartoons and jokes concerning him were extremely puerile, his [protracted exposure to public ridicule] – ridicule that embraced his clothes, his writings and his treatment of Regine – had a shattering effect on his life. Whereas extended casual walks had previously been his chief recreation, he was now painfully aware of the looks, sneers and sniggers of passers-by and the streets became a place of torment rather than relaxation. (We must remember that the atmosphere of Copenhagen then was, as Kierkegaard himself put it, much more like that of a provincial market town than the international metropolis it is today.[7]) He was also hurt by the fact that none of those leaders of public opinion whom he regarded as his natural allies came to his support. Thus he came to see the whole affair as a manifestation of the evil power of the media in managing public opinion and subverting personal responsibility in modern society and when Kierkegaard spoke of his opponents in this debate as representing 'rabble-barbarism' he was not primarily indicting the *sans-culottes*, but the 'reading public', the bourgeois and petty-bourgeois, whose silence counted as tacit support for the campaign of vilification waged against him.

The whole incident epitomized the cultural shifts that he described in *Two Ages*, an extended literary review he published at this time in which he analysed the present age as an age that no longer has the all-consuming passion of the age of revolution but that no less surely, if underhandedly, evades the requirements of religious and social authority. It is, as he describes it,

> a *sensible, reflecting age, devoid of passion, flaring up in superficial, short-lived enthusiasm and prudentially relaxing in indolence ... it lets everything remain but subtly drains the meaning out of it; rather than culminating in an uprising, it ... lets everything remain and yet has transformed the whole of existence into an equivocation ...* The established order continues to stand, but since it is equivocal and ambiguous, passionless reflection is reassured. We do not want to abolish the monarchy, by no means, but if little by little we could get it transformed into make-believe, we would gladly shout 'Hurrah for the King!' ..[we are willing to keep Christian terminology but privately know that nothing decisive is supposed to be meant by it.[8]]

The true roots of this attitude are cowardice and envy: the refusal to stand up and be counted coupled with the repudiation of anyone who does so. In a word, it is what Kierkegaard calls 'levelling', the reduction of social difference to an average conformity.

Kierkegaard certainly did not lose all contact with society after *The Corsair* Affair, and he went on to write some of his most significant works – *Works of Love, Christian Discourses, Training in Christianity* and *The Sickness Unto Death* – yet from 1846 until his death in 1855 he was increasingly isolated. However, in the very last year of his life he once more stepped out onto the public stage. In 1854 the Primate of the Danish Church, Bishop Mynster, died. Mynster had been the Kierkegaards' family priest and Kierkegaard himself had often written of his high estimation for Mynster's religious writings. None the less he came to the view that, in practice, Mynster compromised the gospel in his desire to make it acceptable to the middle and upper classes. Mynster's preaching was preaching without the essential possibility of scandal – a possibility that, for Kierkegaard, was the hallmark of all true Christian preaching. After Mynster's death a memorial sermon was preached by Hans Lassen Martensen, a theologian who had at one time been strongly influenced by Hegelianism and who had served as Kierkegaard's tutor for the study of Schleiermacher. In Kierkegaard's eyes, Martensen's address was little more than a pretext to promote himself as Mynster's successor (which, in fact, he became). Moreover, when he referred to Mynster as a 'witness to the truth', Kierkegaard was outraged, since he himself had used this expression in a very precise sense to mean those Christians who witness to the truth of the gospel by enduring persecution and even martyrdom for its sake – something that was certainly not the case with Mynster! A real 'witness to the truth', according to Kierkegaard, was someone whose life

> is unacquainted with everything which is called enjoyment ... [experiencing] inward conflicts ... fear and trembling ... trepidation ... anguish of soul ... agony of spirit ... a man who in poverty witnesses to the truth – in poverty, in lowliness, in abasement ... unappreciated, hated, abhorred, and then derided, insulted, mocked ... scourged, maltreated, dragged from one prison to the other, and then at last ... crucified, or beheaded, or burnt, or roasted on a gridiron, his lifeless body thrown by the executioner in an out-of-the-way place ... or burnt to ashes and cast to the four winds, so that every trace of the 'filth' (which the Apostle says *he* was) might be obliterated.[9]

Kierkegaard proceeded to write a series of articles and pamphlets in which he charged the Church with being hopelessly compromised by its incorporation into the political status quo in such a way that to be a Christian simply meant being born in a 'Christian' country. Chief amongst his targets in this attack were the payment of the clergy by the state (rather than by the freewill offerings of the congregation) and the way in which marriage, baptism and confirmation merely sanctified rites of reproduction rather than marking initiation into Christian discipleship.

In the midst of this attack, he died – aged 42.

II

As we turn from Kierkegaard's life to his thought we shall begin by examining the critical aspect of his thought, i.e. the way in which, as a thinker, he worked out his own position polemically, as the critique of the prevailing patterns of intellectual, cultural and social life.

Kierkegaard is, perhaps, best known in the history of ideas as a leading critic of Hegel. Bearing in mind a number of comments already made, however, we need to realize that the issue was never merely one of pure philosophy. The faults of Hegel's system, as Kierkegaard saw them, led directly to many of the most vicious aspects of contemporary life. In this respect, Kierkegaard regarded the radical 'Young Hegelian' left as being the authentic interpreters of Hegel, and also as acting upon the implications of the master's philosophical formulations. The abolition of the principle of difference which Kierkegaard saw as the central element in Hegelian philosophy thus led straight to the political and social levelling he so deprecated.

Kierkegaard's critique can, however, be traced back to a difference concerning the scope of logic. As Kierkegaard understood him, Hegel claimed that whereas all other disciplines – history, empirical science, philology or whatever – necessarily made certain assumptions regarding both method and content, philosophy was able to suspend all such presuppositions and determine its content purely on the basis of self-evident logical truths. Kierkegaard, closely following the German Aristotle scholar Adolf Trendelenburg, saw this claim as making demands on logic that logic itself could not possibly fulfil. Logic, as Kierkegaard understood it, was simply incapable of integrating the illogical complexity of actual existence – let alone generating existence out of its own resources! Acknowledging that while it is indeed possible to conceive of a logical system, Kierkegaard claimed that it was impossible to conceive of an existential system.

> A system of existence cannot be given. Is there, then, not such a system? That is not at all the case. Neither is this implied in what has been said. Existence itself is a system – for God, but it cannot be a system for any existing spirit. System and conclusiveness correspond to each other, but existence is the very opposite... Existence is the spacing that holds apart; the systematic is the conclusiveness that combines.[10]

there cannot be an existential system

Only a human being could write the perfect system – but the very fact of being human disqualifies one from writing it. However, the problem is not just that the existing human being has, as such, a strictly limited view on the universe and is consitutionally incapable of getting an overview on the whole. The problem is also, more fundamentally, to do with the kind of being that the existing human being is. An existing individual, Kierkegaard asserts, is one whose existence is of supreme interest: *that* he exists and *how* he exists and *what he is living for* are matters that are of inexhaustible interest to him. 'Abstraction' – i.e. the kind of thought involved in any attempt to have a systematic overview of the world – 'is disinterested, but [to exist is the highest interest for an existing person]... For the existing person, existing is for him his highest interest, and his interestedness in existing is his actuality.'[11] Exploiting the etymology of the term 'interest' as 'inter-esse', i.e. 'being-between', Kierkegaard describes reality or existence as that state in which, contrary to the principle of identity embraced by idealism, thought and being are always separated. Thus, 'God does not think, he creates; God does not exist, he is eternal. A human being thinks and exists, and [existence separates thinking and being,] holds them apart from each another in succession.'[12] Whereas abstract thought 'is thought without a thinker', thought that takes existence seriously orients itself from the passionate concern of the individual thinker in what concerns his own existence. That is to say: existential thought is *ethical* because it always concerns the subject in his free responsibility for becoming what he is. That the situation of existence inherently arouses in me the passion of freedom is, according to Kierkegaard, 'the *interest* of metaphysics and also the interest upon which every metaphysics comes to grief ...'[13]

The question of <u>temporality</u> provides an important focus for Kierkegaard's critique of idealism. In the *Philosophical Fragments*, for instance, he explores the Socratic question as to whether truth can be learned by showing how, on the Socratic/Platonic model itself, the learner always already knows the truth implicitly in such a way that the process of learning is simply bringing to consciousness what is already latent within it. For Plato, of course, the truths of mathematics provide a paradigmatic case: to understand mathematics one does not need to acquire new information – one only has to unpack what the mind itself already understands. Even if subsequent forms of idealism do not adopt the Platonic mythology of the pre-existent soul, the principle of recollection, according to Kierkegaard, remained determinative for them. We have already noted Hegel's dictum concerning the Owl of Minerva which flies only at dusk; and even though Hegel extended the scope of philosophy to embrace history, his philosophical approach to history can only interpret what is already past and can only understand history to the extent that it conforms to a logical structure that is in some sense prior to any particular historical events. As Kierkegaard understands it, it follows that nothing new ever really comes to pass. Everything that can be known has already been. When, therefore, Hegel claims to incorporate a principle of movement into philosophy, this means one of two things. Either he has pulled a sophistical trick and illegitimately imported an understanding of movement derived from other sources into logic – or what Hegel calls 'movement' is merely an appearance: (there is no real change, only a change in perspective on the part of the thinker) (as when I 'discover' for myself the truth of Pythagoras' theorem: the theorem itself is not essentially altered by my discovery of it).

Kierkegaard, following (Trendelenburg,) appeals to Aristotle and, in particular, to Aristotle's categories of possibility and actuality. For, according to Aristotle, ('movement' is precisely the transition of something from possibility to actuality.) But such a transition, such a movement, necessarily involves both discontinuity and time – neither of which idealism allows for: 'abstractly thought, there is no break, but no transition either, because viewed abstractly everything *is*. However, (when existence gives movement time,) and I reproduce this, then the leap appears in just the way a leap can appear: it must come, or it has been.'[14]

In opposition to the principle of recollection, Kierkegaard set up his own principle of 'repetition'.

> Just as [the Greeks] taught that all knowing is a recollecting, modern philosophy will teach that all life is a repetition ... Repetition and recollection are the same movement, except in opposite directions, for what is recollected has been, is repeated backward, whereas genuine repetition is recollected forward.[15] (R 131)

Repetition is therefore a way out of the threat of chaos that a radical acceptance of the temporality of existence and of the reality of movement would entail. Repetition allows for continuity in the midst of change, but this continuity depends on activating the ethical passion of the existing subject. Repetition is not simply the internalization of an idea of meaning that already exists independently of the subject. Repetition is precisely the act by which the knowing subject expresses its interest in its own existence. Nor can the insight gained by repetition then become a 'result', for it must be appropriated over and over again in ever-renewed acts of repetition.

Repetition also plays an important role in the construction of selfhood in Kierkegaard's thought, and our discussion here is limited to its critical function over against the Hegelian and idealist principle of recollection.

A third important element in Kierkegaard's critique of Hegel has already been alluded to at several points and hinges on the sharp distinction drawn by Kierkegaard between subjectivity and objectivity. As Kierkegaard sees it, Hegelian philosophy abstracts from the existing individual thinker, passionately concerned in their own existence. In looking at existence objectively it fails to do justice to the living subject of knowledge. In contrast to this, Kierkegaard, in his most succinct formulation of the matter declared that 'truth is subjectivity'. How did he distinguish between the two? Here is how he puts it in *Concluding Unscientific Postscript*.

> When the question about truth is asked objectively, truth is reflected upon objectively as an object to which the knower relates himself. What is reflected on is not the relation but that what he relates himself to is the truth, the true. If only that to which he relates himself is the truth, the true, then the subject is

in the truth. When the question about truth is asked subjectively, the individual's relation is reflected upon subjectively. If only the how of this relation is in truth, the individual is in truth, even if he in this way were to relate himself to untruth.[16]

Or, as he goes on to say, '*Objectively the emphasis is on what is said, subjectively the emphasis is on how it is said.*'[17] Truth thus becomes '*An objective uncertainty, held fast through appropriation with the most passionate inwardness …*'[18]

Note here the emphasis on appropriation: what matters is not an objective account of how the world is really constituted, but how I come to know about it, how I experience it, how I understand it from my standpoint of living in it as an existing individual.

Kierkegaard's appeal to the 'how' of truth signals another dimension of his dissatisfaction with Hegelian philosophy. We saw that Feuerbach had attacked Hegelian philosophy for its professorial style as well as for its content. Kierkegaard too never ceased to amuse himself at the style of professional and professorial philosophy, ridiculing its pomposity, its lack of irony and humour and, as he saw it, the comical consequences resulting from the way in which it overlooked the standpoint of the existing individual. The systematic philosopher, he said, is like a man who builds a castle, but lives in the hovel next door – his own life can never match up to the grandeur of his philosophical speculations. At one point he sketched a dialogue between Socrates and Hegel in the underworld, in which Socrates (who, of course, left no written works) makes fun of Hegel's 21 volumes of collected works, none of which, as Socrates makes clear, has helped him to understand the most elementary problems of philosophy. Again and again we find Kierkegaard privileging the Socratic, dialogical way of doing philosophy over against the systematic, encyclopaedic style of the German professors. Like Socrates, Kierkegaard did not set himself up as the teacher of a finished doctrine but sought to be a midwife, bringing others' thoughts to birth – or a gadfly, stinging them into an ever more urgent pursuit of truth.

III

Hegel was not the only target of Kierkegaardian critique. No less important to Kierkegaard was his debate with Romanticism.

Romanticism had by no means ceased to be a vital intellectual and cultural force in Kierkegaard's time, despite the Hegelian attack on it. Figures from the early years of Romanticism, such as Schleiermacher and Schelling, continued to play a significant role in the 1830s – it was, after all, to hear Schelling (ten years after Hegel's death) that Kierkegaard went to Berlin and, in 1833, Schleiermacher's visit to Copenhagen had been an unqualified triumph.

Indeed, the contemporary significance that a thinker such as Schleiermacher had for Kierkegaard's generation was signalled by the way in which Karl Gutzkow, a leading writer from the left, re-issued an early work by Schleiermacher, *Confidential Letters on Schlegel's Lucinde* (in 1834), in order to try to claim Schleiermacher as an ally in the fight against repressive bourgeois morality. The continuing vitality of ideologies of the aesthetic in the period also testify to the importance of Romanticism in the overall shaping of modernity.

Kierkegaard's early journals can themselves be interpreted as a significant piece of Romantic writing. Yet even here he is already criticizing some of the fundamental tenets of Romanticism. His ambivalence towards the Romantic celebration of poetry and art is well brought out in a journal entry concerning the nature of the poet and the poetic:

> The poetic ... is the cord through which the divine holds fast to existence. Therefore one could believe that they are blessed, those gifted individuals, those living telegraph wires between God and men. But this is most certainly not true ... their lot ... [is] annihilation of their personal existence as being incapable of enduring the touch of the divine ... his [the poet's] fate: to know a thirst which is never satisfied. [The poetic life in the personality is the unconscious sacrifice]. it is first in the religious that the sacrifice becomes conscious and the misrelationship removed. *(JP* 1027)

Such a statement could be taken as belonging to Romanticism itself, in so far as Romanticism too embraced the agony of the artist who has become aware of the meaninglessness of his work. Yet it also shows [Kierkegaard struggling to articulate a standpoint that has gone beyond that of Romanticism.]

His dissertation *On The Concept of Irony* also seems to put Kierkegaard on the side of the Hegelians in their critique of

Romanticism as a one-sided doctrine, which has failed to engage with the complexity of reality. Focusing on the early Romantic writers in Germany (writers such as Friedrich Schlegel, whose novel *Lucinde* celebrated the freedoms, including the sexual freedoms, of the poetic lifestyle), Kierkegaard accuses them of floating several degrees above reality and of cultivating a kind of subjectivity that, far from expressing the individual's concern with his existence demonstrates his detachment from it. The stance of ironic superiority adopted by the Romantics is described as leading to a completely arbitrary attitude towards the world:

> irony acted just as Hercules did when he was fighting with Antaeus, who could not be conquered as long as he kept his feet on the ground. As we all know, Hercules lifted Antaeus up from the ground and thereby defeated him. Irony dealt with historical actuality in the same way.[19]

But, according to Kierkegaard himself, 'actuality (historical actuality) stands in a twofold relation to the subject: partly as a gift that refuses to be rejected, partly as a task that wants to be fulfilled.'[20] Unless it is rooted in actuality, life loses continuity and the ironist who imagines himself to be poetically superior to the world ends up by drifting purposelessly from mood to mood – 'At times he is a god, at times a grain of sand' – and finishes in a state of boredom, an 'eternity devoid of content'.[21]

Although Hegelian professors and Romantic ironists superficially cut very different figures, Kierkegaard's analysis suggests that they share a common problem: neither does justice to the actual existential situation of the individual. Both the system and poetic fantasy abstract from the reality of life to the point of delusion.

If Kierkegaard had at one point been tempted by Hegelianism, the temptation of the aesthetic went far deeper: throughout even his most critical discussions of the aesthetic there reigns a profound ambivalence. He rejects art with the passion of an artist. In this we can see another aspect of his method of indirect communication, for his critique of Romanticism and of the aesthetic attitude promoted by the Romantics is carried through in his authorship especially in those works that themselves read most like works of Romantic fiction: *Either/Or*, *Repetition* and *Stages on Life's Way*. Here Kierkegaard sets out to show from within the contradictions of a life based on aesthetic values, how such a life culminates in despair – and how the individual must then set about retrieving himself from the terminal nothingness of a failed aesthetic existence.

IV

Just as there is a profound congruence between Kierkegaard's critique of Hegelianism and his critique of Romanticism, so too there are important continuities between both of these and his critique of society since contemporary society is itself a manifestation of the totalizing and rationalizing tendency of the system and is also said by Kierkegaard to be essentially aesthetic.

The connections between bourgeois society and idealist philosophy had, of course, been made by the Hegelians themselves. Hegel's own thought was widely understood as claiming that the existing social and political order was the most adequate expression of the idea ruling history, a conclusion famously summed up in the dictum, 'The real is the rational and the rational is the real.' (Although this is, in fact, a misleading misquotation.) H. L. Martensen, the Hegel-oriented theologian (whose eulogy on Bishop Mynster was to be the immediate occasion of Kierkegaard's attack on the established Church), wrote of the contemporary world that 'it is the period of systems, not only in the more strict sense of philosophical and scientific systems, but of religious, poetic, political, yes, even industrial and mercantile systems.'[22]

Speaking of the political tendency of his age, Kierkegaard describes it in terms essentially identical to those in which he attacks Hegelianism and Romanticism:

this tendency is guilty of an attack on the given actuality; its watchword is: Forget the actual (and this is already an attack) ... Like Hegel, it begins, not the system but existence, with nothing, and the negative element, through which and by virtue of which all the movements occur ... is distrust ...[23]

This prejudice against the given actuality, however, was not merely a failing of the left: it was also the secret of the bourgeois establishment, and we have already seen how Kierkegaard described this as simply a façade, maintaining the outward forms of authority – monarchy and Church – but draining away all meaning from them. Kierkegaard's own experiences at the hands of *The Corsair* reinforced his view that the press was an integral part of this process, a process leading to the rule of 'the public'. But,

> The public ... is an abstraction ... The public is not a people, not a generation, not one's age, not a congregation, not an association, not some particular persons ... Composed ... of individuals in the moments when they are nobodies, the public is a kind of colossal something, an abstract void and vacuum that is all and nothing ... the most dangerous of all powers and the most meaningless.[24]

Politics carried on in the name of this public is the 'deification of statistics', the rule of 'the numerical' – and it is this that Kierkegaard regards as the real contemporary 'opium of the people' (cf. *JP* 2980). As such it is politics without responsibility and, consequently, politics is continually on the brink of war. Kierkegaard quotes Schelling approvingly: '"When it comes to the point where the majority decided what constitutes truth, it will not be long before they take to deciding it with their fists"' (*JP* 4112). In his view the revolutions and nationalist wars of 1848 confirmed this diagnosis.

In the face of such a society, Kierkegaard explains his own task as being to lure the individual away from the crowd: to individualize and bring each one, singly, to a sense of their own responsibility. However, precisely because all external forms of authority have been undermined, anyone who seeks an authentic reformation must accept 'unrecognizability' as an integral part of their strategy. To become a 'leader', an 'authority' or a 'guru' is precisely to absolve the individual from decision and responsibility. The best such a contemporary teacher can hope for is rejection and suffering.

The aesthetic aspect of contemporary society is emphasized in Kierkegaard's apologia for his tactic of indirect communication, *The Point of View for My Work as an Author*. Here he explains that the reason why he had to write aesthetic books was because of the pedagogical requirement to start where the learner himself is. Simply to launch a frontal attack on 'Christendom' would be to invite dismissal as an extremist or crank: 'an illusion can never be destroyed directly, and only by indirect means can it be radically removed.'[25] Instead, the indirect communicator works from within – but this means first identifying very clearly the illusion against which he is operating. This illusion is 'Christendom' itself,

i.e. that 'Christendom = Christianity'. But for K
dom is no longer a matter of life and death,
the truth in the face of violent persecution, b
an aesthetic game: 'If, then, according to
greater number of people in Christendom or
to be Christians, in what categories do they live? They
thetic, or, at the most, in <u>aesthetic-ethical categories</u>.'[26] And, as he
was to say in his final 'Attack on "Christendom"', the priests themselves are no more than poets, habituating the people to their sickness, instead of curing them – whilst church services themselves are
mere <u>theatre</u>, with the disadvantage that you can't ask for your
money back if you don't like the show!

Social, political and religious life, then, like Hegelian philosophy
and Romantic aesthetics, have essentially lost touch with the reality
of human life. They no longer express real human interests or
real human needs. Moreover – and this is a crucial element in
Kierkegaard's critique of the age – there are no ready alternatives,
for every alternative that can be offered, every opposition movement, is itself entangled in the same dialectic that reigns throughout. All authority has been destroyed and individuals are radically
isolated in their quest for truth.

Kierkegaard did not himself proclaim the death of God, as
Nietzsche was to do, but it is clear that, for him, the life of the
individual in society was a life denied the resources of religious
tradition since even those insitutions and systems of thought that
claimed to represent tradition were profoundly anti-traditional. We
can no longer believe on the basis of what the Church teaches or
what our fathers have taught us. Kierkegaard's world is not atheistic, but it is atheous: there is no immediate presence of God in the
world, no recognizable, unambiguous focus for religious belief. We
are each thrown back on ourselves and challenged to find truth by
finding it first in ourselves.

It is, then, to Kierkegaard's construction of what it means for the
individual subject to exist as his or her own truth that we now turn.

V

Kierkegaard's anthropological descriptions were to provide key
elements of the analysis of *Dasein* in Martin Heidegger's *Being
and Time* and so to prove a seminal influence on the development

...stentialist philosophy in the twentieth century. However, ...reas several of the leading representatives of existentialism ...ok an atheistic or agnostic stance towards religion, Kierkegaard's own depiction of the human subject is inseparable from the religious question in which, as he sees it, the whole dynamics of selfhood are rooted and grounded – 'every life is religiously planned', as he put it in *The Concept of Anxiety*.

However, Kierkegaard does not use any single 'plan' to account for the complexities of the subject's resolution of the religious issue at the heart of its existence, but uses a whole range of models to explore what would be involved in such a resolution. We shall concentrate here on two of these models. The first is that of developmental psychology, tracing the growth of the personality from childhood to adulthood, with particular emphasis on the moment of adolescence, when the child prepares to step out onto the stage of adult life. The second is that of the three stages: the aesthetic, the ethical and the religious.

The theme of the transition from childhood to adult life is one that has been central to the culture of modernity. The perennial popularity of coming-of-age novels and movies witnesses to this. Nor should this be surprising, since the experience is not only profoundly important for each individual, it also re-enacts modernity's epochal quest to put aside dogma and authority and establish reason and moral responsibility as the determining centre of social, scientific and cultural organization. In this respect we are still very much the heirs of Kant, who, in his essay *What is Enlightenment?*, defined Enlightenment in terms of the development of autonomy, as the subject emerges from the tutelage of others and takes command of its own life.

In Kierkegaard's writing the transition is both described in narrative terms and made the subject of conceptual analysis. We have already referred to the journal recording a holiday in northern Sjælland, when Søren, or his fictionalised alter ego, reflects on how to find the idea for which he will live and die. In the course of these reflections his mind runs over the multitude of possibilities from which he can choose: a life of pleasure or of knowledge, of science or of religion. Which is it to be?

In *Repetition* he shows how this situation has an inner affinity with the nature of theatre. Theatre, he argues, is essentially about the representation of possible roles or personalities that the spectator is able imaginatively to enter into. Because the world of the theatre is fictional, we are able to explore aspects of the personality that are forbidden in the 'real' world. We can try out what it might be like to be a Don Juan, a Macbeth, a Romeo, a Hypochondriac or a Hamlet, an Antigone, a Juliet or a Donna Elvira. The shadows of the stage are essentially shadows cast by the imaginations of the audience. The drama, tragic or comic as the case may be, is the exposition of what belongs to their own possibilities. All this, of course, is only in the realm of imagination: 'the personality is not discerned, and its energy is betokened only in the passion of possibility ...'[27] One role succeeds another in a kaleidoscopic blaze: in the world of the theatre (or film or TV) we can be anyone and everyone.

According to Kierkegaard's pseudonym Constantin Constantius, all this is just fine as long as it takes place at the right time, the time of youth, and is kept separate from the sphere in which moral responsibility should hold sway. It is, however, disastrous if we start to live our lives as if they were merely roles we can change at will, ignoring the claims others make upon us and shrugging off the need to be consistent. But, of course, it is extremely difficult to take responsibility for who we are and to become a distinct, determinate personality. Faced with the magnitude of the task we shrink back in anxiety.

In *Either/Or* Kierkegaard sets up two contrasting ways of life, the aesthetic and the ethical (to which we shall return) and makes it clear that there is an essential affinity between, on the one hand, the aesthetic life and the time of youth and, on the other hand, between the ethical life and adulthood, with all its claims and responsibilities. The crucial element in making the transition from the one to the other is that we actually choose who we are to be. In this act of choice the self identifies itself with its situation and its history, accepts its particular limitations and chooses from amongst its multitutde of possibilities. Precisely because human adult life is life lived on the basis of freedom it can only come about by an act of free self-determination. Authentic adulthood cannot be simply a matter of biological maturity. Some biological adults fall far short of being adults in the full, moral sense.

An example of such failure, according to Kierkegaard, is Nero, and he demonstrates how Nero's criminality is precisely rooted in his anxious fear of freedom.

I picture, then, that imperial sensualist ... I imagine him as a somewhat older person; his youth is past, his buoyant disposition has drained away, and he is already familiar with every imaginable pleasure, already sated with them ... Now he snatches at pleasure; all the ingenuity of the world must devise new pleasures for him, because only in the moment of pleasure does he find rest, and when that is over, he yawns in sluggishness. The spirit continually wants to break through, but it cannot achieve a breakthrough ... Then the spirit masses within him like a dark cloud; its wrath broods over his soul, and it becomes an anxiety that does not cease even in the moment of enjoyment. This, you see, is why his eyes are so dark that no one can bear to look into them, his glance so flashing that it alarms, for behind the eyes the soul lies like a gloomy darkness. This is called the imperial look and the whole world quakes before it, and yet his in most being is anxiety ... He is as if possessed, inwardly unfree, and that is why it seems to him as if every glance would bind him. He, the emperor of Rome, can be afraid of the look of the lowliest slave. He catches such a look; his eyes dispatch the person who dares to look at him that way.[28]

Terrifying, monstrous Nero is essentially someone who has failed to grow up. And so, paradoxically, Kierkegaard goes on to note that such a character can take a child's delight in 'trifling things': 'A matured personality cannot enjoy in this way, for although he has retained his childlikeness he nevertheless has ceased to be a child.'[29] Moreover, although Nero's anxiety is acted out on the grand scale – in the imperial manner – the basic features of his psychological predicament belong, potentially, to us all. That is why he continues to fascinate: 'Even after his death Nero causes anxiety, for however corrupt he is, he is still flesh of our flesh and bone of our bone, and there is something human even in an inhuman wretch.'[30]

Kierkegaard underlines the universality of the crisis of anxiety when, in *The Concept of Anxiety*, he sets it in the context of the biblical narrative of Creation and Fall and describes it as pivotal in the emergence of humanity in the full sense. He imagines the primitive state of the first humans as one of innocence. This innocence is that of an almost animal-like nature. Humanity has not yet discovered its capacity for freedom (or: spirit). And yet, humanity is what it is only and precisely in relation to this capacity. Even in the state of innocence we are not simply animals.

In this state there is peace and repose, but there is simultaneously something else ... What, then, is it? Nothing. But what effect does nothing have? It begets <u>anxiety</u>. This is the profound secret of innocence, that it is at the same time anxiety. Dreamily the spirit projects its own actuality, but this actuality is nothing, and innocence always sees this nothing outside itself.[31]

This may sound mystifying, but it can be related to certain very simple considerations regarding the nature of freedom: free actions are precisely actions that are not determined by anything other than the free agent – in other words, they are *in*determinate or determined by nothing. They cannot be explained by any concatenation of cause and effect but only by the free will itself. But this is exactly why we experience our possibility of freedom in the mode of anxiety. As a free subject I can no longer take refuge in the excuse that I do what I do because I have been made that way, or because I am obeying the laws of my tribe [I, and only I, decide.] — *Causes anxiety*

In the state of anxiety, however, I have not yet acted. My freedom is only a future possibility. I stand on the threshold. If I am Nero, I fail to cross it – and life takes its revenge by subjecting me to the compulsive repetition of the crisis of anxiety. If, on the other hand, I do act, I freely choose myself and become who I am, then I take *if I act I choose myself and* upon myself the burden of being <u>guilty</u>. Guilt, as marking the moment of transition beyond anxiety into freedom, becomes a crucial term in Kierkegaard's vocabulary, although we should remember that for Kierkegaard, writing in Danish, the expression 'guilt' *take on burden of guilt* does not have exclusively forensic connotations. The root meaning of the word 'skyld'[32] has to do with being indebted, so that it is possible for Kierkegaard to move between the sense of 'guilt' as having to do with moral wrong-doing and 'guilt' in the sense of being *we are accountable* accountable or answerable. Thus, even when (as in *Repetition* or the second part of *Stages on Life's Way*) the question of guilt is focused on the predicament of a young man who breaks off an engagement and is then tormented by the question of his responsibility for the sufferings of his former fiancée, the key issue is that of responsibility and of accepting all the consequences that flow from one's free actions.

Taking one's guilt upon oneself in this sense is also expressed in *self-acceptance take and guilt you choose* *Either/Or* by means of the concept of <u>repentance</u>, understood as the total act of <u>self-acceptance</u> and <u>self-commitment</u>. As the pseudonym <u>Assessor William</u> puts it, the individual who chooses himself both isolates himself completely by the intensity of his free resolve and also, by the very same act, 'is most radically sinking himself into the root by which he is bound up with the whole ... He repents

[handwritten margin note: repents of back into the race]

himself back into himself, back into the family, back into the race, until he finds himself in God. Only on this condition can he choose himself.' To repent is freely to choose one's self, lovingly, 'from the hand of the eternal God'.[33]

It would, however, be a mistake to think of this as something one does once and for all, like being converted at an evangelistic rally. The act of freedom by which we exist as free and responsible adults is an act that is repeated in each and every action of our lives for which we consent to be held responsible. It is in this context, then, that we are to understand Kierkegaard's insistence on the concept of 'repetition'. On the one hand, there is the compulsive repetition of a Nero, on the other hand, even freedom itself can only exist as repetition and renewal. It can never be an achievement or result that I take for granted, but is something that meets me anew in each new situation that demands my action. Continuity through time can be attained only by repetition – like the repetition practised by married people, who renew their love on a daily basis in and by means of how they actually behave towards each other. Maturity is not something defined biologically: it is a task for freedom, a task that can only be fulfilled under the sign of repetition.

The plotting of the crisis of freedom in terms of the transition from childhood to adult life has provided us with much of the terminology of Kierkegaard's second model of becoming-a-self: the three stages of the aesthetic, the ethical and the religious. Indeed, the aesthetic stage can to a very considerable extent be regarded as the form of life that results from the self's failure to be itself in freedom. In this sense, Nero is an archetypal 'aesthetic' figure. The life of the aesthetic self is depicted in many ways by Kierkegaard as a kind of permanent adolescence. He is by no means blind to the attractive and appealing features of such a life, but his view of it is that fundamentally it is based on despair, since it is a loss of nerve in face of the challenge of its basic possibility of free self-commitment. The aesthetic personality, no matter how brilliant or witty his public persona might be, is a fugitive from himself. His self-indulgence in erotic adventures is a way of masking his inability to sustain serious involvements that would demand commitment and responsibility. Even when he acknowledges that his life is based on despair, he refuses to take the next step and seize his freedom. Instead, he prefers to atrophy in despair, rather than risk the insecurity of action. Brooding on death, he none the less refuses to confront himself seriously. When one set of pleasures,

[handwritten marginalia: aesthetic personality stays on surface]

pursuits or relationships begins to bore him, he moves on to another, always staying on the surface, never going into the depths.

'One ought to be a riddle not only to others but also to oneself. I examine myself; when I am tired of that, I smoke a cigar for diversion and think: God knows what our Lord actually intended with me or wants to make of me.'[34] In such aphorisms and in a string of essays and narratives, Kierkegaard provides a definitive critique (which is great precisely because it is also self-critique) of the attitude of Romantic aestheticism. Above all, *The Diary of the Seducer* in *Either/Or*, Part I shows what a life lived on such a failure to grasp the crisis of freedom might look like. Yet, although the Seducer appears in his own eyes as someone who consciously and deliberately manipulates both his own life and the lives of all about him in order to extract the maximum of pleasure, he is exposed by Kierkegaard as someone who is essentially defined by his flight from freedom and responsibility. *[handwritten: avoids freedom + responsibility]*

To such Romantic narcissism and escapism Kierkegaard opposes the ethical view of life. This is the view represented chiefly by Assessor William, whom we have already met as promoting the merits of choice and repentance in the formation of the personality, and to whom we owe the analysis of Neronian anxiety. According to William, the outcome of the choice of selfhood is, generally speaking, entry into the ranks of adult life: marriage, vocation, citizenship. Yet – although many Kierkegaard commentators clearly find William's bourgeois tastes and habits a bit too *Biedermeier* for their liking – he is not simply advocating bourgeois conformism for its own sake. As we have seen, choice is the *sine qua non* of his existential project, and he also insists that such choice is not an act of Romantic self-creation but a religiously motivated grounding of the self in what it owes to God. None the less, choice does not exist in a psycho-social vacuum and so, for William, the necessity of choosing oneself and the duties of citizenship cohere in a unitary vision of the good life. It is certainly no accident that Kierkegaard has made him a legal official.

Despite his insistence on social obligation, William's constant reiteration of the need for the self to choose itself in order to become what it is marks him out as distinctively modern. None the less, there are also difficulties with his position to which he does not entirely face up.

For a start, we might think of the point made by another of Kierkegaard's pseudonyms, Frater Taciturnus, writing in *Stages on*

Life's Way. In a lengthy analysis of (yet another) story about a broken engagement, it is shown that there are situations in which it is
far from clear what our real duty is. Moreover, although the problem of balancing conflicting duties has been a part of the moral
landscape for a long, long time, the typical characteristics of modernity involve an internalising of such conflicts to a hitherto unparalleled degree. For the typical person of modern times is neither a
simple 'child of nature', whose actions are immediately expressive
of natural instincts, nor is such a person readily disposed to submit
to any external source of authority in determining moral duties.
The nature of modernity means that every moral situation is therefore subject to intense reflection and is potentially ambiguous. The
self that freely chooses itself cannot appeal to any external, objective validation for that choice. It is exposed to a loneliness unlike
that experienced by previous generations, a loneliness that intensi-
fies what is at stake in the choice and that can therefore lead to
paralysis in the face of freedom. When this happens we come up
against the paradox that it is precisely anxiety in face of its own
freedom that has rendered the subject incapable of acting. In the
opinion of Frater Taciturnus, the ethical position is therefore unable
to provide a satisfactory solution to the crisis of the aesthetic personality. If the age of poetry is past, he writes, then we must choose
the religious. Nothing in between will do.

William himself approaches the issue in the light of what he
calls the question of the exception. Already in *Either/Or* he is honest enough to append to the letters that set out his ethical point of
view a sermon by a friend of his who is a pastor in a remote Jutland
parish. The dominant thought of the sermon is that over against
God we are always in the wrong. Thus it raises the question
as to whether the kind of self-choice and self-affirmation recommended by William can in fact be carried out in its entirety. In
Stages on Life's Way (where William reappears as the author of
an extensive treatise on the subject of marriage) he admits that
maybe not everyone is called by God to a life of dutiful citizenship.
Perhaps there is a duty to God that is higher than the duty to society. Perhaps there are some whose choices will lead them beyond
what counts as valid for the generality of humanity. Although he
surrounds this possibility with a number of cautions and scarcely
admits whether or not there may be such individuals, the theme
itself is taken up in what is arguably Kierkegaard's most influential
work, *Fear and Trembling*.

Fear and Trembling focuses on the predicament of Abraham, called by God to sacrifice his only son, Isaac, and yet, simultaneously, obliged to believe God's promise that through Isaac he would become the father of many nations. One aspect of this predicament that Kierkegaard explores is the sheer incommensurability between what Abraham is asked to do and the requirements of human moral law. Abraham has to step outside the universal moral principle – 'Thou shalt commit no murder' – for the sake of his obedience to God. The faith of Abraham cannot therefore be like the faith of Assessor William. Whereas William's religious commitment brings him into conformity to the universal, Abraham's leads him beyond it.

But Abraham's faith is not identical with his willingness to submit to the inscrutable will of God (a willingness that Kierkegaard calls 'resignation'). Its really astonishing characteristic lies in Abraham's conviction that – against all reason – he will get Isaac back. Faith is neither living in the world in the manner of the average sensual man nor does it mean world renunciation. What constitutes faith is living in the world as if not of the world.

> The dialectic of faith is the finest and the most extraordinary of all; it has an elevation of which I can certainly form a conception, but no more than that. I can make the mighty trampoline leap whereby I cross over into infinity; my back is like a tightrope dancer's, twisted in my childhood, and therefore it is easy for me. One, two, three – I can walk upside down in existence, but I cannot make the next movement, for the marvellous I cannot do – I can only be amazed at it.[35]

Thus Kierkegaard's pseudonym Johannes de silentio, insisting that faith is neither reducible to nor comprehensible in terms of any general principles or concepts. The real exception, the really extraordinary person of faith, then, is not the one Kierkegaard calls the 'knight of resignation' who renounces the world for the sake of heaven. He is a 'knight of faith', who lives in the world like the rest of us, but does so in each and every moment by virtue of his utter dependence on God, 'by virtue of the absurd'. Imagining himself face to face with such a knight, Johannes de silentio sets about examining him.

> I move a little closer to him, watch his slightest movement to see if it reveals a bit of heterogeneous optical telegraphy from the

infinite, a glance, a facial expression, a gesture, a sadness, a smile
that would betray the infinite in its heterogeneity with the finite.
No!... he belongs entirely to the world; no bourgeois philistine
could belong to it more... He resigned everything infinitely, and
then he grasped everything again by virtue of the absurd. He is
continually making the movement of infinity, but he does it with
such precision that he continually gets finitude out of it, and no
one ever suspects anything else.[36]

The nature of the religious question at the heart of every human
life is far from simple. Indeed, despite having offered us the map of
the three stages of the aesthetic, the ethical and the religious,
Kierkegaard goes on to show that of these three positions the religious can be further refined and subdivided. In the *Concluding Unscientific Postscript*, for example, Kierkegaard distinguished between
what he calls Religiousness 'A' and Religiousness 'B'.

Religiousness 'A' is a category comprising the kind of religiousness
we have examined so far. It incorporates the subjectivity of the individual's self-concern and the intensification of that subjectivity in the
light of the recognition that (in the words of the sermon from
Either/Or) 'over against God we are always in the wrong'. In the
Postscript Kierkegaard illustrates this position by taking the example
of a man who hears in church on Sunday that a human being can do
nothing of himself and must depend entirely on God in all things. But
how does this work out in practice? What, for example, does it mean
in the situation of a Copenhagen citizen contemplating the prospect
of an outing to a popular amusement park? Can a person who has
really taken to heart his utter dependence on God in all things lower
himself, as it were, to indulge in such a popular pastime? And, if so,
what does his dependence on God mean in such a context?

Kierkegaard manages to fill 30 pages with reflections on these
questions, the outcome of which is that the individual does go to
the park, but with a thorough understanding that even such an
innocent diversion is something he can only participate in and enjoy
by the grace of God. For the spirituality of such guilt-consciousness
(as Kierkegaard calls it) is not that of world-renouncing religious
heroism: like the spirituality of the knight of faith it means living in
the world whilst not being 'of it'.

Our religious person chooses the way to the amusement park,
and why? Because he does not dare to choose the way to the

monastery. And why does he not dare to do that? Because it is too exclusive. So he goes out there. 'But he does not enjoy himself,' someone may say. Yes, he does indeed. And why does he enjoy himself? Because the humblest expression for his the relationship with God is to acknowledge one's humanness, and it is human to enjoy oneself. [37]

Such a programme of self-annihilation before God may seem strenuous, but Kierkegaard curiously refers to it as the standpoint of humour. Why humour? Because the religious individual understands that what concerns him in the depths of his 'hidden inwardness' is completely incommensurable with their social persona: having an absolute commitment to God cannot be fitted into any category of worldly behaviour and there will therefore be a perpetual mismatch between such a person's inner and outer identity. Although such a person will take their obligation to God infinitely seriously, they will never take themselves seriously in any particular detail of their lives, since they will know that no particular action or relationship can ever adequately express what they believe to be at stake in the God-relationship.

All this, Kierkegaard says, is an essential precondition of the dialectic of Religiousness 'B' – but of itself it still falls short of 'B'. Religiousness 'A' can exist in paganism, but Christianity requires something more, and this 'more' is the necessity of finding salvation through faith in the historical event of the Incarnation. But what makes this 'more' necessary? Why is the standpoint of a totalized guilt-consciousness sustained in hidden inwardness not adequate?

The problem seems to concern the fact that even though the practitioner of Religiousness 'A' understands the necessity of total self-emptying and reliance on God in all things, this understanding is something he achieves by virtue of his own reflection upon the circumstances of his life. To count myself as nothing before God is still, in the parlance of theology, a matter of 'works', not faith. It is based on the conviction that we can come to know the truth about ourselves recollectively by gaining a total view on who we are and ordering our lives in relation to that view – even if, as in this case, 'the truth' is conceived in negative terms. But, as the *Fragments* argued, if we are fundamentally in error, then we will never even get round to realizing that we are in error: the condition for knowing that we are in error must be given to us from outside. We do not

need a Socrates to remind us maieutically of what we already
implicitly know, we need a Saviour who will give us a capacity for
truth that we otherwise cannot attain.

This is what Christianity proclaims in the doctrine of the Incarnation, understood not as the manifestation of a universal truth of
reason but as a singular historical event: the God-man present in a
single human individual – a position that Kierkegaard adopts polemically against the left-Hegelian view represented by Feuerbach and
David Friedrich Strauss that the Incarnation is merely the symbolic
representation of the identification of the collectivity of the human
race with God.

The doctrine of the Incarnation, therefore, strikes reason as a
paradox, seemingly antithetical to reason's universal claims. Yet
Kierkegaard also suggests that it is the supreme passion of reason
itself to seek out and to know its own limits, 'to want to discover
something that thought cannot think'.[38] It is precisely the totalizing
nature of Hegelian claims on behalf of reason that, in its hubris,
is truly unreasonable. Yet we should not play down the 'scandal'
of Kierkegaard's position too rapidly. For the interplay between
the necessity of the paradox and the total character of our being
in error means that the proclamation of the gospel always carries
with it the possibility of offence. This is not just because its claims
are unprovable but also because it exposes our life-situation as
being radically in the wrong. The error that is spoken of here is no
longer mere guilt-consciousness, the consciousness of our being
always already obligated to the power that gives us being, it is
sin-consciousness. Regarded under the rubric of sin our situation
is not to be understood merely negatively, as not having the fullness of truth within us, but positively, as a state of active rebellion
against God: 'defiance', as Kierkegaard calls it in *The Sickness
Unto Death*. Here, our failure to be what God would have us be is
not simply a matter of shortcoming or of incompleteness: it is
a determined and culpable refusal of God's will. Without faith,
we are in despair and, Kierkegaard asserts, 'no human being ever
lived and no one lives outside of Christendom who has not
despaired, and no one in Christendom if he is not a true Christian,
and in so far as he is not wholly that, he still is to some extent in
despair.'[39]

Our salvation, then, consists in having faith in the Incarnation
and faith that, in the Incarnation, the forgiveness of sin is made
available to us.

The realm of the religious has been subdivided into 'A' and 'B', with 'B' being defined as the decisively Christian standpoint, but Kierkegaard now gives one more twist to the plot. Having reached the position that salvation is by faith in the paradox alone – or, as he puts it, becoming contemporary with Christ – he is then troubled in case this is read simply as an excuse for passivity. For such paradoxical faith is still very much a matter of inwardness and of the inner intention of heart and mind. In other words, it can too easily be accommodated to the prevailing ethos of Christendom – just as the Lutheran insistence on justification by faith alone has led to the conflation of the duties of citizenship with the duties of Christianity.

In Kierkegaard's later thought, therefore (and in parallel with the increasing bitterness of his attacks upon Christendom), there is an attempt to reopen the question of 'works', without impugning the finality of grace. We cannot, the argument goes, claim to be Christian unless and until we shall have *done* all that is in our power to do and beyond in order to bear witness to Christ – even if (as we have seen) this means persecution and martyrdom. Kierkegaard finds himself returning to the medieval and early pietistic emphasis on imitation: Christ is the pattern or prototype of the individual life and the individual Christian must be conformed in his or her life to the sufferings of Christ and re-enact in that life His experiences of being despised and rejected.

In this emphasis on imitation Kierkegaard seems to be moving away from those aspects of his thought that were to shape the history of existentialism, religious and secular, in the twentieth century. Even here, however, there are continuities, for the image of the disciple that Kierkegaard creates in his writings on radical discipleship reinforces his general picture of the believer as outsider, as an anti-establishment, marginal figure, standing out on the strength of conscience alone for the sake of truth and inviting the calumny of the world to fall upon him. This motif of the individual *contra mundum* was, of course, to be integral to the whole culture of existentialism, even if it was to be manifested in quite different ways by religious and anti-religious existentialists.

VI

It is almost inevitable that a short overview of Kierkegaard's thought will give the impression that it was in fact far more doctrinaire and

more systematically ordered than is the case. Kierkegaard is very
aware that the problematization of knowledge has important
consequences for the way in which Christian communication happens. His appreciation of Socrates' maieutic method and his own
tactic of indirect communication has been noted, but it is very hard
to give a real sense of the extent to which the implications of this
are worked out on virtually every page of his authorship. The use
of pseudonyms is only one aspect of this: irony, lyric, metaphor,
parable and polemic are just some of the ways in which he lures or
provokes readers into thinking for themselves – not just about the
meaning of what he wrote, but about the meaning their own lives
should have. His passionate and constant endeavour to find an
appropriate way of communicating a faith that, he believed, could
not be understood by reason suggests one final comment. Against
those who regard Kierkegaard as a thorough-going individualist or
even a philosophical solipsist, it has to be said that, once the centrality of the question of communication has been grasped, it
becomes clear that Kierkegaard's life-work was not just about
becoming subjective but about how to exist inter-subjectively and,
as the title of one of his religious meditations has it, how to remain
in the debt of love.[40]

NOTES

1.   S. Kierkegaard, *The Journals*, trans. Dru (London: Oxford University
     Press, 1938), p. 146. Howard V. and Edna H. Hong translate the
     Danish term as 'curlew' (cf. *JP* 5842). Even if Dru is less correct, how-
     ever, his translation makes for a more powerful image.
2.   It is in this connection that we can discern the continuing significance
     of existentialism in the culture of postmodernity. Existentialism is
     often dismissed by postmodernists as simply a by-product of moder-
     nity. However, its critical distance from modernity gives it the poten-
     tial to offer a way of constructing meaning 'after modernism' that
     could offer an important alternative to much of what passes for post-
     modernism. For a further discussion of this issue see chapter 12,
     below.
3.   P. M. Møller, *Efterladte Skrifter* (Copenhagen: Reitzel, 1856), Vol. 5,
     p. 134. For further discussion of Møller, see my *Kierkegaard: The
     Aesthetic and the Religious* (Basingstoke: Macmillan, 1992), pp. 26–34.
4.   P. M. Møller, *Efterladte Skrifter*, Vol. 5, p. 41.
5.   Reported in R. Meyer (ed.), *Sören Kierkegaard und sein Verhältnis zu 'ihr'*
     (Stuttgart: Juncker, 1905), p. viii.

6. *The Corsair's* articles and cartoons, as well as Kierkegaard's published and unpublished responses, are collated in S. Kierkegaard, *The Corsair Affair*, trans and ed. Hong and Hong (Princeton: Princeton University Press, 1982).
7. For Kierkegaard's view of the city see my '*Poor Paris!*' *Kierkegaard's Critique of the Spectacular City* (Berlin: Walter de Gruyter, 1998).
8. S. Kierkegaard, *Two Ages: a Literary Review* (Princeton: Princeton University Press, 1978), pp. 68, 77, 80–1.
9. S. Kierkegaard, *Attack upon 'Christendom'* (Princeton: Princeton University Press, 1944), p. 7.
10. S. Kierkegaard, *Concluding Unscientific Postscript* (Princeton: Princeton University Press, 1992), p. 118.
11. Ibid., pp. 313–14.
12. Ibid., p. 332.
13. From unpublished journal notes quoted in S. Kierkegaard, *Fear and Trembling* and *Repetition* (Princeton: Princeton University Press, 1983), p. 324.
14. Kierkegaard, *Postscript*, p. 342.
15. *Fear and Trembling/Repetition*, p. 131.
16. *Postscript*, p. 199.
17. Ibid., p. 202.
18. Ibid., p. 203.
19. S. Kierkegaard, *The Concept of Irony* (Princeton: Princeton University Press, 1989), p. 277.
20. Ibid., p. 276.
21. Ibid., pp. 284–5.
22. H. L. Martensen, 'Fata Morgana af J. L. Heiberg', in *Maanedskrift for Literatur* (19) 1838, p. 367.
23. S. Kierkegaard, *Early Polemical Writings* (Princeton: Princeton University Press, 1990), p. 64.
24. *Two Ages*, pp. 92–3.
25. S. Kierkegaard, *The Point of View* (London: Oxford University Press, 1939), p. 24.
26. Ibid., p. 25.
27. *Fear and Trembling/Repetition*, p. 154.
28. S. Kierkegaard, *Either/Or* (Princeton: Princeton University Press, 1992), Vol. 2, pp. 186–7.
29. Ibid., p. 188.
30. Ibid.
31. S. Kierkegaard, *The Concept of Anxiety* (Princeton: Princeton University Press, 1980), p. 41.
32. Like the cognate German term *Schuld*.
33. *Either/Or*, Vol. 2, pp. 216, 217.
34. Ibid., Vol. 1, p. 26.
35. Kierkegaard, *Fear and Trembling/Repetition*, p. 36.
36. Ibid., pp. 39–41.
37. Kierkegaard, *Postscript*, pp. 440–1.
38. S. Kierkegaard, *Philosophical Fragments* (Princeton: Princeton University Press, 1985), p. 37.

39.   S. Kierkegaard, *The Sickness Unto Death* (Princeton: Princeton University Press, 1980), p. 22.
40.   For recent works that emphasize the theme of communication in Kierkegaard's work, see my *Kierkegaard: the Aesthetic and the Religious*; also R. Poole, *Kierkegaard: the Indirect Communication* (Charlottesville: University of Virginia Press, 1993); M. Strawser, *Both/And. Reading Kierkegaard from Irony to Edification* (New York: Fordham University Press, 1997).

4

What Russian Boys Talk About

The year is 1849. The sun has just lifted above the horizon on a hazy December day in St Petersburg. A procession of 23 black carriages is starkly silhouetted against the foot-deep snow, as it comes to a halt in the middle of the large military parade ground known as the Semyonovsky Square. Out of each carriage steps a bewildered prisoner, accompanied by an armed guard. Nearly all are emaciated, dishevelled and unshaven. Looking about them they begin to recognize comrades whom they have not seen for the eight months since their arrest. They are members of a network of reading and discussion groups concerned with radical ideas and, in some cases, with plans to print and disseminate forbidden literature. In the middle of the parade ground is a large wooden platform, near to which are four stakes driven into the ground. After a brief moment in which the prisoners are allowed to greet each other, they are lined up and led past a large contingent of troops to the platform. They are made to stand in two rows as an official passes along the rows, reading out to each man singly the indictment against him and the sentence passed. Although there is some variation in the charge, the same sentence is repeated again and again: 'The Field Criminal Court has condemned all to death by firing squad, and on 19 December His Majesty the Emperor personally wrote: "Confirmed."' This process takes half an hour. The prisoners are then invited to make their confession – in other words, to repudiate their 'crimes' – but all refuse, although they kiss the cross held before them by the priest. Finally, the first three men are seized and led away to be tied to the stakes, including Mikhail Butashevich-Petrashevsky, the leader of the group and the one by whose name they are collectively known – 'The Petrashevsky Circle'. Petrashevsky pushes back the hood that has been pulled over his head and stares defiantly at the firing squad which now takes aim. After what seems like an interminably long silence a drum-roll strikes up. But what is being beaten is a retreat. The guns are lowered, the three men untied and returned to the company of their comrades. A horseman arrives at the gallop and reads out to the prisoners that their sentences have been commuted by an act of imperial clemency and that, instead, they are to serve varying terms of hard labour and exile. Yet their humiliation is not quite finished. Each must kneel and have a sword broken over his head to symbolize the loss of civil rights. Then they must put on convict clothes and, finally, the chains that they will have to wear for the term of their sentence are unceremoniously heaped onto the platform and although it will not be until Christmas Day, three days later, that they have to put them on, Petrashevsky once again performs an act of defiance by stepping forward and fixing his own chains.

On the scale of both pre- and post-revolutionary government terror in Russia this incident does not perhaps rank highly. The reason that it has become one of the most widely-known instances of Tsarist oppression is that one of those who suffered this mock execution was to become one of Russia's greatest writers: Fyodor Mikhailovitch Dostoevsky. Dostoevsky's crime had been to participate in the discussion evenings organized by Petrashevsky and, in particular, to have read aloud a letter written by the critic Vissarion Belinsky to the writer Gogol. In his letter Belinsky had lambasted Gogol for defending serfdom and had bitterly denounced the role of the Orthodox Church in legitimating Tsarist autocracy. Dostoevsky was also suspected of being amongst those who were preparing to set up an illegal press. Not surprisingly, the whole event marked Dostoevsky for life. Many years later, in his novel *The Idiot*, he gave an only slightly fictionalised account of his experiences and thoughts on that day.

He wanted to realize as quickly and clearly as possible how it could be that now he existed and was living and in three minutes he would be *something* – someone or something. But what? Where? He meant to decide all that in those two minutes! Not far off there was a church, and the gilt roof was glittering in the bright sunshine. He remembered that he stared very persistently at that roof and the light flashing from it; he could not tear himself away from the light. It seemed to him that those rays were his new nature and that in three minutes he would somehow melt into them ... The uncertainty and feeling of aversion for that new thing which would be and was just coming was awful. But he said that nothing was so dreadful at that time as the constant thought, 'What if I were not to die! What if I could go back to life – what eternity! And it would all be mine! I would turn every minute into an age; I would lose nothing, I would count every minute as it passed, I would not waste one! (*I*, pp. 56–7)

The situation of the individual consciousness, brought to the brink of death and face-to-face with the impenetrable uncertainty as to whether what awaited him was simple extinction or some other kind of life was to be a recurrent theme in Dostoevsky's writing. So too was the world of violence and crime with which he became familiar during his four years' penal servitude, and the following four years as a soldier without civil rights in Semipalatinsk (a semi-frontier town in Central Asia). For whatever convergences there were between their intellectual passions and commitments, Dostoevsky's life-experience was of a very different kind from that of Kierkegaard. As with Kierkegaard, however, the legend of Dostoevsky's life has contributed crucially (and often misleadingly) to the reception of his work. Let us therefore look briefly at this life, at the sequence of events that brought him to the edge of the scaffold and at what happened afterwards.

Dostoevsky was born in 1821 – and it is striking in this connection that, although only eight years younger than Kierkegaard, the circumstances of his imprisonment and exile meant that the works for which he is best known run from the 1860s through to 1880, a generation later than Kierkegaard's key works (nearly all from the 1840s). Dostoevsky's father was a doctor at a hospital for the poor in Moscow who, during Dostoevsky's childhood, acquired the status of minor nobility and purchased a small estate. Dostoevsky, together with his brother Mikhail, was sent to the Military Engineering School in St Petersburg, shortly after the death of their mother. In 1839 they were to receive the further news that their father had died. It seemed at the time – (and they both believed it – that he had been murdered by the peasants on his estate) Many commentators see in this the roots of the theme of parricide that was to be so central in *The Brothers Karamazov*.

Throughout his childhood and schooldays, Dostoevsky was an enthusiastic and promiscuous reader. Victor Hugo, Georges Sand and Balzac were strong influences (he translated *Le Père Goriot* from

French into Russian), as well as Sir Walter Scott and Friedrich Schiller. Along with Schiller he imbibed other sources for German idealism which entered into Russian intellectual life in the 1830s and 1840s. After graduating from the Engineering School he left the army in 1844 to devote himself entirely to writing and in 1845 saw his first novel, *Poor Folk*, published. It was a considerable success and received the very favourable attention of Vissarion Belinsky, the critic, and N. A. Nekrasov, another leading writer. This reception gave Dostoevsky an entrée into fashionable literary circles and exposed him to the radical end of contemporary Russian thought. However, he seems to have made a bad impression on many of the *literati* and quarrelled particularly with Turgenev. His second novel, *The Double* (1846), although now seen as anticipating many of the most important psychological themes of his later work, was not a success.

It was in this period that Dostoevsky began his association with the Petrashevsky circle, where the ideas of the French utopian socialist Fourier were the main focus of conversation, along with such figures as David Friedrich Strauss and Feuerbach. Dostoevsky was probably drawn to the more extreme edge of the Petrashevsky circle and was associated with a sub-group known as the Palm-Durov circle who were perhaps planning some form of direct action against the autocratic government and the institution of serfdom. At four o'clock in the morning on 23 April 1849, however, their plans were dashed, as Dostoevsky and the others were arrested in a series of dawn raids. Months of imprisonment and interrogations followed before the mock execution and exile.

The state of Dostoevsky's religious convictions throughout this period has been much discussed. Although the contents of Belinsky's letter to Gogol (the letter that Dostoevsky's judges found so offensive) contained a damning indictment of the Orthodox Church, many of those in the Petrashevsky Circle held to a kind of quasi-humanist Christianity, interpreting the figure of Christ and the gospel message in a manner amenable to their egalitarian and utopistic views (Christ as the first socialist) Yet, as the account of the mock execution in *The Idiot* suggests, Dostoevsky had no clear views regarding the ultimate destiny of the individual at this time.

A significant moment in the course of Dostoevsky's journey into exile occurred when he was given a New Testament by one of a group of remarkable women whose husbands, known as the Decembrists, had been exiled in an earlier uprising and who devoted themselves to bringing aid and comfort to prisoners en route to Siberia. This New Testament was to be virtually all the reading that Dostoevsky had over the next four years, and is physically described in a crucial scene in *Crime and Punishment* when Raskolnikov forces the prostitute Sonia to read the story of the raising of Lazarus to him. The experience of prison also transformed his understanding of the Russian people. Much of the theory of his fellow 'conspirators' involved an extremely naive belief in the goodness of the common people, a belief that looked on their criminality and drunkenness as products of their environment. Dostoevsky's own novel *Poor Folk* can be read as a part of this tendency. In prison, however, living alongside them in crowded barracks, he experienced at first hand the brutality of many of these 'common people' – as well as the utter contempt in which the peasants regarded intellectuals such as himself. In the face of this reality there could be no sentimental glorification. Yet, paradoxically, it was immediately in the wake of a particularly brutal brawl in the barracks that Dostoevsky had a kind of conversion experience through which he did come to believe in the profound goodness and humanity that coexisted with the coarseness and cruelty of peasant life. Most of what he wrote subsequently about the poor – urban or rural – reflects this profound ambiguity. On the one hand, Dostoevsky enters far more deeply than Tolstoy into the reality of the lives of the poor and hides nothing of their moral failings. On the other hand, there is none the less a deep faith in the people, which, in his final years, acquires an almost Christological significance, as the Russian people come to be envisaged in some mysterious way as Christ-bearers. It is, moreover, a striking feature of many of his novels (and one to which we shall return) that many of the most 'Christian' thoughts are put into the mouths of the most debased characters. For Dostoevsky as for Kierkegaard degradation and suffering come to be seen as a mode of the incognito of Christ, although far more graphically portrayed than in Kierkegaard.

Another significant development in the course of Dostoevsky's imprisonment was the onset of epilepsy. Again, his experience of epilepsy was to contribute to his wrestling with religious questions. Especially in *The Idiot* (whose eponymous hero, Prince Leon Myshkin, is also a sufferer) Dostoevsky explores the question as to whether the extraordinary feelings of insight into the meaning of life that he experienced immediately before an attack were really visions of a higher reality – or merely symptoms of sickness.

After his release Dostoevsky had to serve a period of military duty in the remote region of Kirghizstan. During this time he began to write again and entered on what was to prove a disastrous marriage to the widow Maria Dmitrievna Isayeva. Apart from the fact of her having given favourable attention to another suitor, she turned out to be extremely unstable and irritable – it is not unlikely that the character of the hysterical Katerina Ivanovna Marmeladova in *Crime and Punishment* is in part based upon her. Additionally, her son by a previous marriage was to make financial demands on Dostoevsky for many years after his mother's death.

In 1859 Dostoevsky returned to St Petersburg and began to establish a second career as a writer and journalist. His fictionalised memoirs *From the House of the Dead* were successful and the novel *The Insulted and the Injured* proved acceptable, if not a triumph. The political situation was still unstable and although Dostoevsky was now a supporter of tsardom his status as a former political prisoner meant that journalism was an extremely insecure career. During this time there was a wave of arson attacks in St Petersburg and the radical Feuerbachian writer Chernyshevsky was arrested and sent to prison. Chernyshevsky's novel *What is to be Done?* set out the vision of a scientifically managed democratic future, in which people would live collectively in open relationships in 'phalansteries', glass and steel constructs modelled on London's Crystal Palace. Dostoevsky's critique of such visionary imaginings was to be famously enshrined in his novella *Notes from Underground*, but before this he embarked upon an extended period of travel, visiting Western Europe (an experience that strengthened his nationalistic feelings) and indulging in an impossible affair with Apollinaria Suslova, a young woman of strong radical views, whom Dostoevsky pursued to Paris and Italy only to be refused. In the midst of this his wife, whom he had left ill in Moscow, finally died, a death followed later that year (1864) by that of his supportive and trusted brother, Mikhail.

In the midst of these personal crises he published *Notes from Underground*, a short work, but one which many see as the beginning of his mature authorship and one which introduces the existential anti-hero onto the stage of European literature. This is how the underground man introduces himself:

I am a sick man ... I am a spiteful man. I am an unattractive man. I believe my liver is diseased. However ... I refuse to consult a doctor from spite. That you will probably not understand. Well, I understand it, though. Of course I can't explain who it is precisely that I am mortifying in this case by my spite: I am perfectly well aware that I cannot 'pay out' the doctors by not consulting them; I know better than any one that I am only injuring myself and no one else. But still, if I don't have treatment, it is from spite. My liver is bad, well – let it get worse!¹

As his monologue continues we learn how his 'spite' has manifested itself on other occasions: how he forced himself on a group of old acquaintances and made a complete fool of himself at their reunion and how he humiliated a prostitute whom he had led to believe he was in love with. We also have from him an indictment of the utilitarian optimism of Chernyshevsky and he offers the example of his own 'spite' as proof of the impossibility of any purely humanistic utopia.

Despite the importance of *Notes from Underground* in Dostoevsky's development and in the development of modernist literature, it did little in the short term to alleviate Dostoevsky's increasingly chaotic financial circumstances, aggravated by a passion for roulette developed on his travels in Europe. *Crime and Punishment* was published in 1866 and met with enormous success, but by this time Dostoevsky's predicament was truly horrendous and he had entered into an extraordinarily risky contract with his publisher to the effect that unless he delivered a new novel by 1 November 1866 he would lose the rights to all his previous work. By the beginning of October he had made little progress and was persuaded to take on a young stenographer, Anna Grigorievna Snitkina. She recalls that at her interview Dostoevsky offered her a cigarette, which she refused – this was in fact a test to see whether she was perhaps a nihilist, smoking being a badge of left-wing views amongst young Russian women in the 1860s! Luckily, Anna Grigorievna did not smoke and was therefore given the job. The manuscript – of the novella *The Gambler* – was finished within hours of the deadline. No less importantly, Dostoevsky shortly afterwards proposed to Anna Grigorievna and was accepted.

Even with her support, however, he was unable immediately to conquer his gambling habits, and during the extended period which the couple now spent abroad they were often reduced to the most abject penury on account of his losses at the roulette table.

This further spell abroad reinforced Dostoevsky's suspicion of the West, which he came to identify with the spirit of scientific materialism in intellectual and in political life.

During this time Dostoevsky completed *The Idiot*, perhaps his darkest and most tragic novel, and it was not until 1871 that he returned to Russia, having finally broken his gambling habit. Dostoevsky worked on his next novel, *The Possessed* (also known as *The Devils*), as Anna Grigorievna worked on bringing their financial and household affairs into order. In 1875 Dostoevsky published *A Raw Youth* and in 1880 *The Brothers Karamazov*. Through the 1870s his stature as one of Russia's major writers was becoming ever more secure, helped by his newspaper column *The Diary of a Writer*, in which he discussed literary, political and a variety of social issues, strongly slanted in the direction of nationalism on political issues, yet also containing sometimes generous appraisals of literary opponents as well as short stories that contain some remarkable moments of existential psychology. In 1880 he delivered a public address on the occasion of festivities in honour of Pushkin that caused a tremendous stir and made him the literary hero of the hour. He died in January 1881, holding the New Testament given to him by the Decembrist wives. Tens of thousands followed his body to its final burial.

Dramatic in a way that Kierkegaard's was not, Dostoevsky's life befits his impassioned yet complex exploration of the shadow side of the human situation and his search for God in that darkness. None the less, we must beware of painting too lurid a picture of that life. The mock execution, the time of imprisonment and exile, gambling, poverty and a number of unfortunate relationships with women were all real ingredients of it. Yet there is a whiff of mythology about aspects of Dostoevsky's life that needs to be dispelled. There has, for instance, been an occasional tendency to seek biographical roots not only for the motif of parricide but also for the allusions to the sexual abuse of young girls that feature in several novels. There is however no more real evidence for such allegations than there would be to ascribe the crimes of a Macbeth or a Richard III to Shakespeare or (perhaps more relevantly) of a Bill Sykes to Charles Dickens.[2] It is scarcely surprising that, given the life he in fact lived and those amongst whom he lived in prison, Dostoevsky should have been deeply fascinated with the limit-situations of crime and punishment and should have made of them the stage on which he was to explore 'the eternal questions, of the existence of God and immortality', the things that Ivan Karamazov declared to be the sole topics of interest to 'the most original Russian boys' (*BK*, p. 239).[3]

II

As with Kierkegaard, we shall begin by looking at the critical aspect of Dostoevsky's thought. As we do so we shall find that many of Kierkegaard's targets reappear as the targets of Dostoevsky's criticism also, if somewhat mutated in their transposition to Russian soil. Yet, as we have seen, although Russia was regarded by its own intelligentsia and by many in the West as hopelessly backward, the ideas of the German idealists and their radical critics, as well as the Romantic literature of Germany and France and the thought of French socialists were known to intellectuals in Russia and, as Dostoevsky himself argued in books such as *Notes from Underground* and *The Possessed*, were having a decisive impact on the very fabric of society in Russia, as well as redefining the context in which 'the eternal questions' were asked.

Like Kierkegaard, Dostoevsky was extremely critical of the belief that human beings could be understood purely in terms of reason and rationality. This was no less true when rationality took a materialistic, as opposed to an idealistic, form. What was inadequate was any approach that objectified the human subject to the point where its actions were understood as quantifiable – and therefore also predictable and manipulable.

Against those who believe that human actions are explicable in terms of the laws of nature that are as consistent as the laws of mathematics and no less indifferent to the wishes and aspirations of human subjectivity, the underground man exclaims:

> what do I care for the laws of nature and arithmetic, when for some reason I dislike those laws and the fact that twice two makes four? Of course I cannot break through the wall by battering my head against it if I really have not the strength to knock it down, but I am not going to be reconciled to it simply because it is a stone wall and I have not the strength.[4]

The utopia of Chernyshevsky and those who share his views is, however, a utopia built precisely on belief in the total explicability

of human behaviour *à la* mathematical science. Putting words in the
mouths of his opponents the underground man continues:

> Then ... new economic relations will be established, all ready-
> made and worked out with mathematical exactitude, so that
> every possible question will vanish in the twinkling of an eye,
> simply because every possible answer to it will be provided.
> Then the 'Palace of Crystal' will be built. Then ... In fact those
> will be halcyon days.[5]

Behind this view the underground man sees the ancient principle
of Platonic philosophy: that reason is virtue and that the only
impediment to living the good life is ignorance as to the nature of
the good. But, he asks, can all human interests be known? Aren't
there perhaps some things that matter essentially to us that resist
all systems of classification – a good that consists precisely in that
which 'breaks down all our classifications, and continually shatters
every system constructed by lovers of mankind for the benefit
of mankind.'[6] Even were the perfect society to be established, he
predicts that

> in the midst of general prosperity a gentleman with an ignoble,
> or rather with a reactionary and ironical, countenance were to
> arise and, putting his arms akimbo, say to us all: 'I say, gentle-
> men, hadn't we better kick over the whole show and scatter ratio-
> nalism to the winds, simply to send these logarithms to the devil
> and to enable us to live once more at our own sweet foolish will!'[7]

What, then, is this 'highest good' that insists on being the thorn
in the flesh of all systems of rational classification and calculation?
It is, the underground man says, 'One's own free unfettered choice,
one's own caprice, however wild it may be, one's own fancy
worked up at times to frenzy – is that very "most advantageous
advantage" ... which comes under no classification ...'[8] Even if he is
faced with the counter-claim that what looks (and perhaps even
feels) like the exercise of such free volition is itself no more than the
by-product of the laws of nature, he insists that a man has the right
to claim to be able to act stupidly against his own best interests for
the sake of his free volition.
    In any case, he asks, what is the evidence for claiming that
human history exhibits some rational idea? War and cruelty are

endemic and even enlightened nations and individuals are as capable of crimes against humanity as Attila or Stenka Razin.[9]

It would be premature to identify Dostoevsky himself with the views of the underground man, yet his insistence on the impossibility of understanding the human situation in terms of what Dostoevsky elsewhere called 'the Euclidean mind' is a pervasive theme in his writings. (Even if Dostoevsky himself hoped that the darkness of this capricious will could be opened up to the light of the gospel and the love of God, he could not see such a conversion as deriving from any sort of rational or historical or psychological necessity.) (Here we may reflect on the principle previously alluded to, that Dostoevsky often puts important truths in the mouths of his most flawed characters. The fact that Dostoevsky himself in an important sense can 'see through' the underground man – and allows us as readers to 'see through' his pathetic self-dramatization – does not justify us in rejecting everything the underground man says.)[10]

The case against utilitarian calculation is not simply that it fails to explicate either the best or the worst in humanity. It is that it can itself be used to legitimate violence and murder, and the logic involved in such legitimation becomes a key issue in *Crime and Punishment*.

Rodion Raskolnikov, the central character of this novel, is sitting in a bar listening to a conversation between a student and a young officer. They are talking about an old woman, known to Raskolnikov, who makes her living as a pawnbroker. The student argues that with the money made in such a cruel fashion by such a heartless and selfish and socially superfluous old woman many, many lives could be vastly improved:

> Hundreds, thousands perhaps, might be set on the right path; dozens of families saved from destitution, from ruin, from vice . . Kill her, take her money and with the help of it devote oneself to the service of humanity and the good of all. What do you think, would not one tiny crime be wiped out by thousands of good deeds? For one life thousands would be saved from corruption and decay. One death, and a hundred lives in exchange – it's simple arithmetic![11]

As fortune would have it, this conversation precisely mirrors the course of Raskolnikov's own thoughts. Indeed, it encapsulates the argument of an article he has had published in which, as he explains it himself, he argued that

> an 'extraordinary' man has the right ... that is not an official right, but an inner right to decide in his own conscience to overstep ... certain obstacles [although] only in case it is essential for the practical fulfilment of his idea (sometimes, perhaps, of benefit to the whole of humanity).[12]

In fact, he regards this as typical of the behaviour of those such as Lycurgus, Solon, Mohammed and Napoleon who come to be regarded by subsequent generations as benefactors of humanity.

The course of the novel – in which Raskolnikov kills the old woman but also, unintentionally, her sister, whose mistreatment at the hands of the old woman was ironically one of his arguments in favour of committing the murder in the first place – demonstrates that this logic is no more than a mask for a profound selfishness that, in the closing pages of the novel, is depicted as a terrifying plague in which men are attacked by microbes with intelligence and will:

> Men attacked by them became at once mad and furious. But never had men considered themselves so intellectual and so completely in possession of the truth as these sufferers, never had they considered their decisions, their scientific conclusions, their moral convictions so infallible.[13]

In *The Idiot* the absurd drunkard Lebedev goes further and arouses the laughter of his companions when he ascribes to the Devil the utilitarian logic for which self-preservation is the highest good. This implication is, in fact, fundamental to the whole conception of *The Possessed,* in which the political manifestation of scientific utilitarianism in Russian nihilism is seen through the lens of the biblical story of Jesus casting out the legion of devils from the possessed man in the region of the Gerasenes – and it is this story that governs the conceptual logic of the novel.

It is, curiously, the Devil himself who, in conversation with Ivan Karamazov, best explains how the vision of a universal scientific utopia gets entangled with individual hubris. His arguments are taken from a piece of Ivan's own writing called 'The Geological Cataclysm' and he begins by reminding Ivan of the vision of a future atheistic society, the society of the man-god who, untrammelled by thoughts of immortality or transcendence, extends 'his conquest of nature infinitely by his will and his science' (*BK*, p. 688). But then the problem is raised as to how society will make the transition from its present state of unenlightened ignorance to such a future. According to 'The Geological Cataclysm', it soon becomes obvious that 'owing to man's inveterate stupidity, this cannot come about for at least a thousand years'. So what is someone who lives in the midst of the present disorder and is surrounded by superstition and yet who already understands how society *should* be regulated to do? Why should he not, even now, 'legitimately order his life as he pleases, on the new principles. In that sense, "all things are lawful" for him'. He is thus justified in arrogating to himself the role that collective humanity is envisaged as enjoying in the utopian future and so this 'new man' may – 'even if he is the only one in the world' – become the man-god, 'and promoted to his new position, he may light-heartedly overstep all the barriers of the old morality of the old slave-man, if necessary' (*BK*, p. 689). But as the Devil caustically comments, 'That's all very charming; but if you want to swindle, why do you want a moral sanction for doing it?' (*BK*, p. 689). Like Raskolnikov, Ivan must learn through the events of the novel that the theoretical justification of the liberty of the extraordinary man has terrible existential consequences, consequences that lead directly to the murder of his father and his own breakdown.

But the ideology of the man-god does not merely have moral and political consequences. It also has religious consequences – precisely because its deepest roots are in the spirit of Luciferian rebellion.

These religious (or anti-religious) roots are powerfully stated by the nihilist Kirillov in *The Possessed*. Kirillov's 'idea' is that human beings are held back from realizing their true freedom by the fear of death. It is this fear – a fear directed both to the pain of death itself and to the prospect of a punishment for sin after death – that ultimately keeps humanity in thrall to religious belief and prevents it from living out its potential liberty. God, according to Kirillov 'is the pain of the fear of death'.[14] He claims therefore that 'There will be full freedom when it will be just the same to live or not to live. That's the goal for all.' When Kirillov's interlocutor objects that people fear death simply as the obverse of their love for life, Kirillov snaps back that this is simply an illusion: 'Life is pain, life is terror, and man is unhappy.'[15]

But how can this be changed? All it needs, according to Kirillov, is that one man should have the courage to commit suicide for the sake of freedom *and for no other reason whatsoever.* 'He who dares to kill himself has found out the secret of the deception. There is no freedom beyond; that is all and there is nothing beyond. He who dares kill himself is God.'[16] If, that is, he kills himself simply as a demonstration of his own freedom of action and not because he is ill, unhappy or afraid or serving some political or religious idea (which, in Kirillov's view, accounts for all previous suicides). We should also note that it is crucial to his case that it is not a matter of simple atheism. It is a matter of man becoming himself a new or an alternative god. Later he is to declare, 'I can't understand how an atheist could know that there is no God and not kill himself on the spot. To recognize that there is no God and not to recognize at the same instant that one is God oneself is an absurdity ...'[17]

Once again, the unfolding of the novel demonstrates the problematic nature of such deceptively simple logic. In Kirillov's final speeches he reveals an important source of his own deep unhappiness: that even Christ, whom he describes as 'the loftiest of all one earth ... that which gave meaning to life' had to suffer death and final extinction; therefore, he says, 'all the planet is a lie and rests on a lie and mockery'.[18] His will to set himself up as the man-god, then, is itself the reflex of a disappointed faith. Moreover, even though he does shoot himself, the manner in which this happens is far from heroic and his final act – writing a suicide note falsely taking responsibility for the murder of Shatov – is rendered useless by the subsequent confession of another member of the nihilist circle. His death is both miserable and in vain.

It is, however, Ivan Karamazov who is Dostoevsky's best-known representative of religious nihilism. Ivan shows himself to be well aware of the mismatch between the visions of the utopists and the reality of the world, nor is he able to believe in a future state in which this discord could be resolved – or, rather (and as he puts it himself), 'though all that may come to pass, I don't accept it. I won't accept it' (*BK*, p. 241). Therefore, he says, it is not God he cannot accept – it is the world created by God. He cannot think together the reality of a world in which there is the kind of suffering that he so eloquently and passionately details to his brother Alyosha and the idea of a supremely good divine creator. 'I have a Euclidian earthly mind ... Even if parallel lines do meet and I see it myself, I shall see it and say that they've met, but still I won't accept it'

(*BK*, pp. 240–1). The upshot is, as he puts it, 'It's not God that I don't accept, Alyosha, only I most respectfully return Him the ticket' (*BK*, p. 251).

Once more, however, Dostoevsky does not leave his character's world-view unquestioned. Over against Ivan's own statement of the case there is a steadily accumulating weight of evidence in the novel to suggest that – although one half of him desperately longs to believe (so that, like Kirillov, he may be described as an unhappy lover of religion) – he is himself implicated in the murder of his father and that his pose of being a critical observer is itself a self-deception. He is an actor, not an observer, and it is only as and when the standpoint of actor is recognised and accepted as one's own standpoint that the religious questions can be seen in their proper light. Even Ivan, for all the passion of his protest against the injustice of the suffering of children, is a nineteenth-century ratio-nalist whose thought is determined by his adherence to what Kierkegaard could have called the objective point of view, that is, the point of view of a detached and calculating observer, one who fails to take account of his own subjective involvement in what he observes.

Dostoevsky's critique of utilitarian reason then, is not simply limited to utilitarianism in the narrow sense. It is a critique of theory as such. What makes the theory of his radical contemporaries especially problematic, however, is precisely that it is a theory that it privileges the scientific approach to a hitherto unequalled degree.

Two further aspects of Dostoevsky's critique of reason may usefully be highlighted at this point.

The first is that although Dostoevsky's major novels target the radical left as chief culprits in the propagation of the ideology of the man-god, he makes it plain that they are, in effect, simply imple-menting the superficially more benign, more romantic, more senti-mental form of idealism popular in an earlier generation.

This is exemplified with particular clarity in the figures of Stepan and Peter Verkhovensky in *The Possessed*. Stepan, the father, is intro-duced as a failed historian of romantic and idealistic provenance, dedicated to 'lofty and exceptionally noble' ideas, which he sees exemplified in fifteenth-century European chivalry. Indeed, he has even had an article on the subject published 'in a progressive monthly review, which translated Dickens and advocated the views of George Sand ...'[19] Although Stepan continues to believe himself to be the guardian of a poetic view of life in the midst of an ever harsher and more abrasive intellectual and social milieu, we are put on our guard against the ultimate implications of these ideals by the narrator's description of one of Stepan Trofimovich's youthful poetic works.

> I find it difficult to describe the subject, for I really do not understand it. It is some sort of allegory in lyrical-dramatic form, recalling the second part of 'Faust'. The scene opens with a chorus of women, followed by a chorus of men, then a chorus of incorporeal powers of some sort, and at the end of all, a chorus of spirits not yet living but very eager to come to life.[20]

However, the conclusion, despite its absurd mixture of heterogeneous mythological elements anticipates the doctrine of the man-god:

> And finally, in the last scene we are suddenly shown the Tower of Babel, and certain athletes at last finish building it with a song of new hope, and when at last they complete the topmost pinnacle, the lord (of Olympia, let us say) takes flight in a comic fashion, and man, grasping the situation and seizing his place, at once begins a new life with new insight into things.[21]

Yet when Stepan Trofimovich is faced with the nihilistic cynicism of his son Peter he is affronted and, until the final dénouement of the novel, is incapable of recognizing the affinity between Peter's programme of political terror and his own 'Romantic' celebration of the powers of man. Such 'Schillerism' is also critiqued in *The Brothers Karamazov*, yet although Dostoevsky is ruthless in unmasking what he sees as the ideological implications of Schillerian idealism, he is never cynical about the aura of enthusiasm and hope expressed in it, and it is typical that it is to Stepan Trofimovich that he gives the task of naming the true character of the demonic possession that is afflicting Russia – albeit in a scene rich in comic elements.

The second comment is that, just as Kierkegaard (following Poul Martin Møller) seems to have recognized the irresistibility of levelling, so too Dostoevsky sometimes appears to suggest that the fever of nihilism will have to reach a crisis point before it is seen for what it really is. Perhaps it may be necessary for faith in God to disappear and for the godless society to come to pass before the truth of

religious faith can be reappropriated as a social reality. Although
the text is suggestive rather than definitive, something like this may
be the implication not only of Raskolnikov's dream of a new plague
devastating Europe, but also the vision of a new golden age enunci-
ated by the highly ambiguous aristocrat Versilov in *A Raw Youth*. In
this vision Versilov pictures a time when 'war is at an end and strife
has ceased'. Yet there is a melancholy tone in this utopia, for
although universal peace has finally arrived,

> men are left alone, according to their desire: the great idea of old
> [i.e. belief in God and immortality] has left them; the great source
> of strength that till then had nourished and fostered them was
> vanishing ... it was somehow the last day of humanity, and men
> suddenly understood that they were left quite alone, and at once
> felt terribly forlorn.

In this situation, he muses, they

> would begin to draw together more closely and more lovingly;
> they would clutch one another's hands, realizing that they were
> all that was left for one another! ... all the wealth of love lavished
> of old upon Him, who was immortal, would be turned upon the
> whole of nature, on the world, on men, on every blade of grass.
> They would inevitably grow to love the earth and life as they
> gradually became aware of their own transitory and finite
> nature ... On awakening they would hasten to kiss one another,
> eager to love, knowing that the days are short, and that is all that
> is left them ... Every child would know and feel that every one on
> earth was for him like a father or mother. 'To-morrow may be my
> last day,' each one would think, looking at the setting sun; 'but
> no matter, I shall die, but all they will remain and after them their
> children,' and that thought that they will remain, always as
> loving and as anxious over each other, would replace the thought
> of meeting beyond the tomb.

Yet, precisely when humanity will thus have learned to live without the old consolations of religion Versilov speaks of a new
epiphany of Christ:

> I always complete my picture with Heine's vision of 'Christ on
> the Baltic Sea'. I could not get on without Him, I could not help

imagining Him, in fact, in the midst of His bereaved people. He comes to them, holds out His hands, and asks them, 'How could they forget Him?' And then, as it were, the scales would fall from their eyes and there would break forth the great rapturous hymn of the new and last resurrection.[22]

The significance of this vision is hard to read, yet it gives an intriguing edge to Dostoevsky's critique of utopian socialism: for it suggests not only that it is founded upon rebellion, but also that, even if realized, it will not be able to provide an abiding framework for human existence. Even the advent of the planned society could not preclude a future new age of faith and it would therefore be premature to identify such a society as marking the end or fulfilment of history. Indeed, the fully humanistic society might itself prove to be only the forerunner of a new age of faith.

The critique of rationality is closely linked in Dostoevsky's work with the critique of the West. Although, curiously, Raskolnikov's dream speaks of a new plague spreading across Europe from the East, it is typical for Dostoevsky that the West is identified as the source of the new thinking that is responsible for the deracination and corruption of the Russian spirit. As suggested previously, his own unhappiness at having to live so long abroad on account of his financial problems exacerbated his hostility towards the West, and he especially disliked the way in which some Russians – notably Turgenev – took the part of the West against Russia. At times, especially in his journalism, this antipathy finds almost fantastic expression. Although he himself speaks, obscurely, of Russia as being charged with a salvific mission towards Europe, the way in which he draws the contrast between the spiritual integrity of Russia and the decadence of Europe invites a highly nationalistic interpretation. Such prejudices express themselves in many of the details of his novels. Smerdyakov, the Karamazov half-brother who kills the father and steals the money, is an enthusiastic Europhile, who wants to use the money to set up a restaurant in Paris. Stepan Trofimovich, as we have already seen, draws his inspiration from ideals of European chivalry. The image of the 'phalanstery', the Crystal Palace, is, of course, derived from the Great Exhibition in London and there are many other allusions to the European origin of many of the ideas critiqued in the novels.

On the other hand, although Dostoevsky verges at times on a semi-mystical view of the Russian people, several of his characters represent evil in a peculiarly Russian form – thus Rogojin in *The Idiot* and Murov in *The Landlady* (both, interestingly, characters connected by Dostoevsky to the sect of the Old Believers).

Dostoevsky's views on the relationship between East and West have a special resonance in the context of his comments on the Church and the contrast he draws on several occasions between Roman Catholicism and Orthodoxy. Although, notoriously, his Grand Inquisitor is a character drawn from the history of Roman Catholicism, perhaps his harshest words against the Roman Catholic Church are put in the mouth of Prince Myshkin:

> Roman Catholicism is even worse than atheism itself, in my opinion ... Atheism only preaches a negation, but Catholicism goes further: it preaches a distorted Christ ... it preaches the Antichrist ... Roman Catholicism cannot hold its position without universal political supremacy, and cries *'Non possumus!'* To my thinking Roman Catholicism is not even a religion, but simply the continuation of the Western Roman Empire, and everything in it is subordinated to that idea, faith to begin with ... they have bartered it all, all for money, for base earthly power! And is this not the teaching of Antichrist? How could atheism fail to come from them? Atheism has sprung from Roman Catholicism itself. (*I*, p. 546)

Although Myshkin quickly emphasizes that he is not speaking about individual Roman Catholics but about the *idea* or *essence* of Roman Catholicism, there can be no underestimating the seriousness of the charge.

It is a charge that is, of course, repeated at length in Ivan Karamazov's 'Poem of the Grand Inquisitor'. In this 'poem' Christ is depicted returning to earth and, more precisely, to Seville at the height of the Inquisition. He is recognised by the multitude and raises a girl from death, only to be immediately arrested by the Grand Inquisitor, who later visits him in prison and explains why it is that the Church has now taken upon itself the duty of burning heretics in apparent contradiction of the spirit of the gospels. The Inquisitor reminds Christ of the temptations in the wilderness and suggests that it was, after all, the tempter who had right on his side. Human beings, he claims, are not strong enough to subsist only on the Word of God, they need earthly bread, and whoever gives them bread will not only satisfy their physical hunger, he will also satisfy the need of the multitude to have someone to look up to, someone, even, to worship. The person who gives earthly bread delivers the people from the anxiety of freedom. As the Inquisitor puts it to Christ:

> I tell Thee that man is tormented by no greater anxiety than to find someone quickly to whom he can hand over that gift of freedom with which the ill-fated creature is born. But only one can appease their conscience can take over their freedom. In bread there was offered Thee an invincible banner; give bread, and man will worship thee, for nothing is more certain than bread. (*BK*, p. 261)

By refusing the temptation of earthly bread, Christ not only refused to deliver humanity from freedom: he made the burden of freedom still heavier. 'Didst Thou forget that man prefers peace, and even death, to freedom of choice in the knowledge of good and evil?' asks the Inquisitor (*BK*, p. 261).

The theme is rammed home in the Inquisitor's view of the second temptation. The temptation to perform a public miracle by throwing himself down from the Temple would have been an infallible way for Christ 'to conquer and to hold captive for ever the conscience of these impotent rebels for their happiness' (*BK*, p. 262). The three powers offered Christ in this temptation were miracle, mystery and authority. Yet Christ refused to require a faith that would be based solely on miracles, desiring only the faith that would be bestowed freely. In this, the Grand Inquisitor says, he has grossly overestimated the capacities of mankind. Far from making humanity happy, Christ's high standards have made them unhappy – until, that is, the Church intervened,

> to teach them that it's not the free judgement of their hearts, not love, that matters, but a mystery which they must follow blindly, even against their conscience...We have corrected Thy work and have founded it upon *miracle, mystery* and *authority*. And men rejoiced that they were again led like sheep, and that the terrible gift that had brought them such suffering [i.e. the gift of freedom] was, at last, lifted from their hearts. (*BK*, p. 264)

The ultimate secret of this 'correction' of Christ's work is then whispered by the Inquisitor: 'Listen, then. We are not working with

Thee but with *him*' (*BK*, p. 264). Even the revolt against religion, he suggests, provided that it does not result in the destruction of mankind through the war of all against all, will lead the survivors back to cower under the banner of the earthly Church that has given itself over to 'him'.

> We shall show them that they are weak, that they are only pitiful children, but that childlike happines is the sweetest of all ... And we shall take [their sins] upon ourselves, and they will adore us as their saviours who have taken on themselves their sins before God. (*BK*, pp. 266–7)

Ivan's poem seems exclusively to indict Roman Catholicism. Yet, just as Kierkegaard's attack upon the established Lutheran Church of Denmark contained a warning to all the Churches of Christendom, so too Dostoevsky's Grand Inquisitor is a warning to institutional Christianity as such – not excluding Russian Orthodoxy itself. Although Dostoevsky's own faith is distinctively Orthodox in colouring, there are many clues throughout his work that the Church *qua* Church (including the Orthodox Church) cannot resolve the spiritual crisis of contemporary humanity. In this respect it is important to notice that what Dostoevsky cites as the crucial element in the apostasy of the Roman Catholic Church – its willingness to wield the sword of Caesar in defence of religious doctrine – was applicable also to the Orthodox Church, integrated as that was into the structure of the state. After all, one of Dostoevsky's own 'crimes' was having read out Belinsky's Letter to Gogol, a letter that particularly attacked the Orthodox Church. To this it might be replied that the principal bearers of religious values in his novels – characters like Father Zossima in *The Brothers Karamazov* and Bishop Tikhon in *The Possessed* – are clearly identified with Orthodoxy. Yet this is only partially true. It is a recurrent theme of *The Brothers Karamazov* that although Zossima is both a genuinely saintly figure and a priest, his position is highly suspect within the ecclesiastical community. This is partly to do with his status as a *starets*, an elder, since, as Dostoevsky points out, the phenomenon of such elders was not fully favoured by the Church authorities. Even within his own monastic community there are those who regard Zossima as, in effect, too 'liberal'. Many are more inclined to regard the crazy but heroically ascetic Father Ferapont as the monastery's true saint. Ferapont is, however, depicted by

Dostoevsky as insane, subject to bizarre hallucinations in which he sees devils everywhere, and declaring that Zossima is himself possessed.

The issue comes to a head when Zossima dies. His supporters hope that God will give a sign of his sanctity by preserving his body from decomposition. When, however, the process of decomposition begins and the room where the body is being kept fills with the nauseating odour of decay, the Ferapont party sense triumph. Zossima was no saint and his success as spiritual counsellor merely a cult of personality. It is no coincidence that Zossima's wish for his pupil Alyosha is that Alyosha leave the monastery and live in the world without the support of monastic discipline and ritual. For Zossima understands that the external forms of monastic life can no longer determine or constrain the movement of the Spirit. In a similar vein, we should note that when Stavrogin, the evil genius of *The Possessed*, finally seeks spiritual advice from Bishop Tikhon, Tikhon – another saintly man in the mould of Zossima – is unable to give him clear direction. Indeed, precisely to the extent that he, Tikhon, acknowledges Stavrogin's freedom and responsibility, he has to leave Stavrogin to make his own ultimate decisions for himself.

To the extent that Orthodoxy is affirmed in Dostoevsky's writings, it is not as an institutional power but because of its participation in the humiliation of Russia and of the Russian people. In several of his works Dostoevsky alludes to the legend of Christ wandering through Russia, a legend enshrined in a poem by Dostoevsky's contemporary Tyutchev and quoted by Ivan:

> Bearing the Cross, in lavish dress
> Weary and worn, the Heavenly King
> Our mother, Russia, came to bless,
> And through our land went wandering.

(*BK*, p. 254)

Towards the end of his Pushkin speech, Dostoevsky returned to this legend: 'Let our land be poor, but this destitute land "Christ in a serf's garb, has traversed, to and fro, with blessing." Why shouldn't we embrace His ultimate word? Wasn't He Himself born in a manger?'[23] Allusion has already been made to Dostoevsky's habit of presenting truth concealed under a contrary exterior and we shall be exploring further examples of this later: but the point in this context is that it is precisely not the Church as a part of the conglomerate of State-and-Church that Dostoevsky regards as Christ-bearing, but the Church in its humiliation, in marginal representatives such as Father Zossima, and always in the closest proximity to the poor.

For Dostoevsky, as for Kierkegaard, then, the religious predicament of nineteenth-century humanity is shaped not only by the prevalence of a materialistic, objectifying and strictly this-worldly philosophy of life, but by the fact that anything – such as the Church – that might claim to offer an alternative to this philosophy is itself ambiguous. No public institution or external authority can deliver the individual from the terrible responsibility of freedom. To the extent that the underground man identifies freedom as the locus of the most crucial question facing contemporary humanity he is indeed the spokesman for Dostoevsky himself. Yet the underground man's conception of freedom seems to be purely negative. It is the freedom to say 'no' to progress, no to a utopia of phalansteries, technological management of the environment and open marriages. But can a genuinely Christian understanding of freedom limit itself to such a negative and reactive view? And, if not, what form might it take?

In turning now to explore how a freely chosen Christian faith might establish itself on a ground determined by the situation of nihilism we begin – paradoxically perhaps – with what for Dostoevsky is the supreme anti-value: death, death in its absolute finality, against which (if nihilism is correct) there can be no appeal. Yet it is precisely in such a confrontation with death that the task and the contours of a renewed and post-nihilistic faith begin to emerge.

[handwritten margin note: "public external authority delivers the individual from responsibility / possibility of freedom"]

[handwritten note below: "post-nihilistic faith emerges in confrontation w/ death"]

III

Given his own experience of mock execution, it is scarcely surprising that the theme of death and the terror of extinction should pervade Dostoevsky's work to the extent that it does. Allusions to this event are scattered throughout his authorship. So, for example, Prince Myshkin speaks of his abhorrence of the death penalty:

But the chief amd worst pain may not be in the bodily suffering but in one's knowing for certain that in an hour, and then in ten

minutes, and then in half a minute, and then now, at the very
moment, the soul will leave the body and that one will cease to
be a man and that that's bound to happen; the worst part of it is
that it's *certain*. (*I*, p. 19)

However, it is much more than mere autobiographical reminis-
cence, since it defines a crucial moment in Dostoevsky's whole
construction of the problematic of religious faith.

Nowhere is this more strongly expressed than in *The Idiot*, where
the question is focused on the image of Holbein's painting of the
dead Christ in the tomb, a painting that Dostoevsky had himself
seen on his travels in the West. When Prince Myshkin visits the sin-
ister Rogojin at the latter's house, he is struck by a reproduction of
this painting, '"Why,"' he exclaims, '"that picture, might make
some people lose their faith"' (*I*, p. 217). It also makes a profound
impact upon the anguished young nihilist, Ippolit Terentiev.
Terentiev acknowledges that Christian doctrine has always theoretically affirmed the reality of Christ's bodily suffering and death on
the cross – but Holbein's unflinching depiction of the saviour of the
world as, simply, a corpse, gives this dogmatic assertion a quite
different import. '"The question instinctively arises,"' says Ippolit,

if death is so awful and the laws of nature so mighty, how can
they be overcome? How can they be overcome when even He did
not conquer them, He who vanquished nature in His lifetime,
who exclaimed ... 'Lazarus, come forth!' and the dead man came
forth? Looking at such a picture, one conceives of nature in the
shape of an immense, merciless, dumb beast, or more correctly ... in the form of a huge machine of the most modern construction which, dull and insensible, has aimlessly clutched,
crushed and swallowed up a great priceless Being, a Being worth
all nature and its laws, worth the whole earth, which was created
perhaps solely for the sake of the advent of that Being. This picture expresses and unconsciously suggests to one the conception
of such a darl, insolent, unreasoning and eternal Power to which
everything is in subjection. (*I*, p. 410)

Ippolit goes on to speculate not only on the impact of Christ's physical death on his disciples, but also on how Christ Himself might
have acted if he had foreseen such an actuality: would he, Ippolit
wonders, have consented to mount the cross as he did?

And if such is the case with such an exceptional being, so much the more will death overwhelm and obliterate ordinary mortals. The sheer inexorability of the impersonal force revealed in the absoluteness of death drives Ippolit to a despair in which he anticipates the logic of Kirillov: to assert his freedom in the face of death in the only way left him – by suicide.

But the terror of death is not just a matter of the individual faced with extinction. That would be no more than infantile selfishness. The terror is, however, heightened by the realization that death freezes the brokenness of human relationships. If love is unfulfilled or betrayed in this life, then there will be no other chance for fulfilment or reconciliation. This is the implication of the ending of *The Insulted and the Injured*. One of the stories running through the novel is that of Nellie, a young girl whose mother was abandoned by her aristocratic seducer. Dying in abject poverty the mother asks Nellie to take a note to the father after she has died, imploring him to care for Nellie. If he does this, she says, '"perhaps then I shall forgive you, and at the judgement day I will stand before the throne of God and pray for your sins to be forgiven."'[24] But Nellie's hatred for the man who has caused her mother's suffering is too strong and she never takes the note, even though she herself is left defenceless on the streets of St Petersburg and is on the verge of being drawn into child prostitution. Her death seals the impossibility of reconciliation.

A similar point is made in the short story *The Meek One*. The story is in the form of a monologue spoken by the widower of a young wife who has killed herself by jumping out of the window of their apartment, driven to it by the way in which he has tormented her. As he tells the tale, it emerges that although his behaviour towards her was sadistic and dominatory, she was in fact the only person to give any meaning to his life. Loving her, he was unable to express that love except as cruelty. And now it is too late.

> Oh, nature! Men on earth are alone – this is the calamity! 'Is there in the field a living man?' – shouts the valiant Russian knight. I – not a knight – am shouting too, and no one responds. People say that the sun vivifies the universe, and look at it – isn't it a corpse? Everything is dead, and everywhere – nothing but corpses. Only men and, around them, silence – such is earth. 'Love each other.' – Who said this? Whose covenant is this? The pendulum is swinging insensibly and disgustingly. It's night – two o'clock. Her little

shoes stand by her dear little bed, as if awaiting her...No, seriously – tomorrow, when they carry her away, what will I do?[25]

The prospect of utter obliteration can, then, lead to despair, with regard both to the extinction of one's own consciousness and to the impossibility of mending the brokenness of human relationships in the face of death.

But this is not the end of the story. For Dostoevsky also suggests that it is when we come face to face with death that we can best realize the value of life. Recall that the most terrible thought in the mind of the one condemned to death is the thought that life might be returned to him, because each moment of life would then be charged with such an immense weight of significance. It is as illustrative of this idea that Father Zossima recalls the death of his brother, at a time when he, Zossima, was far from Christian faith. The brother, Markel, is a student of philosophy who regards religion as superstitious nonsense. Taken ill with consumption it becomes clear that death is imminent. He ignores his mother's pleas to take the sacrament until, suddenly, on the Tuesday of Holy Week, he agrees to go to church with her – only for her sake, he insists. But, then, as his illness rapidly worsens, a spiritual change comes over him. He allows his old nurse to light the candle in front of the icon: "'Light it, light it, dear,'" he says. "'I was a wretch to have prevented you doing it. You are praying when you light the lamp, and I am praying when I rejoice seeing you. So we are praying to the same God'" (*BK*, p. 296). He goes on to speak of the joy of life, and when asked how he can talk of joy in the midst of so much suffering, he tells his mother that "'...life is paradise, and we are all in paradise, but we won't see it, if we would, we should have heaven on earth the next day.'" He tells the servants that he does not deserve to be waited on by them: "'If it were God's will for me to live, I would wait on you, for all men should wait on one another'" (*BK*, p. 297). His sense of obligation towards others reaches extraordinary levels:

> 'every one of us has sinned against all men, and I more than any...believe me, everyone is really responsible to all men for all men and for everything...why do we quarrel, try to outshine each other and keep grudges against each other? Let's go straight into the garden, walk and play there, love, appreciate, and kiss each other, and glorify life.'

He even turns to the birds:

> 'Birds of heaven, happy birds, forgive me, for I have sinned against you too … there was such a glory of God all about me; birds, trees, meadows, sky, only I lived in shame and dishonoured it all and did not notice the beauty and glory … If I have sinned against everyone, yet all forgive me, too, and that's heaven. Am I not in heaven now?' (*BK*, pp. 297–8)

Death, then, can teach us the urgency of spiritual renewal – an idea touched on in Versilov's vision of a future golden age in which humanity is united in mutual care and love *precisely by virtue of a collective consciousness of mortality.*

It is in this context, perhaps, that we should read the ending of *The Brothers Karamazov*, as Alyosha addresses the friends of the dead boy Ilusha:

> there is nothing higher and stronger and more wholesome and good for life in the future than some good memory … and if one has only one good memory left in one's heart, even that may some time be the means of saving us … however bad we may become – which God forbid! – yet, when we recall how we buried Ilusha, how we loved him in his last days, and how we have been talking like friends all together, at this stone, the cruellest and most mocking of us – if we do become so – will not dare to laugh inwardly at having been kind and good at this moment! … and who has united us in this kind, good feeling which we shall remember all our lives? Who if not Ilusha, the good boy, the dear boy, precious to us for ever! Let us never forget him. May his memory live for ever in our hearts from this time forth! (*BK*, pp. 819–20)

Ilusha had earlier been an outcast, tormented by the other boys on account of his father's grotesque behaviour, but Alyosha's speech sums up a process of reconciliation that has given the boys a new consciousness of the implications of their mortality and the need to practise love and compassion.

Yet the moral conversion of Zossima's brother and Alyosha's appeal on behalf of mutual charity fall short of a full answer to the ultimate absurdity of death: that we shall each of us dissolve back into inanimate matter. Even if believers and unbelievers can unite in acknowledging the urgency of practising forgiveness and love in the face of their common mortality, believers still have to face the question of those sufferings that cannot be resolved by such practice. The question left unanswered is that of theodicy: how can we believe in the final vindication of a good, creator God in the light of the cruelty and horror of life in the world? The moral improvement of some individuals can never be enough to justify the suffering that we see and, unless we are able to believe in some future state, those failed relationships that are rendered final by death will never find reconciliation.

It is Ivan Karamazov who most eloquently represents the case on behalf of suffering humanity against God. Although he lists examples of cruelty on a grand scale, the essence of his argument requires no more than a single instance such as that which he tells at length about a small boy torn to death in front of his mother by his master's hounds for the crime of having thrown a stone that accidentally hurt the paw of the master's favourite dog. 'Listen!' he says to Alyosha,

> I took the case of children only to make my case clearer. Of the other tears of humanity with which the earth is soaked from its crust to its centre, I will say nothing. I have narrowed my subject on purpose ... Men are themselves to blame, I suppose; they were given paradise, they wanted freedom, and stole fire from heaven, though they knew they would become unhappy, so there is no need to pity them ... But then there are the children, and what am I to do about them? ... If all must suffer to pay for the eternal harmony, what have the children to do with it? ... I understand solidarity in sin among men. I understand solidarity in retribution too; but there can be no such solidarity with children. And if it is really true that they must share responsibility for all their fathers' crimes, such a truth is not of this world and is beyond my comprehension. (*BK*, pp. 249–50)

His conclusion is that not even the mother of the boy torn to pieces by the dogs has the right to forgive the murderer: justice outweighs harmony and the sufferings of the insulted and the injured not only render the visions of an earthly utopia ridiculous, they also falsify the prospect of any future, other-worldly utopia. Even if there is to be a final 'hallelujah', a final state of bliss that is more beautiful and glorious than anything we can now conceive, it cannot, in Ivan's opinion, compensate for what some must suffer on earth. Certainly, from our perspective now, on earth, such a final state cannot be anything other than speculation. We can have no knowledge of it. It is hidden from us behind the impenetrable incognito of death – and as we have seen, even Christ is subject to death, and even the body of a saint such as Zossima is subject to corruption and decay. Not even religion can offer any objective guarantee that all shall be well.

If we are to speak of any kind of final reconciliation, therefore, it can only be in the language of myths, dreams and visions, in stories that, as Dostoevsky tells them, are as absurd as they are edifying.

One such absurd story is the one made up by Ivan as a schoolboy and recited by the Devil in the course of their bizarre, schizoid conversation. It concerns a Russian atheist who has long since given up belief in God and immortality and who is deeply shocked to find on dying that he is indeed alive in another world. He still refuses to believe the evidence of experience, however, because it is against his principles. For this refusal he is sentenced to walk a quadrillion kilometres in the dark before he is admitted to heaven. Once again, however, he refuses. He simply lies down and, as the Devil tells the tale, stays there for a thousand years. At last, he gets up and for the next billion years or more walks his quadrillion miles and, then,

> the moment the gates of Paradise were open and he walked in, before he had been there two seconds, by his watch (though to my way of thinking his watch must have long dissolved into its elements on the way), he cried out that these two seconds were worth walking not a quadrillion kilometrees but a quadrillion of quadrillions, raised to the quadrillionth power! In fact, he sang 'hosannah' and overdid it so, that some persons there of lofty ideas wouldn't shake hands with him at first – he's become too rapidly reactionary, they said. (*BK*, p. 683)

As with 'The Geological Cataclysm', it is typical of Dostoevsky's method of presenting the truth under a contrary exterior that the hope of a final state of bliss in which all the sorrows and sufferings of the world are made good is put in the mouth of a Devil who is, in any case, probably no more than an apparition in the rapidly disintegrating mind of Ivan. In face of the impenetrability of death such testimony – the demonic vision of a madman – is as good as any other.

No less ambiguous is the vision of Alyosha as he stands by the body of Zossima. The gospel story of the wedding at Cana of Galilee is being read over the corpse, and as Alyosha drifts off into sleep he has a vision of the wedding feast and suddenly he sees, amongst others, Zossima himself. Zossima speaks to him:

> 'Yes, my dear, I am called too, called and bidden ... We are drinking the new wine, the wine of new, great gladness; do you see how many guests? here are the bride and bridegroom, here is the wise governor of the feast ... Do you see our Sun, do you see Him?'
>
> 'I am afraid ... I dare not look,' whispered Alyosha.
>
> 'Do not fear Him. He is terrible in His greatness, awful in His sublimity, but infinitely merciful. He has made Himself like unto us from love and rejoices with us ...'
>
> Something glowed in Alyosha's heart, something filled it till it ached, tears of rapture rose from his soul ... He stretched out his hands, uttered a cry and waked up. (*BK*, pp. 377–8)

The vision of Christ, moving amongst his people in a blessed afterlife, is – just a dream. Meanwhile, the body continues to decompose and Zossima's detractors are undeterred from their view that his sanctity was a sham.

One final example: the short story *A Little Boy at Christ's Christmas Tree*. Here Dostoevsky describes how, one Christmas Eve, a small boy leaves his mother, who is dying painfully of consumption in a filthy basement, to wander the streets of St Petersburg, where he sees shop windows with displays of mechanical toys and other wonders and through the windows of wealthy houses he sees Christmas parties, with children dancing around Christmas trees and tables laden with cakes. Jostled by a mob of other children he goes off in the biting cold and falls asleep behind a pile of wood in an courtyard. In his mind he seems to be transported into another, more beautiful world. His mother is there, and there too is the most dazzling, most beautiful Christmas tree he has ever seen – only this time, he too is invited to the party. The other children there tell him that this is Christ's Christmas tree, and their stories, like his, are stories of suffering, but now 'they are all here, all like little angels, and they are all with Christ, and He is in their midst, holding out His hands to them and to their sinful mothers ...'[26] Then, suddenly, the vision ceases, and we are informed in the simplest of narrative voices: 'Next morning, down in the courtyard, porters found the

tiny body of a little boy who had hidden behind the piles of kin-
dling wood, and there had frozen to death. They also found his
mother. She died even before he had passed away.'[27]

A sentimental, perhaps even a pious tale? But not quite: the brutal simplicity of the account of the finding of the dead body under-
mines any sense of conviction that the heavenly vision might have
induced – and Dostoevsky goes on to problematize his own narrative. 'Why,' he asks,

> did I invent such a story … But the point is that I keep fancying
> that all this could actually have happened – I mean, the things
> which happened in the basement and behind the piles of kindling
> wood. Well, and as regards Christ's Christmas Tree – I really
> don't know what to tell you, and I don't know whether or not this
> could have happened. Being a novelist, I have to invent things.[28]

This acknowledgement of the limitations of literature in the
face of 'the eternal questions' is of the utmost importance for our
understanding of Dostoevsky. Quite apart from the fact that within
his novels images of a final resolution of the conflicts and discords
of this world are offered only in visions, dreams and other such
ambiguous forms, the very form of fiction itself makes it impossible
to deliver any authoritative view as to the 'answers' to the eternal
questions. Here it is perhaps appropriate to suggest an analogy
with Kierkegaard's strategy of indirect communication and
Kierkegaard's understanding of the writer as being obliged, ultimately, to leave readers to make their own judgements on the
aporia raised by the text. Here too we might also mention the
extremely important line of Dostoevsky interpretation opened up
by the Russian critic Mikhail Bakhtin. According to Bakhtin,
Dostoevsky is the pre-eminent example of a dialogical writer, that
is, a writer who refuses to subordinate his characters and narratives
to the viewpoint of the author but, instead, leaves the characters
arguing amongst themselves and within themselves as to the final
significance of their lives and actions. Thus, in *The Brothers
Karamazov*, the rebellion of Ivan is contrasted with the faith of
Zossima and of Alyosha, but even Alyosha, we learn, recognizes
within himself the brutal Karamazovian nature; he too feels the
force of Ivan's indictment of God and has no ready answer to it.
Even Zossima makes it clear that the monastic form through which
his own faith has been chanelled will not necessarily work for

others, and we are repeatedly reminded that a number of the other characters within the novel are unable to recognize Zossima's sanctity. It is no accident that a crucial section of the novel is headed 'Pro and Contra' – and, as with Kierkegaard's *Either/Or*, each opposing point of view is explored and exposed from within and is not merely subjected to the 'final word' of the author.[29]

But it is not only the novelist *qua* novelist who is limited with regard to providing answers to ultimate religious questions. In the situation of modernity the authority of Church, state or reason is equally unable to give an unambiguous and universally compelling vision of how things are or of what the final end of all things will be, for all alike are bounded by the impenetrable frontier of death.

In this situation, the only 'answer' that counts is the answer of the heart – as he awoke from his vision of Cana of Galilee, we are told that 'Something glowed in Alyosha's heart'. That experience, that 'glow', is the only assurance that Alyosha is ever to get. And when Alyosha has experienced his vision of Cana *of* Galilee he runs out into the garden of the monastery where, we are told, he

> stood, gazed, and suddenly threw himself down on the earth. He did not know why he embraced it. He could not have told why he longed so irresistibly to kiss it, to kiss it all. But he kissed it weeping, sobbing and watering it with his tears ... In his rapture he was weeping even over those stars, which were shining to him from the abyss of space, and 'he was not ashamed of that ecstasy'. There seemed to be threads from all those innumerable worlds of God, linking his soul to them, and it was trembling all over 'in contact with other worlds'. He longed to forgive everyone and for everything, and to beg forgiveness. Oh, not for himself, but for all men, for all and everything ... he felt clearly and, as it were, tangibly that something firm and unshakeable as that vault of heaven had entered his soul. (*BK*, pp. 378–9)[30]

It is characteristic of this emotional and experiential resolution of the eternal questions that in response to the cynicism of the Grand Inquisitor's accusation that He has made the burden of freedom too heavy for men to bear, Christ says nothing at all. All he does is to kiss the Inquisitor. At the level of reasoned argument there is no answer to be made. Conversely, in his conversation with Ivan Karamazov the Devil expresses his fondness for spiritualism, precisely because the spiritualists are convinced of the possibility of material and scientific proof for the reality of another world.

From the perspective of those whom Kierkegaard would have called 'existing human beings' there can be no direct and unambiguous experience of transcendent reality and no objective proof of such reality either. The truth comes to us concealed under a contrary exterior and in the utter ambiguity of life itself, bounded by the impenetrable incognito of death. The strongest expressions of Christian hope are uttered in situations or by persons that undermine any claim that they might be binding either for the characters in the novel or for us, the readers. Such, as we have seen, are the Devil's reflections on redemption, Alyosha's vision and ecstatic experience, and the fairy-story of Christ's Christmas Tree. In the same vein is the speech of the grotesque drunkard Marmeladov (in *Crime and Punishment*) in which he speaks of Christ coming to save the poor and outcast. Likewise the absurd interpetations of the Book of Revelation by the buffoon Lebedev in *The Idiot* and the tragi-comic 'conversion' of Stepan Trofimovich Verkhovensky in *The Possessed* in which he retells the story of the demoniac of Gerasa as a parable of Russian nihilism. But perhaps most powerful of all is the character of Prince Myshkin, the 'idiot'. Critical opinion remains divided as to the extent to which Dostoevsky intended Myshkin to represent a perfectly good man and thus, also, a possible Christ figure. Without entering into such debates, however, we may say that no matter how flawed Myshkin himself may be, he is given a number of Christological attributes as the representative of an all-forgiving, utterly tender, utterly compassionate love. Yet it is also possible to see him as no more than an 'idiot', a pathetic victim of some unnamed degenerative psychosomatic illness of which his epilepsy is only one symptom. Indeed, the novel begins with his return to St Petersburg from a long sojourn in a Swiss sanatorium, and ends with his readmission to the sanatorium in a state of complete and irremediable mental collapse. In the course of the story it has been made plain that, far from bringing redemption to the lives of those he meets, he is in fact the catalyst for the tragic sequence of events that lead to the terrible murder that ends the main action of the novel. *The Idiot* is the bleakest, the darkest and the most psychologically disturbing of all Dostoevsky's novels – and yet it is also profoundly Christological. Once more like Kierkegaard, Dostoevsky can only envisage a presence of Christ in the world in which the divine love is concealed beneath a figure of lowliness and humiliation that is not illumined by any divine aura or betrayed by any display of supernatural power.

* K + D can only imagine Christ in the world in which the divine love is concealed beneath a figure of lowliness + humiliation.

Kierkegaard was, as he himself put it, a private thinker, 'without authority', and Dostoevsky was a novelist. But what can Christian theology make of their dark visions? For doesn't theology require a commitment to objectivity and doesn't it make doctrinal assumptions that claim somehow to break through the kind of ambiguity or incognito in which Kierkegaard and Dostoevsky clothe the fundamental questions of religious belief?

But before we turn to see what the theologians have made of the existential gospel of these doubting believers, we must call on one more voice from the margins of nineteenth-century culture: that of Friedrich Nietzsche, who was to assert the impossibility of faith in a manner that, on the one hand, takes to an extreme the logic of Kierkegaard and Dostoevsky and yet, paradoxically, can also be said to represent the conclusion of precisely those tendencies in modernity against which they wrote – a paradox that precisely mirrors their continuing commitment to faith even in a situation in which they are compelled to accept that the cumulative force of modernist ideology has rendered that faith undemonstrable.

NOTES

1. F. M. Dostoevsky, 'Notes from Underground', in *White Nights and Other Stories* (London: Heinemann, 1918), p. 50.
2. On the question of sexual abuse, see R. L. Jackson, *Dialogues with Dostoevsky. The Overwhelming Questions* (Stanford: Stanford University Press, 1993).
3. Stewart Sutherland regards the references to the Russian boys' interest in the God-question as ironic, and suggests that it is part of Ivan's complex strategy to attack a way of presenting that question that is especially vulnerable to being reduced to atheism. See S. Sutherland, *Atheism and the Rejection of God. Contemporary Philosophy and* The Brothers Karamazov (Oxford: Basil Blackwell, 1977).
4. Dostoevsky 'Notes from Underground', pp. 58–9.
5. Ibid., p. 68.
6. Ibid., p. 66.
7. Ibid., pp. 68–9.
8. Ibid., p. 69.
9. A Cossack atman of legendary brutality.
10. In this lies the truth and the falsehood of the narrowly 'existentialist' reading of Dostoevsky. Shestov and Berdyaev are examples of those who read the underground man as a spokesman for Dostoevsky's own views. For an opposite approach see Joseph Frank, *Dostoevsky. The Stir of Liberation. 1860–1865* (London: Robson, 1987).

11. F. M. Dostoevsky, *Crime and Punishment* (London: Heinemann, 1914), p. 61.
12. Ibid., p. 237.
13. Ibid., p. 489.
14. Idem., *The Possessed* (London: Heinemann, 1914), p. 102.
15. Ibid.
16. Ibid., p. 103.
17. Ibid., p. 563.
18. Ibid.
19. Ibid., p. 3.
20. Ibid., pp. 3–4.
21. Ibid., p. 4.
22. F. M. Dostoevsky, *A Raw Youth* (London: Heinemann, 1916), pp. 466–7.
23. Idem., *The Diary of a Writer* (Haslemere: Ianmead, 1984), p. 980.
24. Idem., *The Insulted and the Injured* (London: Heinemann, 1915), p. 345.
25. Idem., *Diary of a Writer*, p. 527.
26. Ibid., p. 171.
27. Ibid., p. 172.
28. Ibid.
29. See M. Bakhtin, *Problems of Dostoevsky's Poetics* (Minneapolis: Minnesota University Press, 1984); also A. Boyce Gibson, *The Religion of Dostoevsky* (Philadelphia: Westminster Press, 1973); and M. Jones, *Dostoyevsky after Bakhtin. Readings in Dostoyevsky's Fantastic Realism* (Cambridge: Cambridge University Press, 1990). Bakhtin is increasingly acknowledged as a major intellectual figure in his own right and there is already a large and rapidly growing secondary literature on his work.
30. The motif of kissing the earth is also found in *Crime and Punishment*, where Sonia instructs Raskolnikov to go to the crossroads and fall on the ground and, kissing the earth, confess his crime. On the theme of 'Mother Earth' in Dostoevsky see, e.g., V. Ivanov, *Freedom and the Tragic Life. A Study in Dostoevsky* (new York: Noonday, 1960), pp. 70–85.

5

A Short Story of the Anti-Christ

On the morning of 3 January 1889, passers-by in Turin's Piazza Carlo Alberto might not have been unduly surprised to see a cab-driver brutally beating his reluctant animal, but they were probably taken aback by what happened next, as a man, distinguished chiefly by his abundant moustaches and burning gaze and recognised by some, perhaps, as a lodger in a nearby *pension*, rushed forward and – in an uncanny acting out of a famous dream-sequence in Dostoevsky's *Crime and Punishment* – flung his arms defensively around the horse's neck, weeping and crying. Taken back to his lodgings, the madman was later escorted home to Switzerland, where, after a period in psychiatric clinics in Basel and, subsequently, Jena, he was handed over to the care of his mother and sister for what was to be a ten-year period of almost complete dissociation from the world about him, an intellectual and emotional paralysis that ended only with his death on 25 August 1900. If those who had witnessed his very public collapse might have been shocked by the incident, his friends, though also shocked and, of course, saddened, could scarcely have been surprised. This was, after all, a man who had been signing his recent letters, variously, 'Caesar', 'Dionysos' and even 'The Crucified'. To one correspondent he had confided, 'Since the old god has now abdicated, I shall be ruling the world,' prophesying that within six months his would be the most famous name in the world.[1] The prophecy was exaggerated – but not totally unfulfilled, for the name of Friedrich Nietzsche has remained one of the most controversial names in modern intellectual history, as his ideas have been imputed to or claimed by a multiplicity of movements and counter-movements: German imperialism, Nazism, avant-gardeism, various species of mysticism and programmes of sexual liberation, and, most recently, postmodernism. Indeed, many of the claims made both by supporters and detractors concerning Nietzsche's importance, have rivalled those made by Nietzsche himself in those last manic months before his final breakdown. Yet if the critical reception of Nietzsche has generated an excess of sound and fury, and if the 'meaning' of Nietzsche's key ideas remains elusive, there are very real lines leading from his extraordinarily beautifully written works to many of the most significant areas of twentieth-century thought and culture.

This is nowhere more so than with regard to questions of religious belief; and if there are those who take Nietzsche at his word and regard him as, to all effects and purposes, an Antichrist (the title of one of his last books), (there are others who see in him the forerunner of a new way of being religious) the progenitor of an authentically postmodern spirituality that has left behind the God of metaphysics. Heidegger once called him 'The one true believer of the nineteenth century'. What is – minimally – clear is that the question of religious belief mattered tremendously to Nietzsche. The struggle with the God in whom and the religion in which he did not want to believe bores into the very heart of his authorship. The attack on religion (or, if one chooses, the reinvention of religion) is a vital and continuing thread running through many of his main works and, whilst acknowledging that he was far from exclusively preoccupied with religious questions, the understanding of his attitude to religion is one of the keys to understanding his work as a whole.

Existentialism itself has been marked by a passionate and often partisan appropriation of Nietzsche – and this is no less true of religious existentialism than of 'secular' existentialists such as Heidegger and Sartre. A clear Nietzsche influence is discernible in Barth, Tillich, Berdyaev, Shestov and others, whilst his method of suspicion concerning the origins of religion, his repudiation of religious other-worldliness, his call for a transvaluation of all values and his prophecy of the death of God all contributed to shaping the horizons within which religious existentialism originated and flourished. This is not to say that religious existentialism was merely 'applying' lessons learned from Nietzsche. In several respects, what they learned from Nietzsche they could have (and, in some cases, clearly had) learned from Kierkegaard or Dostoevsky or yet other sources, where they would also have found arguments against aspects of Nietzscheanism. None the less, Nietzsche's writings brought together and brought to a particularly sharp point many of those strands of nineteenth-century culture that constituted the sharpest challenge to religious belief – thereby also calling for the most creative response. Therefore, although this study has in

Anxious Angels

general chosen to concentrate specifically on those who might be
called *religious* existentialists (in the sense that their thought can
be read as an appeal on behalf of religious commitment), it can
scarcely forgo some engagement with Nietzsche. It should, however, be made clear that what follows is intentionally a partial reading of Nietzsche, focusing on those areas most directly relating to
the main line of this book. We shall look at the following topics, in
order: a vital-ecstatic view of life, the genealogy of religion, the
death of God, nihilism and the call for a revaluation of values, will-
to-power, the aesthetic justification of life and eternal recurrence.

Nietzsche's first major work was *The Birth of Tragedy from the
Spirit of Music* (1872), and although it remains a key text, it is
unrepresentative in several respects. Nietzsche wrote it shortly after
taking up his professorship in Classical Philology at the University
of Basel and although its style is not quite that of a standard academic work, Nietzsche nurtured the hope that it would establish his
reputation in the scholarly world. This hope was not fulfilled, and
Nietzsche was never again to attempt to write primarily for the
academy (in this respect it occupies a not dissimilar place on the
Nietzschean canon to that occupied by *The Concept of Irony* in
Kierkegaard's work). It was also written at a time when he was still
under the influence, philosophically, of Schopenhauer and, artisti-
cally, of Wagner (to whom it is dedicated) – both of whom he was
later to repudiate in the sharpest of terms. Yet there are several
respects in which *The Birth of Tragedy* sets the tone for the works
that were to follow.

This is nowhere more apparent than in Nietzsche's challenge to
the values of rationality and order in favour of an ecstatic and
passionate commitment to life, in all its terrible ambiguity of joy
and pain. In *The Birth of Tragedy* this conflict is conceived of as the
conflict between Apollo and Dionysus. The importance, and the
continuity, of the Dionysian-ecstatic element in his thought is evidenced by his last major piece of purely poetic writing, the
Dionysus-Dithyramb.

In looking to Ancient Greece as a model for artistic, moral and
spiritual values, Nietzsche was entering into a well-established line
of German thinkers: Schiller, Hegel, Hölderlin and others had all
seen in Greece a paradigm for the reformation of Germany. For
the most part, however, the image of Greece that had been put
forward was one in which the Greek spirit culminated in the pursuit of beauty, truth and goodness, in which the ideal of a perfectly

balanced fusion of mind and body, of sense and spirit, of individual and society – in short, of all-round harmony in personal and social development – had been fulfilled as nowhere else on earth before or since. The liberal-progressive dream was for the founding on German soil of a Greek *polis*, incorporating these values. As Nietzsche saw it, however, this idealization of Greek values was essentially fraudulent. The reality of the Greek world was very different. True, the image of Apollo provided an historical focus for aspirations after harmony, balance and order, but Apollo was only one half of the Greek experience. Furthermore, the eventual triumph of Apollo was, Nietzsche maintained, the moment when the real springs of Greek culture lost their formative force and vigour. 'Tragedy' produced under the sign of Apollo was merely a pale vestige of the tragic spirit generated in the encounter with Dionysus.

What, then, is the Dionysian? Not something to be 'understood' by means of a definition, Nietzsche insists. It is, rather, to be experienced in becoming ecstatically open to that realm of primordial feelings that exists before and beyond individuation and conceptualization. Although such experience is the gateway to a joy beyond words, it also demands the loss and dismemberment of everything we customarily regard as making up our individual identity and must appear as terrifying to those who live within the ordered security of the Apollonian world. It cannot be had without a voluntary exposure to the *urschmerz*, the primal agony, of existence. Manifest in the orgiastic rites of early religions, the Dionysian experience is transformed by the Greeks and becomes the basis of early tragedy, of which the fundamental element, according to Nietzsche, is the Dionysian chorus, the chorus of satyrs who represent the primitive collectivity of Dionysian man. The emergence of the individual hero, who acts out the suffering of the individual will that is dismembered and reabsorbed into this primitive state, already reflects the presence of the Apollonian spirit, which gradually gains the ascendancy in the historic course of Greek drama. However, the real antithesis to the Dionysian spirit of drama is not Apollo but Socrates, and the Platonic dialogues represent the beginning of a new kind of hero. No longer is the hero a sufferer who redeems himself by means of suffering; instead, he justifies himself by argument and counter-argument. Dialogue becomes dialectic and passion is supplanted by theory as the dark, chaotic and pain-filled world of Dionysian experience yields to the serene optimism of philosophy. Human beings, in reality characterized by infinite self-contradiction, now conceive themselves in terms of the rational simplicity of the Platonic soul.

But Nietzsche is not simply concerned to trace the rise and fall of tragedy in Ancient Greece. He is driven by a more urgent question, of which the dedication to Wagner gives notice: can the spirit of Dionysian tragedy be reawakened; more particularly: can it be reawakened now, on the soil of contemporary German culture? Nietzsche's hope is that it can. An early sign of such a reawakening was the spontaneous discovery of the Chorale in Lutheran Church music; a further, and powerful manifestation of it, was Beethoven's setting of the *Ode to Joy*; but the greatest hope of such a rebirth, however, is aroused by Wagnerian music drama.

> the German spirit is still alive, and marvelously [*sic*] alive, like a knight who sleeps his enchanted sleep and dreams far underground. From out of these depths a Dionysiac song rises, letting us know that this German knight in his austere enchantment is still dreaming of the age-old Dionysiac myth... One day the knight will awaken, in all the morning freshness of his long sleep. He will slay dragons, destroy the cunning dwarfs, rouse Brünnhilde, and not even Wotan's spear will be able to bar his way.[2]

Nietzsche was to abandon his enthusiasm for Wagner, but the basic antitheses of *The Birth of Tragedy* were to continue to resonate in his work.

One of these was his belief that, at some point in the history of the classical world, humanity had undergone some kind of 'fall' from its natural state. This 'fall' is most clearly evidenced in what were to be counted as the two pillars of Western civilization: reason and religion.

Reason and religion alike portray themselves as offering a picture of reality, of how things 'really' are. Both of them, according to Nietzsche, mistrust the experience of the senses and the voice of the passional self. Instead, they posit the existence of a 'real' world, transcending the world of mere appearance (as they describe the world revealed to the senses). They thereby commit themselves to a consistent denigration of all that belongs to the illusory world of appearance and, above all, they declare war on the life of the body.

In *The Genealogy of Morals* Nietzsche depicts the rise of Christianity as a kind of monumental con-trick perpetrated on the powerful warrior peoples of the ancient world. In early classical culture, the chief aim in life was not goodness in the sense of later morality but goodness in the sense of nobility. The opposite of goodness in this sense is not the morally bad, but the plebeian, the base, the common. The virtue of the noble type is, Nietzsche acknowledges, the virtue of those who are happy in their own strength and confidence, and who give little consideration to the feelings of others. 'Deep within all these noble races there lurks the beast of prey, bent on spoil and conquest,' asserts Nietzsche,[3] as he goes on to speak warmly of their 'boldness', 'so headstrong, absurd, incalculable, sudden, improbable... their utter indifference to safety and comfort, their terrible pleasure in destruction, their taste for cruelty...'[4] – all traits that their victims will no doubt characterize as 'evil' but, in Nietzsche's view, simply the manifestation of the energy and drive of those favoured with health and strength.

The conflict between such an 'aristocratic' view of the world and the attitude of its victims, the conflict between the warrior and the priest, comes to a head, Nietzsche declares, in the conflict between Rome and Israel. Israel is the nation of priests *par excellence* – but it must be pointed out that Nietzsche's real target here is not Judaism: it is the Christian Church, for it was the Christian Church that actually effected the triumph of Israel's priestly values over the warrior values of Rome.[5] And how was this triumph brought about? By the fiction of conscience. Natural man, noble man, has an entirely spontaneous desire to inflict cruelty, to impose his will on the other. With the rise of civilization, however, there developed a complex web of societal relationships and constraints that made it ever more difficult to exercise such desires.

> [L]acking external enemies and resistances, and confined within an oppressive narrowness xand regularity, man began rending, persecuting, terrifying himself, like a wild beast, hurling itself against the bars of its cage. This languisher, devoured by nostalgia for the desert, who had to turn *himself* into an adventure, a torture chamber, an insecure and dangerous wilderness – this fool, this pining and desperate prisoner, became the inventor of 'bad conscience'.

And, Nietzsche goes on,

> the phenomenon of an animal soul turning in upon itself, was so novel, profound, mysterious, contradictory, and pregnant with

possibility, that the whole complexion of the universe was changed thereby. This spectacle ... requires a divine audience to do it justice. Henceforth man was to figure among the most unexpected and breathtaking throws in the game of dice played by Heracleitus' great 'child', be he called Zeus or Chance.[6]

The introduction of the hypothesis of a divine spectator, however, marks a new twist in the story of conscience. The experience of guilt is raised to a new level of intensity and humanity's self-experience becomes circumscribed by concepts of 'God (the divine Judge and Executioner) ... transcendence ... eternity ... endless torture ... hell ... the infinitude of guilt and punishment'.[7] The ideal of divine holiness feeds the individual's sense of worthlessness. Moreover, the logic of this development works most effectively against those who are naturally strongest, for the measure of their natural strength becomes the measure of the punishment they now inflict on themselves in the terrors and trials of guilt and self-condemnation.

If religion is one source of this corruption of natural innocence, philosophy is another. Like religion it is a sign of perversion and degeneration. Socrates, in Nietzsche's estimation, epitomizes the life-view of the rabble, of those whom a member of the aristocratic warrior caste would regard as base. Amongst other evidences for this Nietzsche adduces Socrates' ugliness, claiming this to be a sign of decadence and criminality. Socrates is essentially a buffoon who was taken seriously. His dialectical virtuosity is not a sign of superiority but is 'a *last-ditch* weapon in the hands of those who have no other weapon left'.[8] Those who have the strength to enforce their rights do not need dialectics, but a dialectician, for all his physical inferiority, can devitalize his opponent. The Socratic equation, 'reason = virtue = happiness', Nietzsche says, means no more than 'one must imitate Socrates and counter the dark desires by producing a permanent *daylight* – the daylight of reason'.[9] But the whole thing, Nietzsche insists, is a misunderstanding. The way of rationality is not really the way to truth: it is a form of sickness. 'To *have* to combat one's instincts – that is the formula for *décadence*: as long as life is *ascending*, happiness and instinct are one.'[10]

The world-historical triumph of Christianity and Socratism, conjoined under the single rubric of 'Platonism for the people', had, according to Nietzsche, completely dominated the intellectual, moral and cultural presuppositions of Western civilization for two millennia. So complete was their triumph that the

Christian–Platonic world-view had come to be accepted by most people as a simple and straightforward representation of how things really are. The vilification of the senses in the realms of knowledge and of morality alike had led to a withering up of humanity's natural impulses and powers in favour of the greater glory of Christianity's pale and other-worldly God. But, as Nietzsche believed his genealogical account of the origin of religion showed, this God was not Himself a power of nature: He was the product of an historical manifestation of the will-to-power of a particular group, the self-styled wise men and priests. What would be the consequences of coming to see this God as nothing but a human construct? *what if we saw this God as a human construct*

Nietzsche was not, of course, the first atheist in the history of modern thought and he was himself well aware of the kind of reductionist account of religion offered by Feuerbach, amongst others. What is virtually unique in his writing, however, is his vision of the extent and consequences of atheism. To cease believing in God is not merely to strike off a particular item from a list of propositions in which one believes, nor is it exclusively a matter of individual belief. For God is the principle that holds together the whole of the Christian–Platonic way of conceiving the world. If God goes, then everything goes: knowledge, art, morality and forms of government are all alike cast into a melting-pot in which all the old forms, all the old ways of doing things, will perish. It is no wonder, then, that people draw back from following through the implications of theoretical atheism. Instead they claim no longer to believe in God, but continue to believe in beauty, truth and goodness, in liberty, justice and humanity – all of which, according to Nietzsche, are little more than by-products of the conception of God.

This explains something of the peculiar pathos of Nietzsche's parable of 'The Madman', one of the most powerful passages in the whole of his authorship, in which he places the death of God on the agenda of modern European thought.[11] On a 'bright morning' the madman runs into a market-place shouting out that he is seeking God. The bystanders find this very funny, particularly those amongst them who do not believe in God. But then the madman turns and confronts them.

'Where is God gone? ... I mean to tell you! *We have killed him*, – you and I! We are all his murderers! But how have we done it?

How were we able to drink up the sea? Who gave us the sponge
to wipe away the whole horizon? What did we do when we loos-
ened the earth from its sun? Whither does it now move? Whither
do we move? Away from all suns? Do we not dash on unceas-
ingly? Backwards, sideways, forwards, in all directions? Is there
still an above and below? Do we not stray as through an infinite
nothingness? Does not empty space breathe upon us? Has it not
become colder? Does not night come on continually, darker and
darker? ... Do we not hear the noise of the grave-diggers who are
burying God? ... God is dead! ... And we have killed him! How
shall we console ourselves, the most murderous of all murderers? ... Shall we not have to become Gods, merely to seem worthy
of it? There never was a greater event, – and on account of it, all
who are born after us belong to a higher history than any history
hitherto!'

The onlookers, however, are bemused by these words and look at
him uncomprehendingly. He throws his lantern down, declaring
that he has come too early. '"This prodigious event is still on its
way, and is travelling, – it has not yet reached men's ears ... the
light of the stars needs time, deeds need time, even after they have
done to be seen and heard. This deed is as yet further from them
than the furthest star, – *and yet they have done it!*"'[12]
Contemporary atheism, then, has not grasped the full scope of
what it is able to acknowledge on the plane of ideas. In another
parable Nietzsche speaks of how it is claimed that there are caves
in India where the shadow of the Buddha can still be seen. The
shadow of god will linger over our culture for a long time to come –
perhaps millennia – he prophesies. Christian values will continue to
haunt us, but they have lost their basis in reality and can no longer
constitute the foundation for a whole conception and construction
of life.
The situation created by the death of God is, Nietzsche says,
the situation of nihilism. But what is nihilism? His simplest answer
is found in the notes published posthumously as *The Will to Power*:
'What does nihilism mean? *That the highest values devaluate themselves.* The aim is lacking; "why?" finds no answer.'[13] He goes on to
expand on what this means, claiming that nihilism 'as a psychological state' has three phases. The first is when what had long been
believed in as the 'meaning' of events and situations is perceived to
be non-existent. The world, life, our life in the world – these have

no 'meaning' apart from the reality of their actual existence. The second phase of nihilism is when we abandon the supposition that the world constitutes a unified totality 'in' or 'underneath' all events that could serve as the focus for whatever value we ascribe to our own lives. Finally, there comes the realization that there is no 'true' world behind or beyond this one: this world is the only world there is. Summing up, Nietzsche says, 'Briefly: the categories "aim," "unity," "being," which we used to project some value into the world – we *pull out* again; so the world looks valueless.'[14]

How does this realization affect us? In the first instance it is likely to lead to pessimism. This is what Nietzsche calls passive nihilism, something he sees exemplified in Schopenhauer and, in his later thought, in Wagner. Passive nihilism despairs over the meaninglessness of the world and, in face of its final valuelessness, regards the world as not worth getting involved in. This is, in effect, nostalgia for the values of Christian Platonism, living on after the recognition that these values have no objective validity. But there is also what Nietzsche calls the active kind of nihilism. This is nihilism that, fully aware of the objective meaninglessness and valuelessness of the world, none the less throws itself into life, affirming itself and affirming the values and goals it chooses for itself, without making the error of regarding them as true in any objective sense. The nihilistic insight that there is no intelligible heaven in which universal truths and values are eternally inscribed is liberative if we accept the consequence that we are now free to create our own values – to engage in the transvaluation of all values, as Nietzsche put it.

One of the most poetic (and precisely for that reason most concise) of Nietzsche's evocations of the journey through the various stages of nihilism is in the discourse on 'The Three Metamorphoses', which begins the first part of *Thus Spoke Zarathustra*. Here Nietzsche speaks of the spirit passing through three metamorphoses, becoming, in turn, a camel, a lion and a child. The camel is the beast of burden and ship of the desert and represents the spirit that, faced with the uniform meaninglessness of existence, none the less bears with the suffering and tedium of life without indulging in the pathetic fallacy of ascribing any intrinsic beauty, truth or goodness to it. But the camel may undergo a second metamorphosis and become a lion. What is the lion? The lion is the will to be lord of its own destiny. Confronted with what Nietzsche calls

'The great dragon [that] is called "Thou shalt"' the Lion opposes its own will.

> Values of a thousand years glitter on the scales, and thus speaks the mightiest of all dragons: 'All the values of things – glitter on me.
>   'All values have already been created, and all created values – are in me. Truly, there shall be no more "I will"!' Thus speaks the dragon.
>   ... To create freedom for itself and a sacred No even to duty: the lion is needed for that ...[15]

But the power of the lion is limited. It can destroy the edifice of the old order, it can kill God, but its sheer wilfulness cannot itself create new values. Therefore a third metamorphosis is needed, the metamorphosis of the child.

> But tell me, my brothers, what can the child do that even the lion cannot? Why must the preying lion still become a child?
>   The child is innocence and forgetfulness, a new beginning, a sport, a self-propelling wheel, a first motion, a sacred Yes.
>   Yes, a sacred yes is needed, my brothers, for the sport of creation: the spirit now will *its own* will, the spirit sundered from the world now wins *its own* world.[16]

With this turn to an affirmative and self-affirmative mode the spirit enters upon a new phase of its existence. No longer ashamed of its natural vitality and exuberance, the spirit casts off what Nietzsche calls 'the spirit of gravity' and throws itself into the infinitely varied movement of the dance of life. If Zarathustra has a God, he says at one point, it must be a dancing God. No longer taking its orders from others nor yet seeking to legislate for others the spirit has learned to trust and love itself. No longer believing in any one objective 'way' that is 'for all', it is concerned only to find and to be true to its own way, a way that no two individuals can share. Becoming true to the earth, the spirit finds that its own particular earthly way is also the way of self-overcoming, the way to the *Übermensch*, the super- or over-man. Nietzsche nowhere claims that he himself – nor even that his prophetic persona, Zarathustra – is or *has achieved* the status of *Übermensch*, but we can each of us take a step towards that by abandoning the discredited notion of human essence, of a fixed, timeless model of humanity to which we are obliged to conform.

The notion of the *Übermensch* is one of the most difficult and unclear of all Nietzsche's concepts. Is he hinting at some sort of evolutionary transformation of humanity? Or is he, more modestly, speaking of how life will be once we have shed the last illusions of Christian and Platonic humanism? In either case we may well find ourselves thinking that, quite apart from any moral qualms we may have, the idea of the *Übermensch* gives an almost fantastic air to Nietzsche's project. Is there not something almost quixotic about his call to abandon all that we have known and cherished and lived by in favour of such an ill- or even undefined idea? Having unchained the familiar world from its controlling sun, isn't Nietzsche now pulled in all directions by the unmanageable centripetal forces he has unleashed?

The challenge of such questions provides one context in which to approach another of Nietzsche's most problematic formulations: eternal recurrence.

Nietzsche's programme of liberating the spirit for the freedom of reinventing its values does not completely ignore the fact that although there is no 'essence of selfhood', the occurrence of such liberation takes place in and through particular individuals living through the particularity of their historical place and time. Now – and Nietzsche's analysis at this point is reminiscent of Buddhism – one of the motives that drives us to construct the fictions of a permanent self and of an objective order of values is the experience of self-loss that life in time brings with it. As thoroughly temporal beings we experience our lives as ceaselessly slipping away into the past. Equally, we find our present choices constrained by our own past history. I, a middle-aged, moderately unfit British academic, do not have a real option of becoming a candidate for the NASA space programme, no matter how much I might want to. Had I taken some different decisions at the age of 12, however, things might have worked out otherwise. Time both undercuts the sense of self that we (falsely and vainly) cling to and also traps us in the limits of the very particular history of past choices and circumstances that has made us what we are. In this situation even my own self can appear strange and alien to me. Who am I? How did I come to be like this? What can I do about it?

Looking around at his contemporaries, Zarathustra ponders the fact that there are few or even none who have achieved anything like wholeness. The typical human situation is of half-developed, one-sided, partial realizations of a limited range of possibilities. In Zarathustra's phrase, 'fragments and limbs and dreadful chances – but no men!'[17] But, he says, 'how could I endure to be a man, if man were not also poet and reader of riddles and redeemer of chance!' What is needed to create unity out of this array of scattered fragments and stunted possibilities is a new understanding of the relationship between self and time.

'To redeem the past and to transform every "It was" into an "I wanted it thus!" – that alone do I call redemption!' declares Zarathustra. In other words, we are no longer to regard our past as a compelling chain of circumstances beyond our control. If we are to experience ourselves as fully responsible for ourselves in the present, then we must look upon the past – our past – as the result of our own decisions and actions. We are who we are not because of what happened to us but because of what we chose.

But how seriously can we take such a proposal?

Nietzsche's doctrine of eternal recurrence is one answer to that question and can thus be seen as arising out of Nietzsche's new conception of the self. It provides the measure of how serious we are in regarding ourselves as the creatures of our own choices. For how would it be if everything were to recur again – and again, and again *ad infinitum*? Would we still make the same choices? If not, then we cannot really claim that those choices represent our deepest or truest will or intention. Only if we dare to say that we would indeed will the same acts and ends in every possible repetition of the circumstances in which our willing occurred can we really claim 'I willed it thus!'.

The doctrine of eternal recurrence, then, does not distract us from the urgency of the existential moment by directing our gaze away from the world to the infinite cycles of cosmic time. In fact, its aim is the opposite: to make us aware of the absolute import that each moment, because we are what we are only in and through the process constituted by the willed succession of such moments. 'You are the sum of your actions,' as Sartre was to put it. And so, if life no longer has the seriousness that the spirit of gravity gave to it in the past, it none the less has a new kind of seriousness, a seriousness that does not require us to renounce or to denigrate the movement of life but, instead, to go with the flow and catch the rhythm of the dance.

Like Kierkegaard, Nietzsche soon recognised that the new content of his thought could not be articulated in the conventional forms of academic philosophy. Although *The Birth of Tragedy* approximated to an academic form, his subsequent books were almost invariably marked by more or less unsettling literary experiments. Aphoristic, parabolic and poetic, Nietzsche's stylistic virtuosity can seduce where it does not persuade. But the artistry of his work is not a matter of mere form since art is a paradigm of the creative use of will-to-power. In book Three of *The Will to Power* he makes the following declaration.

Art and nothing but art! It is the great means of making life possible, the great seduction to life, the great stimulant of life.

Art as the only superior counterforce to all will to denial of life, as that which is anti-Christian, anti-Buddhist, antinihilist *par excellence.*

Art as the *redemption of the man of knowledge ...*
Art as the *redemption of the man of action ...*
Art as the *redemption of the sufferer ...*[18]

And here we see one way in which the 'cruelty' of Nietzscheanism might be mitigated. To be sure, the accolades heaped upon warrior values and the celebration of cruelty in works such as *The Genealogy of Morals* might seem to justify the reading of Nietzsche that inspired many young German soldiers in the summer of 1914 or that made him a favoured source of Nazi ideology (despite his hostility towards anti-Semitism). If we cannot confidently absolve Nietzsche of all responsibility for facilitating such misreadings, he was not himself historically naive. He knew that the situation of modernity was such that will-to-power cannot take the direct, physical form that it took in Homeric Greece. More important is the arousal and celebration of the values of life-affirmation that we can produce and experience in the world of art. The modern hero does not prove his prowess by feats of arms but by the power of the vision that he is able impress upon the consciousness of his contemporaries. He makes us see and experience the world differently. Whereas for Schopenhauer art was a means to help us detach ourselves from worldly entanglements and ascend to the serene intellectual contemplation of beautiful forms, Nietzsche came to see it instead as a way of giving form, colour, meaning and value to a world that, in itself, lacks all these things. (Famously, he came to see *Carmen* as exemplary in this respect.) Art is, then, in a sense, Nietzsche's 'spirituality': art, he predicts, will do for the humanity of the future what religion did for it in the past, but without requiring us to assent to the (false) beliefs about the world that are intrinsic to religion. The artist knows that his work is but a work of art, and the existential artist of Nietzsche's vision knows that the meaning he gives to his life is but the meaning he gives to his life – and nothing more.

In recent years the British philosopher of religion Don Cupitt has argued that the role ascribed to such an artist by Nietzsche is precisely the role that religion itself must assume in the postmodern world. No longer attempting to claim for itself the ontological validity that Catholic metaphysics and Protestant biblicism claimed in the past, this new understanding of religion will persuade only by virtue of the attractiveness and life-enhancing energy of its forms and expressions. Its 'truth' must be forever objectively uncertain.[19] Although Cupitt sets this up in terms of the situation of postmodernity, however, we can see that in fact the core question goes to the heart of the project of existentialist religion, a project that is quintessentially modernist. It is precisely the question bequeathed also by Kierkegaard and Dostoevsky in their differing ways: what kind of religious faith is still possible in the wake of modernity's destruction of all the traditional arguments and supports for the existence of God and immortality? In an atheous world, a world devoid of any immediate or compelling presence of God, can we go on being religious at all?

Many theologians have, of course, refused to accept the finality of God's death. Many have argued extensively and powerfully against the various forms of critique (including that of Nietzsche) that have militated against belief in God. Many have offered revised versions of what belief is really saying or doing, thereby claiming that its critics have missed the essential point. Even within the community of science there is a continuing willingness among many to debate the possible validity of some religious beliefs. Statistically it would doubtless be unwise to make unqualified claims regarding the final disappearance of religion in the contemporary world. As a social phenomenon, indeed, some would claim it is proving as vital as ever. As a careful reading of Nietzsche's parable of the Madman shows, however, 'the death of God' is not something immediately identifiable with 'atheism' in the popular sense. Not a few of the bystanders who laugh at the madman no longer believe in God. They do not think that his proclamation of God's death adds anything to what they already know. Equally, we may say, the persistence of religious belief does not of itself disprove or invalidate the thrust of the parable. Taking its parabolic form seriously, we cannot say that it is an argument against the existence of God. What it is saying is that irrespective of the state of play of arguments for or against the existence of God and irrespective of the rise or fall of God's popularity in the opinion polls, there is a kind of certainty regarding the basic foundation of all beliefs and all values that can no longer be taken for granted. It is not the *fact of God's non-existence* but the *disappearing of a whole way of conceiving and representing reality* that the parable brings to the fore. Even those who still believe must believe in a manner quite distinct from that in which previous generations believed, confronting the situation that there can be no final or conclusive answer to atheism and that, consequently, the experience of the death or absence or simple non-existence of God is a permanent possibility of modern existence. Living in the presence of radical atheism – neither dismissing nor refuting it but accepting it as an intrinsic part of modernity – is the challenge taken up by the religious existentialists of the twentieth century. For these thinkers, the death of God, of which Nietzsche gives the most dramatic notice, is not an intellectual position or a cultural fact that they experienced as something standing over against them and still less something they just happened to address but could equally well have ignored: it is a part of their condition. How are they able to experience 'this prodigious event' without falsification or denial, and yet go on affirming their Christian or Jewish faith? That is what we shall now try to see.

NOTES

1. On the circumstances of Nietzsche's collapse, see L. Chamberlain, *Nietzsche in Turin. The End of the Future* (London: Quartet Books, 1996).
2. F. Nietzsche, *The Birth of Tragedy* and *The Genealogy of Morals* (New York: Doubleday Anchor, 1956), p. 144.
3. Ibid., p. 174.
4. Ibid., p. 175.
5. *The Genealogy of Morals*, like many of Nietzsche's works, contains some harsh words regarding anti-Semites.
6. Ibid., pp. 218–19.
7. Ibid., p. 226.
8. F. Nietzsche, *Twilight of the Idols* and *The Anti-Christ* (Harmondsworth: Penguin, 1968), p. 32.
9. Ibid., p. 33.

10. Ibid., p. 34.
11. It is now widely accepted that Nietzsche was not the first to broach the idea of the death of God. Jean Paul, Hegel and Heine in Germany and Quinet in France had all anticipated Nietzsche's vision at this point, but none had expressed it as forcefully or as definingly as he was now to do.
12. Nietzsche, *The Joyful Wisdom* (London: Foulis, 1910), pp. 167–9. I have used this older translation as, I believe, it is as yet unmatched in its catching something of the poetic force of the original. The parable is in Book II. 125 of *The Joyful Wisdom* (also translated as *The Gay Science*).
13. Nietzsche *The Will to Power*, trans. Kaufmann (New York: Vintage Books, 1968), p. 9.
14. Ibid., p. 13.
15. Nietzsche, *Thus Spoke Zarathustra* (Harmondsworth: Penguin, 1969), p. 55.
16. Ibid.
17. Ibid., p. 160 (this and the following quotations are taken from the Discourse 'On Redemption').
18. *The Will to Power*, p. 452.
19. See, for example, Don Cupitt, *Radicals and the Future of the Church* (London: SCM, 1989) and *After God: the Future of Religion* (New York: Basic Books, 1997).

6

A Bombshell in the Playground of the Theologians

Kierkegaard, Dostoevsky and Nietzsche, the three nineteenth-century thinkers who did most to define the terms of twentieth-century existentialism, were all thinkers outside the establishments of academy and Church. Most (but by no means all) of those we shall be examining in the remainder of this study held positions of authority in either or both institutions. It is therefore possible to see the religious existentialists of the twentieth century as seeking to incorporate, to legitimate and in some sense, perhaps, to tame the radical insights of the nineteenth century's anxious angels. However, it is no less true that the appropriation of Kierkegaard, Dostoevsky and Nietzsche in twentieth-century theology came about in a context that tended of itself to raise the kind of questioning of the social and intellectual structures underpinning religious belief to which they had been led in their time. At their best the religious existentialists of the twentieth century were not mere epigones, 'applying' the 'results' of others' anguished labours to the questions of academic theology, but were themselves attempting an original rethinking of the basic questions of religious belief in the light of analogous cultural pressures.

A crucial element in this context of reception and questioning is the role of history in religious belief. Hegel had, of course, produced his own vision of history as the manifestation, in time, of the eternal life of the divine trinity. If Hegel's own totalizing tendencies came to be downplayed by subsequent liberal thinkers, his emphasis on history remained a vital part of philosophical and theological thought in Germany. For thinkers such as Dilthey, history provided the context to which all attempts to express or understand the meaning of human life were bound. Others in the social sciences were developing a more reductionist view. This historicizing of

109

thought provided theologians with a challenge they could not
shirk – unless, that is, they took the option of the Catholic hierarchy
and simply turned their backs on the whole of the modern world.
They therefore found themselves compelled to attempt an account
of Christianity that would justify belief as a historical phenomenon.

An important aspect of this engagement with history had, of
course, to do with the fact that Christianity itself had always tied
its truth claims to a series of events that belonged to history and
that were, in principle, open to investigation by historians. Moreover,
the Bible was itself now seen to be, at one level at least, a collection of historical documents comparable to all other historical
evidences.

If the problematizing of metaphysics in post-Kantian philosophy
had removed the need for belief to justify itself at the bar of abstract
reason, historical and social science presented the theologians with
no less arduous a task: the justification of belief at the bar of history.
But was such justification possible without resorting to special
pleading? Or would Christianity have to allow itself to be reshaped
by the historical consciousness, shedding those bits of doctrine and
tradition (and perhaps even of scripture) that did not meet the conditions of historical proof? And, if that was so, how far was it possible to go without compromising the very essence of the faith? On
the other hand, if faith ignores or overrules the challenge of history,
then it seems to be drawn towards something like Kierkegaard's
paradoxical faith: faith by virtue of the absurd. Certainly, as historical and social science became ever more rigorous, such an option
came to look increasingly attractive to many theologians.

The second edition (1921) of Karl Barth's commentary on Paul's
Letter to the Romans is often taken as inaugurating the explosive
impact of radical existential thought on modern theology. The significance of this text – described as 'a bombshell in the playground
of the theologians' – cannot easily be underrated. However, it
should be clear from what has been said that the kind of questions
addressed by Barth were very much part of the theological environment in which he wrote. (Indeed, one could argue that any book
that makes a significant impact, no matter how 'revolutionary' it at
first appears, does so because it is, in the best and deepest sense, 'of
its time'.) Therefore, although Barth's *Romans* must be given a
prominent role in any account of the rise of existentialist theology,
I shall not approach it as if it were the only work of significance in
the period immediately following the First World War, when it first

becomes possible to speak of a coherent movement of existentialist religious thought.

Indeed, 'existential' elements can be seen in a number of theological works from before the First World War itself. A particularly striking example is the conclusion of Albert Schweitzer's classic study *The Quest of the Historical Jesus* (1906). In this book Schweitzer chronicled the rise of the historical approach to the gospels and the attempt by German theologians of the nineteenth century to make of Jesus a credible figure of history, whilst ensuring his survival as a continuing focus of religious authority and faith. The story that Schweitzer tells is, in his own words, the story of 'the greatest achievement of German theology' – and German theology itself, he says, is 'a great, a unique phenomenon in the mental and spiritual life of out time'.[1] And yet the story seems to end in failure. Schweitzer himself concluded that the upshot of the quest of the historical Jesus is the choice between thorough-going scepticism and thorough-going eschatology – and neither of these options is able to secure the results for which the life-of-Jesus project had hoped. Why does the story end this way? Because, Schweitzer says, the kind of textual analysis conducted by scholars such as Wilhelm Wrede has shown that it is uncertain whether Jesus ever regarded himself as Messiah or, indeed, made any of the claims that his followers made for him. We cannot understand the mind or spirit of Jesus because the texts as they stand are determined by their confessional character. Thus, we are confronted with thorough-going scepticism. On the other hand, in so far as an historically credible picture of Jesus does emerge from historical scholarship, the figure who appears is that of a first-century apocalyptic enthusiast, someone whose beliefs and world-view are simply alien to those of modern human beings. Thus, thorough-going eschatology. Schweitzer's dramatic conclusion combines both scepticism and eschatology. As he sees it, 'it is a good thing that the true historical Jesus [i.e. the eschatological Jesus] should overthrow the modern Jesus, should rise up against the modern spirit and send upon earth, not peace, but a sword. He was not a teacher, not a casuist; He was an imperious ruler.'[2] But although this quality of absolute imperiousness is something that the first-century titles of Jesus (Messiah, Son of Man, Son of God, etc.) do express, such titles are meaningless for us, belonging as they do to a thought-world that is simply not that in which we live. 'We can find no designation which expresses what He is for us,' writes Schweitzer. But faith, and discipleship, are still possible, for, although the meaning of Jesus' life and work enshrined in New Testament text and Church tradition is no longer accessible to us,

> He comes to us as One unknown, without a name, as of old, by the lake-side, He came to those men who knew Him not. He speaks to us the same word: 'Follow thou me!' and sets us to the tasks which He has to fulfil for our time. He commands And to those who obey Him, whether they be wise or simple, he will reveal Himself in the toils, the conflicts, the sufferings which they shall pass through in His fellowship, and, as an ineffable mystery, they shall learn in their own experience Who He is.[3]

With theologians such as Schweitzer asserting the claims of a radical, almost fideistic scepticism from within the body of the Church, the liberal theologians could not escape the problematic nature of any grand claims regarding the meaning of history or the meaning of Christianity as a historical religion. If any historical metanarratives – the overarching stories that encompass and determine the particular narratives of historical specialists – were still to be attempted, they would have to be open enough and flexible enough to allow for areas of uncertainty and open-endedness. History being still in mid-course, the end could not be predicted with absolute assurance.

A fine example of the attempt to maintain 'the big picture' in balance with a sense for the complex and ever-changing detail of historical existence is the thought of Ernst Troeltsch (1865–1923) who, as the editors of a recent collection of his papers have written, was branded by the theologians of crisis (Barth and others) 'as the last and most dangerous representative of an idealist theology which they wished to repudiate'.[4] In Troeltsch there is nothing of the systematic completeness to which Hegel aspired. Convergences, connections and affinities between religion and culture abound, but they are all open-ended and revisable. Christian faith must engage with history because, amongst other reasons, it has its goal

> in the creation of a great community of humanity which strengthened and elevated through faith, is at the same time united in a common recognition of the divine will to which it owes its existence and by which it is directed to mutual works of love. Such an ethical community requires means of solidarity and

demarcation. These means can lie only in the realization and common recognition of the historical powers that have brought it into being.[5]

the form in which Christianity is expressed change

Even if Christianity is the absolute religion, its historicality means that the forms in which its absolute truth are expressed are always particular and always liable to change. A liberal and critical attitude toward history, which in its ups and downs sometimes approaches the ideal and sometimes departs from it, must free us from both skepticism and evolutionary progressivism.'[6] The practical consequence of this is that 'For everyone who adopts the modern attitude toward history, the conclusion will be inevitable that the historical connections of faith are to be retained but are to be formulated in a new way.'[7] This even includes the articles of faith enshrined in the creeds: the substance of Christian religious life may be unchanging but 'there is a constant flow of new constructions and interpretations of [this] fundamental substance ...'[8] The formulations of the creed can no longer be regarded as 'articles' of faith' but merely as 'ideas of faith' – 'ideas' open to reinterpretation and reconstruction. Similarly, Christianity remains eschatological in the sense that it looks towards a more perfect realization of 'the eternal worth of the person', but 'its form can no longer remain bound to the biblical myth'.[9] The goal towards which Christianity strives is, indeed, 'a common goal in the Unknown, the Future, perchance in the Beyond' that it shares with all religion.[10] In the meantime, however, 'there are only working, partial, synthetically uniting solutions'. Yet (and this is in 1923, after the First World War and after Barth's *Romans*), Troeltsch remains optimistic that 'the stream of life is always surging upward and onward'.[11] We may not be able to determine the final meaning of history exhaustively nor yet with absolute precision, but we may none the less remain confident that that meaning is commensurable with the actual flow of historical happenings.

If Troeltsch provides us with a characteristic example of those to whom the early dialectical theologians saw themselves opposed, Friederich Gogarten's ground-breaking article 'Between the Times', published in the journal *Die Christliche Welt* (*The Christian World*) in 1920, provides a no less characteristic summary of how and why that opposition arose – Gogarten's essay was itself to provide the title for the journal *Zwischen den Zeiten* that became, in effect, the organ of dialectical theology.

dialectical theology

Gogarten, born in 1887 (a year after Barth), was a pastor in Thuringia, and, in his article, sets out why he finds it impossible to continue in the paths forged by such teachers as Troeltsch. We stand between the times, he wrote, because we are both alienated from the past represented by these teachers and also unable to believe in the utopian future to which, for example, the Religious Socialists still look. To his teachers he wrote,

So we are berated as individualists, grumblers and eccentrics. And we have suffered under this chiding. But we could not do otherwise. Your concepts were strange to us, always strange. When we did think of them and use them, it was as if we were tormented by an inner vacuum. When we heard you, we heard the best and truest of intentions, but they sounded hollow, hollow to our ears ... We never belonged to your period ... We were so far from this period that we had to look outside it; Nietzsche and Kierkegaard, Meister Eckhard [*sic*] and Lao-Tzu, have been our teachers more than you to whom we are indebted for all our intellectual training. (*BDT*, pp. 277–8)

Equally, Gogarten finds himself cut off from the aspirations of Religious Socialists:

Although we feel the allure of the courage, the impartiality, the indifference toward things meriting no consideration, and the youthful vigour exhibited by this period, and although our human sense of justice really draws us toward those ranks ... yet our thoughts and aspirations seek a different goal. (*BDT*, p. 281)

And this goal? It is, simply 'to raise questions about God'. For, 'The times fell asunder and now time stands still. For one moment? For an eternity? Must we not be able to hear God's Word now?' (*BDT*, p. 281). But to be able to ask about God does not help us to solve the problems of society, culture or intellectual life. This hour 'between the times' is not an hour in which to busily ask practical questions – 'We should guard ourselves in this hour from nothing so much as from considering what we should do now' (*BDT*, p. 282) – but an hour, simply, for 'repentance', for realizing that 'We stand not before our own wisdom, but before God' (*BDT*, p. 282).

In a second article, 'The Crisis of our Culture', Gogarten insisted on the irreducibility and exclusiveness of what he called the religious point of view.

> The religious point of view has meaning only insofar as it retains nothing but God, only insofar as everything human disappears from it, only when it crosses the border into a realm different in its very roots, and only when man's busynes ceases and God's activity begins. Therefore, what occurs in this moment no longer belongs to the general relativity of events, nor can it spring from that context of events and man's event-determining energy or passivity; nor can it have any influence – as cause and effect – upon the general development of world history. (*BDT*, p. 286)

The religious point of view, he claims, is therefore both 'a total valuing' and 'a total devaluation' of the world. It is a total valuing because it sees what happens within history as meaningful in and through God's personal act of revelation/incarnation in Jesus Christ. It is a total devaluing because it no longer sees the ebb and flow of historical and cultural life as ultimately significant. Gogarten is no longer concerned, as his teachers were, to claim that religion is the true 'soul' of culture, the obscure referent of each and every meaningful human act. Instead, religion really means the crisis of human culture.

The aftermath of the First World War provided easy pickings for cultural pessimists. The first volume of Oswald Spengler's tone-setting *The Decline of the West* appeared in July 1918, but, Gogarten insists, the kind of crisis *he* is talking about is not the same as the lament over the fragmentation and loss of the Renaissance humanist ideal. It is a crisis – a judgement – that hangs over *every* culture. Even when all is going well, even when it seems natural to speak of religion and culture as converging ever more closely – even then the truth of the situation is that culture stands under the judgement of God and is only truly comprehensible from the religious point of view.

When it comes to saying *what* this religious point of view discloses there is little that can be said. For although the Christian is called 'to see as a man but with the eyes of God ... the situation in which man sees with God's eyes is untenable' (*BDT*, pp. 296–7). Similarly, the question 'What is to be done?' is misplaced, for the only answer is that 'there is nothing to be done' except to hear and to obey the gospel word: 'Repent, for the Kingdom of Heaven is at hand' (*BDT*, p. 300). The Christian message is, in the last resort, non-negotiable and its articles of faith are not translatable into human 'ideals of faith' (as by Troeltsch). The Church cannot surrender the principle of authority within its own sphere. It is not a democratic community and the meaning of its message is to be determined solely in the light of the authoritative preaching of the Word of God. It cannot be validated by argument, proof, history or experience. As it was for the Kierkegaardian apostle, the Word is its own evidence and has no authority apart from its own claim to authority. We can either believe or disbelieve this claim, but it is altogether inappropriate to want to prove it or to establish its probability apart from the act of faith itself. 'The organization of the Church', Gogarten declares, 'is not established by the intimate community of its members, edifying and strengthening each other with their individuality, but by nothing more nor less than the preaching of the Word of God in the Church. Thus, it is not an individualistic, personalistic community, but an authoritative, objective corporate society' (*BDT*, p. 340).

The claims seem, as I have indicated, to be Kierkegaardian. Indeed, Troeltsch referred to Gogarten's position as 'an apple from the tree of Kierkegaard'. But, having eaten of the Kierkegaardian fruit, Gogarten and his sympathizers do not, according to Troeltsch, seem able to accept the 'complete rejection of the church and cultural accommodation' that he believes is the logical consequence. 'In Gogarten's theology of the absolute moment,' Troeltsch says, 'there would be no pastors, no church administration, no mission, and no sermons on education or counseling.' How can Gogarten's 'religious point of view' be contained within 'the narrow Protestant adherence to the Bible and the Creed'? (*BDT*, p. 316). This is an important point, relating back to the question raised at the beginning of this chapter as to how the radical insights of the nineteenth-century anxious angels can be appropriated as foundational for an ecclesiastical or theological programme. Isn't there a crucial element in their work that points beyond all institutional and doctrinal expression and objectivity? We shall return to this question again. None the less early dialectical theology was prepared to go very far in its attack on what most of their contemporaries assumed to belong to the very life-blood of the Church. Nowhere is this attack more powerfully expressed than in Barth's *Romans*, to which we now turn.

The legend of this work has been often told: how the obscure Swiss pastor, scandalized by the public support given by Germany's liberal theologians to the Imperial war effort, steeled by standing alongside the miners of his parish against their bosses, and inspired by the reading of the New Testament, laid the axe to the root of the nineteenth century's theological tree – throwing his 'bombshell' into the 'playground of the theologians'.[12] Especially in its second (1921) and subsequent editions Barth's commentary brought into question the whole scholarly and cultural apparatus that Protestant Europe assumed to be necessary for the interpretation of scripture. In the preface to the second edition, Barth himself listed the reasons behind the radicalization of his position. Principal amongst these is, he says, the continued study of Paul; secondly, the influence of Franz Overbeck; thirdly, the study of Plato, Kant and 'what may be culled from the writings of Kierkegaard and Dostoevsky for the interpretation of the New Testament' (*KB*, p. 4) and, fourthly, the critical response to the first edition.

In terms of the present study, the references here to Overbeck, Kierkegaard and Dostoevsky are of especial interest. Franz Overbeck (1837–1905) was a Professor of Church History at the University of Basel, who had argued that the Hellenization of Christian theology represented a melding with a pagan culture that was fundamentally alien to the gospel. This corruption or confusion had distorted all subsequent Church history. A definitive separation of Church and culture was therefore essential for the assertion of authentic Christianity. Overbeck was also closely associated with Nietzsche, not only as a colleague, but also as a friend. Indeed, it was Overbeck who, when Nietzsche suffered his final collapse into madness, was despatched to Turin to bring him back to Basel. Interestingly, Barth later links Overbeck to Nietzsche as representing an 'anti-religious' coupling analogous to the 'religious' coupling of Luther and Erasmus.

Barth's own evaluation of Nietzsche – who by this time had already exercised an incalculable influence on a whole generation of German thinkers – can be seen in a number of references or quotations. 'Nietzsche,' Barth says, 'when he wildly and passionately rejected God, seems to have seen the issue far more clearly than the thoughtless "direct" believers who condemned him' (*KB*, p. 349). An instance of such perspicacity would seem to be found in Nietzsche's discussion of suffering, to which Barth appeals in commenting on Romans 8.18: 'I reckon that the sufferings of this present time are not worthy to be compared with the glory which shall be revealed to us-ward.' Barth states that 'To overlook suffering is to overlook Christ,' and it is as one who has had the courage to gaze unflinchingly on the horror of human suffering that Nietzsche is enlisted – alongside Luther! – in a couple of quotations: '"He rests not till he finds hopelessness everywhere"', to which Barth adds, 'until he finds hope in this hopelessness – ave crux unica spes mea!'; and, at greater length:

> With great energy the thinkers of old sought happiness and truth; but with deep-sounding, evil voice Nature decreed that they should never know what they perforce must seek. But he who of his own free will seeks falsehood everywhere and pursues misfortune, to him nature perchance draws near and offers her gift – not misfortune, but a miracle; something no words can frame, something of which happiness and truth are forms idolatrous. Maybe the earth lets go its heavy weight; maybe its powers and solid happenings dissolve in dreams, and are transfigured as on some glowing summer eve. And to the man who sees, it is as though his first awakening is girt about with sportive, dreamy, floating clouds, which later disappear, and it is day. (*KB*, pp. 305–6)

These words of Nietzsche are glossed by Barth as follows: 'When we are blind and dumb, then we see and speak; when we are bereft of question and answer, then we ask and find; when they suffer, then the children of God know and love their Father – triumphantly' (*KB*, p. 306). How authentically 'Nietzschean' this articulation of Christian triumph in the midst of suffering may be is clearly open to question. It is by no means intellectually insignificant, however, that Barth shows himself thus willing to take the self-declared 'Anti-Christ' into the service of the gospel – although we may continue to be troubled by Troeltsch's question as to whether such appropriation is ultimately consistent with the continuing commitment to the forms of Church life, including, of course, the understanding of scripture as the authoritative source and criterion of Christian truth.

The importance of Kierkegaard can be gauged from Barth's riposte to one of his reviewers that 'if I have a system, it is limited to the recognition of what Kierkegaard called the "infinite qualitative distinction" between time and eternity, and to my regarding this as possessing negative as well as positive significance' (*KB*, p. 10).

Kierkegaard and Dostoevsky are several times linked together by Barth – as, indeed, he has already linked them in the preface to the second edition. In the commentary on Romans 4.1 they appear, along with Abraham, Jeremiah, Socrates, Grünewald and Luther as representing 'the crimson thread' running through history, which, within history, constitutes a sacred history hidden within the course of secular history and secretly judging it. With regard to Romans 7.9–11 they are listed with Calvin, Overbeck and Blumhardt, and Barth speaks of Kierkegaard's 'dialectical audacity' and Dostoevsky's 'hunger for eternity' (*KB*, p. 252).

The spirit of Barth's image of Dostoevsky is very much that of his friend Eduard Thurneysen, whom he credits with having introduced him to Dostoevsky. Like Barth, Thurneysen continually sees Dostoevsky in conjunction with radical critics of the link between Church and culture such as Kierkegaard and Overbeck. Thurneysen says of Dostoevsky that,

> Without knowing Kierkegaard or Overbeck, he bore in himself *all of them, in of rejection of "Christendom"* the deepest mistrust toward a Christendom that had become church, and he loved in his Russian church just that which is *not* church in it – the reminders, still preserved pure, as he believed, of the early history of Christendom, free from compromise.[13]

The impact of Dostoevsky – not only on Thurneysen and Barth themselves, but on many who were reading him in the wake of the *[they are reading Dost. in wake of War plus Russia Rev.]* world war and the Russian Revolution – is wonderfully, if melodramatically, articulated by Thurneysen. Let this one passage stand for many – a passage in which, again, one feels the force of Gogarten's sense that the world of his theological teachers was no longer a world in which he could feel himself at home:

> Whoever comes to Dostoevsky from the regions of secure humanity, of the pre-war period for instance, must feel like one who has been looking at such domesticated animals as the dog and the cat, the chicken or the horse, and then suddenly sees the Wild before him, and without warning finds himself face to face with the yet untamed animal world, jaguar and puma, tiger and crocodile, the slithering of the snakes and the fluttering of the wings of the eagle and the condor ... He has been led out past the

furthermore border posts, (past the limits of known humanity)
with pounding heart he looks on the unknown face of a man who
shares with him the common name of 'man,' and who yet
appears to live beyond all the concepts tied with this name,
beyond good and evil, wisdom and folly, beauty and ugliness,
beyond even state and family, school and church. And just as one
who returns from the wilderness to domesticated animals redis-
covers in the four-footed creatures who share his house, and
whom he had previously regarded sympathetically, the traces of
original wildness, and sees himself even in his own four walls
confronted at a stroke with dangerous, unsuspected slumbering
possibilities, so there proceeds from an encounter with the world
and the men of Dostoevsky something of hidden trembling and
fear.[14]

At one level, then, Barth's *Romans* can be situated in a line of
writing that takes as its theme the unknown shadow regions of the
human spirit: the underground world that bourgeois society and,
particularly, a bourgeois Church, does not wish to have acknowledged. In this perspective, religious existence does not mean sup-
pressing or rising above or taming this wild side of human nature,
but acknowledging it, entering it, owning it and finding faith in the
very midst of it. If, after the discussion of Paul's introductory
words, Barth immediately embarks on the exegesis of Romans
1.18–end, it is therefore no surprise that he entitles this section
'The Night' – i.e. the shadow side of modernity represented for
contemporary culture by the likes of Nietzsche, Dostoevsky and
Kierkegaard: not that they 'are' the Night, nihilists to be resisted at
all costs, but that they are able to show us just what is afoot in the
darkness.

The first thing we learn, in the exegesis of verse 18, is that what
passes itself off as religion and as the worship of God is, for the
most part the idolatrous self-worship of humanity:

We suppose that we know what we are saying when we say
'God'. We assign to Him the highest place in our world: and in so
doing we place Him fundamentally on one line with ourselves
and with things. We assume that He *needs something*: and so we
assume that we are able to arrange our relation to Him as we
arrange our other relationships. (We press ourselves into proximity with Him:) and so, all unthinking, we make Him nigh unto

ourselves. We allow ourselves an ordinary communication with Him, we permit ourselves to reckon with Him as though this were not extraordinary behaviour on our part. We dare to deck ourselves out as His companions, patrons, advisers, and commissioners. We confound time with eternity. This is the *ungodliness* of our relation to God. And our relation to God is *unrighteous*. Secretly we are ourselves the masters in this relationship. In 'believing' on Him, we justify, enjoy, and adore ourselves. (*KB*, p. 44)

→ Barth as critiquing idea that we make ourselves the makers

The 'infinite qualitative distinction' that should mark all relations between creature and Creator has been forgotten and religion has been made commensurable with humanity's other historical and cultural productions and expressions. Barth throws out a dazzling display of images by which to invoke this distinction and the deleterious consequences that follow when it is forgotten.

[T]he understanding of what is characteristic of God was lost. They had lost their knowledge of the crevasse, the polar zone, the desert barrier, which must be crossed if men are really to advance from corruption to incorruption. The distance between God and man had no longer its essential, sharp, acid, and disintegrating ultimate signficance. The difference between the incorruption, the pre-eminence and originality of God, and the corruption, the boundedness and relativity of men had been confused ... But, on whatever level it occurs, if the experience of religion is more than a void .. it is a shameless and abortive anticipation of that which can proceed from the unknown God alone. In all this ... there is always a revolt against God. For in it we assist at the birth of the 'No-God', at the making of idols. (*KB*, pp. 49–50)

When this occurs, then – naturally – 'The revolt of Prometheus is wholly justified ...' (*KB*, p. 48). The myth of Prometheus had, of course, been reappropriated enthusiastically from the Romantic period onwards as a symbol of the humanist or existential struggle against political absolutism and ecclesiastical obscurantism and, conversely, identified by Christian thinkers as the 'secret' of the iconoclastic and rebellious programme of modernity. So, once more, Barth is signalling his alliance with the radical protest against the Church establishment.

Barth in agreement w/ Prometheus – Church against establishment

If Paul's words in these early chapters can be understood as chiefly concerned with the varying relationship between Jew, Gentile and God, Barth makes it abundantly clear that he is translating them from this historical context and applying them to the contemporary triangle of Church, existential revolt and God. What Paul says about the Law, and about those who pride themselves on the possession of the Law (meaning, in the first instance, his contemporary Jewish community), is applied by Barth unambiguously to the Church (and, of course, very much to the theology of the Church!).[15]

Jew = Church
Gentile = existential revolt

The law is the revelation once given by God in its completeness. The law is the impression of divine revelation left behind in time, in history, and in the lives of men; it is a heap of clinkers marking a fiery miracle which has taken place, a burnt-out crater disclosing the place where God has spoken, a solemn reminder of the humiliation which some men had been compelled to pass, a dry canal which in a past generation and under different conditions had been filled with the living water of faith and clear perception, a canal formed out of ideas and conceptions and commandments, all of which call to mind the behaviour of certain other men, and demand that their conduct should be maintained. The men who *have the law* are the men who inhabit this empty canal. They ... possess the form of traditional and inherited religion, or even the form of an experience which once had been theirs. (*KB*, p. 65)

Paul's 'gentiles', on the other hand, are those whose 'individual lives and ... experiences of history are not stamped by revelation ... They may be named sleepers ... unbelievers ... unrighteous.' They are those whose world is 'disintegrated ... disorganized ... undermined ... where nothing noble can find an entrance; ... where men are incapable of being impressed by anything at all; just in the midst of the last deepest scepticism ...', or else reduced to 'the last stage of human nakedness (Dostoevsky!)' having only 'some last terror before the mystery of death, some final disgusted rejection of the inevitability of the world by a man when he leaves his busy life protesting against its futility' (*KB*, pp. 66–8). If such characters from the Dostoevskian underground are now 'the gentiles', then the Church should note Paul's warning that it is sometimes the gentiles who 'show the work of the law, written in their hearts', who are 'preferred' over the righteous inhabitants of synagogue or church – even if all they 'own' is the honesty of their experience of alienation.

> Revelation is from God; it cannot be compelled to flow between the banks of an empty canal. It can flow there; but it also fashions for itself a new bed in which to run its course, for it is not bound to the impress which it once had made, but is free ... Among the gentiles there is, moreover, a shattering and disturbing awe which those who inhabit the empty canal neither perceive nor understand ... The living water fashions its own course, and the visible pre-eminence of the inhabitants of the canal is destroyed. There has been exposed to view a new rough river-bed, a very unfamiliar and strange impress of revelation, a disturbing form of faith. But who will deny what God alone can deny? (*KB*, pp. 66–7)

"the living water fashions its own course"

Again, Barth's immediate appeal is to the evidence of 'the religion and the experiences of the characters in the novels of Dostoevsky' (*KB*, p. 68).

Clearly, if one is reading Barth from the standpoint of a liberal theology that holds to a belief in the possibility of some kind of convergence or correlation between human culture and divine meaning in history, then his appropriation of the existential tradition with its dramatic subjectivism and its tormented plunge into the shadow-side of existence seems to risk giving up those very certainties or aspirations that make religion a resource for humane living in a complex world. But again, Troeltsch's question to Gogarten is apposite: how far can you go in this direction?

But how far did the dialectical theologians really go? Weren't the risks they took always qualified in advance by the assurance of scriptural authority? Barth may *say* that *everything* is subject to the negative dialectic of the infinite qualitative difference, but hasn't he exempted the authority of the apostle, and of scripture from this otherwise universal wrack? To recall Thurneysen's image of what happens to Dostoevsky readers when they return home: isn't Barth's *Romans* essentially a domesticated version of the wildness visible in the pages of Kierkegaard, Dostoevsky and Nietzsche? The savage gleam is there – but only as reflected in the eye of cat or dog. The acceptance of the authority of scripture or of a dogmatic tradition has always already set up a secure fence between Barth's theology and the desert regions where wild things roam. In this connection it is striking that in the opening article of the first number of *Between the Times* Barth himself defines the locus of the critical questions at the heart of his theology in terms of the parish priest on a Saturday evening considering how he might link the worlds of scripture and contemporaneity.[16] Indeed, as one scans the articles of *Between the Times* one cannot avoid the feeling of a distinct Churchiness.

It was not only liberals such as Troeltsch who sensed this problem. The same complaint is at the heart of an appreciative yet critical response to *Romans* by Paul Tillich. Tillich drew on many of the same nineteenth-century resources as Barth and his understanding of the crisis of Western culture and of the Christian tradition in the West had been heightened by his own experiences during the First World War and the social upheavals that followed. At one and the same time he regards Barth as going too far and yet, paradoxically, not far enough.

Seizing on the concept of the dialectical, Tillich notes that the dialectical theologians claim to see each and every phenomenon at one and the same time in the light of God's 'no' and of God's 'yes', his word of judgement and his word of salvation. It is precisely their perception of the 'no' that has led them to refuse the harmonizing of culture and Church as exemplified in their liberal predecessors. But Tillich's own understanding of dialectics leads him to assert that even a dialectically-oriented thinker has to acknowledge that he too has a position; his 'no' to culture presupposes a 'yes', i.e. a set of values or a viewpoint that determines the course of his thinking. Moreover, not only is the dialectician's negative judgement on the world about him undergirded by his own positive position, but a truly dialectical view would see the world itself and each and every phenomenon in it as containing both positive and negative elements. The dialectical theologians, however, characteristically overlook the positive aspects.

Tillich applies his argument to the relationship between God and nature, and between God, spirit and history. With regard to nature, he maintains that it is not possible to see the natural world exclusively in terms of the violent struggle for existence or of the universality of death. He writes, 'as soon as one speaks of the world or nature or life, in which judgement, irrationality, or death is revealed, the corresponding positions – namely, the world as the unity of form, nature as unity of configuration, life as reality – are presupposed' (*BDT*, p. 136). [With regard to the realm of spiritual reality, Tillich agrees that it is right to be suspicious of the absolutization of conscience, as if human conscience were adequate to decide all issues of right and wrong.] On the other hand, Gogarten's insistence that Christ, not conscience, is the 'place of revelation' 'appears with the gesture of absoluteness'. It is not the values of the autonomous conscience that need to be opposed 'but demonically distorted autonomy' (*BDT*, p. 137). Similarly, Barth's refusal to allow religious significance to the insights of artists, mystics and the creators of cultural values is seen by Tillich as too one-sided. Tillich states that 'there is no profundity that does not see into the depths of the eternal source of things, that is, there is no profundity that is not faith' (*BDT*, p. 138). In other words, the struggles of human beings to find and to express in symbolic activity or in moral action some kind of meaning in life cannot simply be brushed aside without distinction as all equally worthless. Of course, culture should not be absolutized – and Tillich fully shares the suspicion that this has been the tendency of bourgeois society – but neither should it be completely rejected.

The situation is the same in the case of history. Here, however, Tillich sees a major inconsistency in the position of Barth and Gogarten. If his critique has up to this point tended to sound essentially liberal (and Tillich never entirely repudiated his debt to liberal theology), implying that the dialecticians have gone too far in their one-sided attack on culture, he now suggests that in one important respect they have not gone far enough. For, he says, Barth and Gogarten 'delimit in history a unique historical occurrence in which history is transcended and something absolutely new is set up. [What happened in Christ happened completely beyond humanity, yet it occurred in the historical man, Jesus of Nazareth' (*BDT*, p. 140)]] Tillich quotes Gogarten himself to the effect that 'Only here is the No not valid for that in which it appears.' But, in Tillich's view, this is the theology of the absurd and is self-contradictory. It is possible only on the basis of authoritarian and heteronomous assertions that intrude absolute claims into the domain of relative truths where they have no place. But within the parameters of human history, it is not at all possible to exempt *any* slice of history or *any* historical documents (such as the New Testament texts) from the continuous simultaneity of 'Yes' and 'No'. In other words, it is not possible to use the absoluteness of faith to secure empirical or historical claims. As historical event and historical evidence, the life of Jesus and the New Testament must be exposed to exactly the same uncertainties and exactly the same provisionality as characterize all other historical phenomena. Here, then, the dialecticians have not gone far enough, for they have withdrawn their own dogmatic position from the scrutiny of the divine 'no'. As Tillich sees it, however, there is nothing that ever has or ever will appear within the horizons of historical life that can be thus exempted. No matter how painful it may be to theologians, even this last vestige of security must be stripped away. Until that has happened, theology will not have entered fully into the crisis of the age and will be unable to speak to the age the saving word it needs.

NOTES

1. A. Schweitzer, *The Quest of the Historical Jesus* (London: A. and C. Black, 1954), p. 1.
2. Ibid., p. 401.
3. Ibid.
4. Ernst Troeltsch, *Writings on Theology and Religion*, trans. and ed. Robert Morgan and Michael Pye (London: Duckworth, 1977), p. vii.
5. E. Troeltsch, 'Faith and History', in *Reason in History*, trans. J. L. Adams and W. F. Bense (Edinburgh: T. and T. Clark, 1991), p. 135.
6. Ibid., p. 143.
7. Ibid.
8. Ibid., p. 145.
9. Ibid., 'Eschatology', pp. 146–58.
10. Idem., *Christian Thought: Its History and Application* (London: University of London Press, 1923), p. 32.
11. Ibid., p. 128.
12. It is mildly ironic that this image should have gained such currency, given that Barth was the citizen of a neutral country, whereas many of those he attacked were, if not in the front line, far more immediately threatened by the impact of the war than he!
13. E. Thurneysen, *Dostoevsky* (London: The Epworth Press, 1961), p. 10.
14. Ibid., pp. 7–8.
15. It is interesting in this respect to compare Barth's hermeneutical claims with Kierkegaard's concept of contemporaneity. For, just as Kierkegaard held that the believer becomes, in faith, 'contemporary' with Christ in such a way that his faith no longer requires the buttress of historical evidence, so Barth argues for the immediacy with which the New Testament message reaches across the centuries. In a famous comment on Calvin's exegetical work he writes: 'Paul speaks, and the man of the sixteenth century hears. The conversation

between the original record and the reader moves round the subject-matter, until a distinction between yesterday and today becomes impossible' (*KB*, p. 7). It is worth adding that, with regard to the importance given by many of the existentialist theologians to issues of interpretation and communication (rather than, simply, questions concerning the 'truth' or 'falsehood' of Christianity), Barth's *Romans* is also very much concerned with *how* Christianity is communicated and not just with whether it is true.

16. K. Barth, 'Not und Verheissung der christlichen Verkündigung', in G. Merz (ed.), *Zwischen den Zeiten* (Münich: Christian Kaiser, 1923), Vol. 1, p. 5.

7

Faith without Myth

Although Barth's *Romans* sought to separate faith from the realms of inner-worldly history and culture it can with hindsight be seen as a text directly and passionately engaged with the world crisis of its time and has often been cited – in a perhaps unlikely triangle – with Spengler's *Decline of the West* and Heidegger's *Being and Time* as one of the most characteristic works of the 1920s. Although Rudolf Bultmann (1884–1976) was to declare, *contra* Barth, the necessity of contextualizing theology in its contemporary thought-world, his own work, paradoxically, seems far less obviously 'engaged' than that of Barth. Indeed Bultmann himself said of his work, 'On the question of the origin of our theology, I am of the opinion that the internal debate with the theology of my teachers plays an incomparably greater role than the experience of war or the reading of Dostoevsky.'[1] It is perhaps doubly striking that whereas Gogarten speaks of the gulf separating his generation from that of their teachers, Bultmann refers to his critical response to their teaching as part of an 'internal debate'.

If Bultmann's theology is indeed inseparable from the internal debates of German liberal theology, it is further defined by the fact that he was first and foremost a scholar of the New Testament, engaged in the kind of detailed textual work that has characterized New Testament scholarship in modern German theology. Bultmann's work must therefore be understood in the first instance as a critical continuation of the liberal theological tradition within the field of the study and interpretation of the New Testament. In this respect, then, Bultmann would seem to be very much a theologian's theologian, and, indeed, compared with Barth or Tillich, his work has attracted relatively little interest outside the domain of theology. None the less, he is a crucial figure in the history of religious existentialism and, I hope to suggest, a not insignificant figure in the wider history of existentialism.

Although firmly rooted and grounded in the minutiae of New Testament exegesis, Bultmann did not, of course, work solely on that level. Over and above his exegetical work he also gave a systematic presentation of the overall theology of the New Testament and, in a number of essays (and especially in his Gifford lectures, *History and Eschatology*), addressed general theoretical issues about the meaning and interpretation of history. Although these three dimensions are inseparable in Bultmann's own work, we shall be concentrating here exclusively on those aspects of his work that are most relevant to the understanding of religious existentialism.

Bultmann's significance for religious existentialism has generally been approached in the light of his programmatic essay 'New Testament and Mythology', in which he called for the doctrines of the New Testament to be translated into the language and concepts of twentieth-century existentialism. This has often given the impression – which Bultmann's critics have continued to disseminate – that he was somehow taking existentialism as a ready-made body of thought and applying its results to theology in a derivative, second-hand way. Responding to this criticism Bultmann remarked that those who levelled it were 'blinding their eyes to the real problem. I mean, one should rather be startled that philosophy is saying the same thing as the New Testament and saying it quite independently' (*K&M*, p. 25). As Bultmann sees it, the affinity between the understanding of the human situation in the New Testament and in contemporary existentialism is not something that he is reading into or forcing onto the text, but has to do with the nature of the subject. In fact he believes that the existentialist understanding of the human condition derives, via Kierkegaard and Luther, from the New Testament itself. Of course, this leaves open the question as to whether it is possible to 'say the same thing differently' – i.e. to translate the world-view of the first century into the categories of existentialism – without changing the subject-matter itself. The problem is particularly difficult when, as in Heideggerian existentialism (at least in its popular reception in the 1920s and 1930s), the terms into which the theology of the New Testament is to be translated belong to a philosophy that has dispensed with God.

We are beginning to touch on the very nerve of Bultmann's significance in the history of existentialism at a point which, inevitably, involves his relation to Martin Heidegger, whose *Being and Time* (1927) is the defining text of philosophical existentialism (even though Heidegger later repudiated an 'existentialist' understanding of it!).

The view that Bultmann merely 'borrowed' the conclusions of Heideggerian existentialism is increasingly implausible in the light

of what is now generally known about the personal and professional relationship between Heidegger and Bultmann in the years
1922–8 when they were colleagues in the University of Marburg.

Heidegger came from an intensely religious background. Indeed,
his philosophical studies had begun at a time when his career
seemed to be directed towards the Catholic priesthood, and his
training in the Aristotelian scholastic philosophy that was at that
time integral to the curriculum of Catholic theology was to be
a continuing point of reference in his own development. By the
time he arrived in Marburg, however, Heidegger had abandoned
all ideas of ordination and, indeed, Catholicism. He continued
to read deeply and extensively in theology, however, including
Schleiermacher, Meister Eckhart, Teresa of Avila, Rudolf Otto, Luther,
Augustine, Kierkegaard and St Paul (giving lectures on the letters
to the Galatians and the Thessalonians). In Marburg he soon became
a close colleague of Bultmann. The two attended each other's
seminars, ran a joint course on Paul's ethics and at one time met for
an afternoon a week to read St John's gospel together.[2] When
Being and Time was published Heidegger wrote to the philosopher
Karl Löwith that only he and Bultmann would be able to understand it.[3]

Of course, such anecdotal evidence says little as to the substance
of the intellectual relationship between Bultmann and Heidegger,
but there are some obvious areas of shared interest that suggest
how that relationship could spring up. Having abandoned the
highly objectified and essentially static metaphysics of Catholic
scholasticism, Heidegger had become drawn to the question as to
how 'Being' could be understood in a radically historicized view of
the world. For the scholastics, Being was not merely the most universal and the most fundamental concept of philosophy, guarantee-
ing the unity of the whole field of human knowledge, it was also
the best possible definition of God: God's essence is, simply, to be.
But this metaphysically construed Being of God is what it is precisely by virtue of its being removed from and resistant to change,
chance and all the vicissitudes of life in time. Since Hegel, however,
German philosophy had been preoccupied with the question of history. In the light of the opposition between metaphysical Being and
the flux of historical becoming, was it still possible to go on speaking of a single overarching meaning to it all? Hegel's own 'answer'
to this question soon came to seem over-optimistic – and not only
to extreme critics like Kierkegaard and Nietzsche. Following

Schleiermacher, thinkers such as W. Dilthey sought to allow for the ongoing and open-ended nature of history and, while refusing to impose any single general plan onto the historical process, to develop a science of hermeneutics (or interpretation) that would make it possible to go on looking for and talking about meaning in history.

This is to some extent part of Bultmann's own background. In his case, however, the question is focused more specifically on the question regarding the meaning of one particular historical event: the life of Jesus of Nazareth, and the documents recording that event, the New Testament. Could this life and could these texts go on providing a normative understanding of existence in a historicized world?

As we have seen, this is already the question of liberal theologians such as Troeltsch and a question to which Barth's *Romans* provided one kind of answer.

The convergence and overlap of these philosophical and theological concerns is clear and it is by no means surprising that Heidegger and Bultmann should discover a shared agenda. Especially, it is by no means surprising that Bultmann should find in Heidegger's anthropology – itself shaped by the religious sources already mentioned – an appropriate resource for articulating how it might be possible to go on making sense of the New Testament on the far side of the dilemma so succinctly posed by Schweitzer: thorough-going scepticism or thorough-going eschatology.

We shall return to the relationship between Heidegger and Bultmann, because, apart from the similarities between them, their ultimate disagreement is also of profound importance for understanding Bultmann's existentialism. Indeed, in the light of this disagreement I shall suggest that in a certain sense, Bultmann is a far more existential thinker than Heidegger, and closer both to Kierkegaard and, strangely, to Sartre, than Heidegger himself ever was. First, however, we turn to Bultmann's reworking of the crucial question of nineteenth-century liberal theology: the question of the historical Jesus.

Barth, while insisting on the historical facts of the New Testament (including the resurrection as historical fact), brilliantly sidestepped many of the complexities that had haunted the nineteenth-century debate by developing his position through the Letter to the Romans rather than the gospels. Apart from some relatively minor verses, the Pauline authorship of the Letter and the essential unity and

integrity of the text itself had not been called into question. But, as
Bultmann saw it, Barth had simply ducked the serious historical
questions altogether. Barth so identifies faith with the transcendent
act of God that it is a 'faith beyond consciousness'. By asserting as
he does that my human consciousness of my religious feelings is
entirely irrelevant to the question as to whether I 'really' have faith
or not, Barth makes faith itself completely vacuous. Barth speaks of
'the impossible possibility', but, Bultmann says, such faith is 'in
every sense an absurdity' (*BDT*, p. 111). 'My justification and my
faith', he states, 'are not some sort of pseudo other-worldly factors,
but my faith is something definite and precise in my consciousness'
(*BDT*, p. 112). Against Barth, Bultmann insists on the historical rootedness of the human subject. It is only because faith is always only
the faith of particular individuals living at particular times and
places that it is able to acquire content and meaning: if I am asked
what my faith 'means', I have to be able to answer in terms of life-
choices and cultural constructions that are intelligible both to my
interlocutor and myself; only so can I truly say what faith asks of
me. But this acknowledgement of the historical rootedness of the
subject also involves taking seriously the question of the historical
Jesus. Here, however, Bultmann's conclusions seem to be almost
entirely negative. Because our cultural horizons have changed
beyond all recognition in the centuries separating us from the time
of Jesus, his historical life can no longer determine the content of
our historical life.

> [I]t is impossible to see what more was done by the historical
> Jesus who goes to his death in obedient love than was done by all
> those who, for example, in the World War [Bultmann is here
> referring to the First World War, in which one of his brothers was
> killed] took the same road also in obedient love. Their road actu-
> ally means more to us ... because we were associated with them
> as a living *Thou*. To try to create such experiences of encounter
> with a person of the past seems to me to be artificial and to lead
> to sentimentality ... I am not helped at all by reading touching
> stories of how Jesus forgave the sinful woman or Zacchaeus.[4]

And, decisively, 'How things looked in the heart of Jesus I do not
know and do not want to know.'[5]

Bultmann's position here is complex. On the one hand, there are
all the questions concerning the possibility of reconstructing or

re-imagining the personality of Jesus on the basis of the historical record. In this respect Bultmann's own commitment to form-criticism is significant, since form-criticism was precisely a method of exegesis that undercut any attempt to read the gospel text as reportage. But, Bultmann claims, interest in the historical personality of Jesus is in any case entirely irrelevant to faith. This is how he puts it in his 1926 study *Jesus* (English title: *Jesus and the Word*):

> *interest in the personality of Jesus* is excluded – and not merely because, in the absence of information, I am making a virtue of necessity. I do indeed think that we can know almost nothing concerning the life and personality of Jesus ... Except for the purely critical research, what has been written in the last hundred and fifty years on the life of Jesus, his personality and the development of his inner life, is fantastic and romantic. Whoever reads Albert Schweitzer's brilliantly written *Quest of the Historical Jesus* must vividly realize this. The same impression is made by a survey of the differing contemporary judgements on the question of the Messianic consciousness of Jesus, the varying opinions as to whether Jesus believed himself to be the Messiah or not, and if so, in what sense, and at what point in his life. Considering that it was really no trifle to believe oneself Messiah, that, further, whoever so believed must have regulated his whole life in accordance with this belief, we must admit that if this point is obscure we can, strictly speaking, know nothing of the personality of Jesus.[6]

The slogan 'the flight from history' has often been used as a weapon with which to bludgeon Bultmann and his followers. In the sense that he is clearly sceptical as to what can usefully be gained for religion by the historical study of the New Testament alone, the charge is comprehensible. However, if we wish to understand Bultmann (rather than merely to refute him) it is important to see that his scepticism is intertwined with a concern and respect for history, and this in two senses. In the first sense, all claims to certain historical knowledge rest exclusively on the work of the historian qua historian. Ideological commitments cannot dictate the results of historical research. The second sense has to do with the fact that Christian truth is not timeless but historical, and therefore subject to an ever-changing horizon. In this sense the living world of the New Testament has faded beyond the reach of our historical existence. We can understand it – but we can no longer live in it.

What determines our existence as historical beings is the situation that, living in time, we are called to define ourselves by our actions and decisions in the specific context of the here-and-now. If I am to understand my life as religious, it can only be on the basis of the religious demand becoming concrete in the actuality of my contemporary existence. Faith, says Bultmann, 'is a free act of decision. For only in the free act of decision is the being of man as a historical being achieved.'[7] If the Word of proclamation is to be effective, it cannot be as a word 'about' a past event: it must be as a word about 'myself' and my present situation,

> as I live within a definite historical situation ... It directs me to nothing other than my history ... It brings nothing into our life as a new entity. It only opens our eyes to ourselves – though not, of course, for the purpose of self-observation. The hearing is an event in our historical living and becomes an act of decision for this or for that.[8]

The 'content' of historical existence is determined solely by the actuality of history itself: that I am such-and-such a person, living at such-and-such a time, having to make such-and-such decisions. Who I am cannot be separated from this situatedness – facticity, as Heidegger called it. Thus, what Heidegger and Bultmann themselves are for us is inseparable from the fact that they lived in the time they did, were heirs to a particular intellectual culture with all its questions and challenges, and that their thinking had to confront the challenge of world wars and totalitarian politics. There is no 'Heidegger' and no 'Bultmann' who can be separated out from that total yet highly specific historical context.

But does this mean that Bultmann is committing himself to some form of historical determinism? If I cannot escape the facticity over which I have no control, am I then nothing but an effect of hidden historical causes? The challenge of such a question points to a further level at which the meaning of my life is tied up with history. For it now appears that if my life is to have any meaning at all – that is, in a sense that ties meaning to that which I am able to bring about on the basis of my own free decisions – then I must somehow rise above my facticity. Instead of seeing it as the determining ground of my existence, I must be able to see it as the arena within which I exercise my freedom and responsibility. But is this possible?

Bultmann himself put the question well in his 1955 Gifford lectures.

> What is the result of all this? It seems to be a consistent *relativism*.
> The belief in an eternal order, ruling the life of men, broke down,
> and with it the ideas of absolute goodness and absolute truth. All
> this is handed over to the historical process which for its part is
> understood as a natural process ruled not by spiritual, but by
> economic laws. History begins to become sociology, and there-
> fore man is no longer understood as an autonomous being, but is
> seen as at the mercy of historical conditions. His historicity does
> not consist in the fact that he is an individual who passes through
> history, who experiences history, who meet with history. No, man
> is nothing but history, for he is, so to speak, not an active being
> but someone to whom things happen. Man is only a process
> without 'true existence'. The end, it seems, is *nihilism*.[9]

We cannot simply turn our backs on this possibility, Bultmann
believes. Indeed, we must make of historicity itself a new criterion
for testing the truth or adequacy of the various understandings of
life or *Weltanschauungen* in and through which human beings interpret their situation. '"A *Weltanschauung*", we may say, is the more
legitimated the more it expresses the historicity of the human being.
Self-understanding is the more astray the more it fails to appreciate
historicity and flees from its own history.'[10] In the light of this
principle, Christianity emerges as a genuinely historical form of
self-understanding. However, amongst the range of possible historical forms of self-understanding, Christianity has one peculiarity:
'Christian faith believes that man does not have the freedom which
is presupposed for historical decisions.'[11] But Bultmann does not
mean that Christianity is deterministic. The problem, as he sees it,
is that, as historically existing individuals, we are each of us determined by our past, by the history of what we have been and done
that has made us what we now are. This past, although essentially
the history of our own actions, comes to constrain our present freedom. We cannot break loose from it or pretend that it hasn't occurred.
Indeed, Bultmann states, although we may express the wish to be free
from the past, we are generally unwilling to come out from behind its
shelter. In the face of the future and of the decisions we must take
now that will determine that future, we find it easier to qualify our
options by reference to the habits, attitudes and limitations that we

have created for ourselves in the course of our lives up until the present. 'I cannot choose this path or that path,' we say, 'because I am not the sort of person who is capable of that, or because my present situation does not allow me to consider that possibility.' We prefer the safety of the relative freedom that is ours on the basis of our past, to the absoluteness of a freedom in which we would find ourselves altogether and utterly accountable for our future. 'Radical freedom', Bultmann says, 'would be freedom [for man] from himself' – that is, from the identity that we have built up by our past actions on the basis of a received facticity. Our longing for radical freedom is countermanded by our tenacity in clinging to a familiar sense of self, no matter how flawed that self may be.

The connection of this to the New Testament understanding of the human situation – an understanding to be found in the gospels and in the Pauline writings alike – is well brought out by Bultmann in the closing pages of *History and Eschatology*.

> The man who understands his historicity radically, that is, the man who radically understands himself as someone future, or in other words, who understands his genuine self as an ever-future one, has to know that his genuine self can only be offered to him as a gift by the future. And indeed, his very historicity misleads him to this attempt, because his historicity includes responsibility for the future. His responsibility awakes the illusion of having power of disposal. In this illusion man remains 'the old man', fettered by his past. He does not recognise that only the radically free man can really take over responsibility, and that he is not allowed to look round for guarantees, not even the guarantees of a moral law, which take off or lighten the weight of responsibility ... Man has to be free from himself or to become free for himself. But ... he can only receive this freedom as a gift. Christian faith believes that it receives this gift of freedom ... 'Whoever will save his life shall lose it, but whoever will lose his life shall find it.' The truth of this statement is not comprehended as general truth. For man cannot say this word to himself, it must be said to him – always individually to you and me.[12]

In such reflections Bultmann finds himself both close to and yet also significantly distant from Heidegger. For when Heidegger discusses the awakening of conscience in *Being and Time*, he too asserts that the self as it exists in its everyday facticity cannot be the source of the call that comes to us in conscience.

> Indeed the call is precisely something which *we ourselves* have neither planned nor prepared for nor voluntarily performed, nor have we ever done so. 'It' calls, against our expectations and even against our will. On the other hand, the call undoubtedly does not come from someone else who is with me in the world. The call comes *from* me and yet *from beyond me*.[13]

Given that Heidegger insists that his understanding of conscience is quite distinct from anything that could be called theological, it is far from clear what the origin of this call can be. None the less, it is clear that it is something I receive, rather than something I do or produce. Bultmann notes that Heidegger and other existentialist philosophers (in his 'New Testament and Mythology' essay he refers specifically to Wilhelm Kamlah) recognize that 'man has lost his true selfhood' and that 'self-commitment is not the natural disposition of modern man' (*K&M*, p. 27). But, as he understands them, 'these philosophers are convinced that all we need is to be told about the "nature" of man in order to realize it,' and he quotes Kamlah to the effect that '"Since it is the true understanding of Being, philosophy emancipates that self-commitment which is proper to man and enables it to attain to its full stature" – evidently [Bultmann adds], that means: emancipates man for true self-commitment' (*K&M*, p. 27). Bultmann, however, believes that 'the philosophers are confusing a theoretical possibility with an actual one' (*K&M*, p. 29). We cannot make ourselves free. Knowledge is not, of itself, virtue. We can only become free if we are exposed to a power, not ourselves, that offers us the concrete, actual possibility of freedom in the ever-specific situatedness of our personal lives. And this, for Bultmann, is only possible as an act of God, an act that, literally, speaks to us as proclamation, as Word. But, then, what is this Word? Self-evidently, Bultmann does not equate it with the simple written text of the New Testament. Nor is it (as he believes Barth sees it) some sort of timeless or transcendent reality. The call to authenticity, he says, 'becomes an event repeatedly in preaching and faith. Jesus Christ is the eschatological event not as an established fact of past time but as repeatedly present, as addressing you and me here and now in preaching.'[14] As the content of what is preached – rather than merely the Word 'contained' in the historical text of scripture – the Word is always contextualized in the concreteness of the real life meeting of preacher and addressee. Even in the apostolic age itself, for all its proximity to the historical reality of the life, death and resurrection of Christ, the preaching of the Word is what is decisive. 'The real Easter faith', Bultmann says, 'is the word of preaching which brings illumination ... the apostolic preaching which originated in the event of Easter Day is itself a part of the eschatological event of redemption' (*K&M*, p. 42). Only thus does Christ, *can* Christ, become present in the here-and-now, and as one recent study has emphasized, Christ is for Bultmann always the present Christ, 'Christus Praesens',[15] not the 'past' historical Jesus, nor yet the 'future' Christ of apocalyptic fantasy. *History and Eschatology* thus concludes:

> Man who complains: 'I cannot see meaning in history, and there-
> fore my life, interwoven in history, is meaningless', is to be admon-
> ished: ... Always in your present lies the meaning in history,
> and you cannot see it as a spectator, but only in your responsible
> decisions. In every moment slumbers the possibility of being
> the eschatological moment. You must awaken it.[16]

In Bultmann's emphasis on preaching as the mode of presence of the *Christus Praesens*, we can see affinities both to Kierkegaard's concept of contemporaneity and to Kierkegaard's sense for the centrality of the question of communication. The debate about Christ and about faith is not just about historic evidence or descriptive accuracy: it is, vitally, about *how*, in a situation of objective uncertainty, I am called to faith and self-commitment.

I have sought to avoid getting entangled too quickly in the question of demythologizing, a question that, for some, is virtually synonymous with the name of Bultmann, but we must now look at the implications of Bultmann's general position for the reading of scripture. Clearly the kind of *summa* of Bultmannian faith that is to be found in the closing pages of *History and Eschatology* might surprise many Christians. There are no credal claims regarding the 'facts' upon which many believe Christianity to be based: virgin birth, miracles, resurrection, let alone the classic dogmatic formulations of ecumenical councils or Reformation confessions of faith. The radicality of Bultmann's understanding of history has the consequence that not only is the message or *kerygma* of the New Testament separable from the facts (or purported facts) that were its occasion: it is also separable from the form of consciousness or *Weltanschauung* in which its first recipients spontaeously expressed it.

As Bultmann sees it, we just don't share this *Weltanschauung* any more.

> *Man's knowledge and mastery of the world* have advanced to such an extent through science and technology that it is no longer possible for anyone seriously to hold the New Testament view of the world – in fact, there is no one who does. What meaning, for instance, can we attach to such phrases in the creed as 'descended into hell' or 'ascended into heaven'? We no longer believe in the three-storied universe which the creeds take for granted ... It is impossible to use electric light and the wireless and to avail ourselves of modern medical and surgical discoveries, and at the same time to believe in the New Testament world of spirits and miracles. (*K&M*, p. 5)

Precisely because of the principle of facticity it was both inevitable and appropriate that the Christian message should have been articulated in the thought-forms of the first century. For Bultmann, these thought-forms are essentially made up of the eschatological expectations of the early Palestinian community, on the one hand, and the gnostic redeemer myth of the hellenistic community on the other.[17] But just as the personality of the historical Jesus is no longer accessible to us and, in any case, has nothing to say to the specific challenges of our lives, so too these first-century thought-forms are closed to us, except as objects of historical enquiry and interpretation. We ourselves just do not think in those terms.

None the less, these myths, like all historical expressions of the *Weltanschauungen* of diverse times and places, are expressions of the self-understanding of the human beings who produced them and, as such, are open to interpretation.[18] But what is 'interpretation'? It is not trying to find a kernel of timeless truth beneath an alien historical husk. That was the understanding of nineteenth-century liberalism. Rather, interpretation is about gaining an understanding of the text that enables it to address me in my historically situated crisis of decision. Although the interpreter must respect the objectivities of historical research, Bultmann does not regard it as inappropriate for interpretation to be guided by what he calls the '"life-relation" of the exegete to the subject matter with which the Bible is concerned and, together with this relation a preunderstanding'.[19] What this means, Bultmann explains, is that the reader must be 'moved by the *existentiell* question for God – regardless of the form that this question actually takes in his consciousness.'[20] Moreover, 'The understanding of the text is never a definitive one, but rather remains open because the meaning of the Scriptures discloses itself anew in every future.'[21] In other words, with each new intellectual situation and with each new world-view, the form of the question for God will change – and so, therefore, must the understanding of the text.

This is where Bultmann feels it appropriate to call on the categories of Heideggerian existentialism, regarding it as characteristic for contemporary humanity's self-understanding – with the proviso, as we have seen, that (as he understands it) the lineage of these categories is itself ultimately rooted in the New Testament. Thus, where the New Testament speaks of 'this world' or 'aeon', of 'sin', 'death', 'the flesh' or 'powers and principalities', existentialist philosophy speaks of inauthentic existence; and where the New Testament speaks of 'faith', 'grace', 'forgiveness', 'a new creature' and 'redemption', existentialism speaks of authentic existence. We have already seen, however, that whilst Bultmann is prepared to recast the first-century dualism in a new, existential twentieth-century form, such that the Christian challenge is to pass from inauthentic to authentic existence, existentialist philosophy of itself is unable to explain how this transition is to be made – and, as Kierkegaard had already insisted, that is the decisive question.

But is Bultmann correct in drawing the analogy he does between New Testament mythology and Heideggerian existentialism?

Certainly, the analogies are striking. But no less striking is the fact that Heidegger himself repeatedly declared that when he spoke of the human situation in terms of 'falling', he was not making the kind of judgement involved in Christian assertions concerning the universal sinfulness of the human condition.

His own entanglement in theology – and the plausibility of what he regarded as a theological *mis*reading of *Being and Time* – made it inevitable that at some point Heidegger would have to settle his philosophical accounts with theology, something he attempted to do in the lecture *Phenomenology and Theology*, a text dedicated to Bultmann and one that goes a considerable way towards clarifying the intellectual relationship between Heidegger and Bultmann and thus towards clarifying the question as to the nature of Bultmann's own existentialism. Let us then, briefly, look at Heidegger's lecture.

Heidegger makes a fundamental distinction between that science, ontology, which deals with Being as such and those sciences, all the rest, which are concerned with 'beings' (*das Seiende*) at what Heidegger calls the 'merely' ontical level, i.e. beings as we encounter them in our everyday dealings with the world. Theology is said to belong to this latter group of sciences and therefore to be closer to chemistry or mathematics than it is to philosophy, because like them, it has a particular domain or class of beings as its object, and not Being as such. The particular ontic field of a science Heidegger calls its 'positum'. And what is the positum of theology? It is, he says, Christianity (Ger.: *Christlichkeit*); that is, Christianity not in the sense of the sum total of Christian history nor even the systematic whole of historical theology, but Christianity as that is given in and to faith, *faith* being understood as 'a mode of existence of human Dasein'.[22] Faith, thus understood, comprises both that which is revealed in this mode of existence (i.e. Christ, the crucified God) and also the total transformation of the existing Dasein itself in the light of this revelation (i.e. 'faith = rebirth').

Theology, as science, can be constructed only on the basis of faith and its content is determined exclusively and exhaustively by faith. It does not itself yield or have as its object 'speculative knowledge of God' that could be separated from faith. On the other hand, faith (and the consciousness of God given in and to faith) are not the 'objects' of theology in the way that animals are the objects of research in zoology, for although faith belongs – as do animals – to the domain of ontic being, that domain is itself divided between those things that exist as objects in the world (like chemical elements or animals) and those things that are invested with subjectivity and characterized by historicity. Faith clearly belongs to the latter kind of ontic being, which Heidegger calls '*existentiell*'.

How, then, does faith relate to philosophy? The fundamental question of philosophy, as has been said, is the question of Being. Being is not one more domain of the ontic, like animals, numbers or faith. Being determines the scope of our existential possibilities in a manner prior to any particular ontic determinations. Yet this does not mean that Being is some kind of super-essence or Platonic idea, the 'truth' behind appearances. The ontological dimension, the dimension of Being, is more like an *a priori* in the spirit of Kant's *a priori* structures of perception – only whereas Kant is concerned to give an account of knowledge of the world, Heidegger is concerned to understand the ways in which we actually exist in the world. To understand existence in the light of ontology (that is, in Heidegger's terminology, to understand it existentially) is to understand what makes possible the various forms of our being-in-the-world.

The example that Heidegger gives in *Phenomenology and Theology* relates to the categories of guilt and sin. Heidegger, in this respect like Kierkegaard, regards sin as a strictly dogmatic concept. That is to say, the judgement that the world is subject to sin or that we are all conceived and born in sin is only possible on the basis of Christian doctrine, i.e. on the basis of the specific ontic domain of faith. But this possibility is itself only possible on the basis of a yet more fundamental understanding of human Dasein as being-guilty, i.e. being indebted for its existence in the minimal sense of not being its own foundation. (As is clear from the discussion of the call of conscience, Heidegger does not want to speak at this point of another to who we are indebted for our being.) This existential-ontological concept of being-guilty is not to be regarded as the *cause* of sin in any way. Heidegger's point is rather that speaking of human beings as sinful only makes sense if we already assume that human beings are the kind of beings in relation to whom it is appropriate to make such judgements. The point might be simpler if we look at a non-religious analogy: political alignment. Political alignment is characteristic of only one form of entity: the citizens of democratic societies. It makes no sense to say, for example, 'The mulberry tree is left-wing' or 'The corn-crake is right-wing'. The application of certain concepts is relevant only within certain domains of being. In the same way, Heidegger is saying, sin, even when it is spoken of as universal and all-embracing, is only relevant to one particular ontic domain. Ontology, however, asks ('more primordially', as Heidegger repeatedly puts it) what it is that makes this particular ontic domain what it is, so that judgements concerning sin (or salvation) can be made about it.

Theology, then, is a positive science, based on and limited to faith and what is disclosed in faith at the level of the ontic-*existentiell*, and unable, of itself, to attain the more primordial dimensions of Being that are the object of ontological enquiry. Remembering that this lecture has a particular bearing on Bultmann, it is interesting that Heidegger's critique of theology here is essentially identical with his critique of Kierkegaard and other theological writers in

Being and Time. Although he acknowledges that some of the crucial categories of *Being and Time* (categories such as anxiety, existence and 'the moment') derive from theological writers, his attitude towards these 'sources' is typified in the following note:

> In the nineteenth century, Søren Kierkegaard explictly seized upon the problem of existence as an existentiell problem, and thought it through in a penetrating fashion. But the existential problematic was so alien to him that, as regards his ontology, he remained completely dominated by Hegel and by ancient philosophy as Hegel saw it.[23]

Existential religious thought, then, remains on the level of the *existentiell*, concerned with the particularities of concrete life-decisions and, in Heidegger's technical sense, unable to grasp the existenti*al* or ontological Interpretation of Being. Curiously, this is strongly analogous to the critique Heidegger later makes of Sartrean existentialism in his 1946 *Letter on Humanism*. Sartre and the theologians, in other words, are too close to the detail of existence at the *existentiell*-ontic level to gain the kind of global view that only ontology can give. Now Heidegger is well aware that the attainment of such a view is highly problematic and that it is all too easy to succumb to the kind of hubris with which his opponents have typically charged Hegel, in other words, to mistake one's own partial perspective for a total view of the whole. None the less, it is towards such a view – an understanding of Being and not merely of beings – that his intellectual enterprise is directed.

But Bultmann's failure – and the failure of all theology – to address the question of Being in an ontologically fundamental manner is only 'failure' in a strong sense if Heidegger's understanding of philosophy is accepted. While it may be tempting to want to argue on behalf of Bultmann, Kierkegaard and theologians generally that they are really just as ontological as Heidegger and no less committed than he to addressing what it is that really makes human beings the kind of beings they are,[24] it may in fact be one of the strengths of Bultmann's and Kierkegaard's *religious* existentialism that it is not tempted by the ontological project. Again and again, as we have seen, Bultmann insists that the Word can only be addressed to and received by individuals in their actual existence, you and me in the concrete decisions concerning relationships, work, politics and ethics that make up the very specific content of our lives.

Already in 1930 Bultmann set out just such an argument in a response to an early critic, G. Kuhlmann, who had accused him of being too dependent on Heidegger, but the article in which Bultmann made this defence could well be read as a response to Heidegger's own *Phenomenology and Theology*. He entirely accepts the distinctions between 'existential/*existentiell*' and 'ontological/ ontic' as made by Heidegger, and even accepts their application to the fields of philosophy and theology respectively. Consequently it is by no means inconsistent of Heidegger to draw on Kierkegaard's *existentiell* analyses in making his own ontological constructions, whilst at the same time rejecting Kierkegaard's Christian faith. The two projects simply have a different aim. Philosophy can never speak the 'Du', the second person singular word of address that faith must speak. Neither can philosophy utter the commandment to love that lies at the heart of the Christian message: '... that would no longer be an ontological statement, because it is facticity that is being spoken about.'[25] For faith and for theology, of course, this (Bultmann claims) is precisely what needs to be spoken about.

We shall be examining forms of religious existentialism – those of Tillich and Marcel, for example – in which the existentialist project is clearly linked to the question of Being. None the less, it may well be that it is the very strength – and the very radicality – of Bultmann's existentialism that it refuses to be deflected from the specificity of actual existence. Like the authority of the text in Barth, the primordiality of Being in Heidegger draws the sting of what Heidegger himself called the 'thrownness' of human beings, abandoned in the midst of the flux of time that has no limit, no end and no meaning outside the decisions they make. To be sure, as Bultmann's 'left-wing' critics pointed out, even he did not abandon talk of the action of God and, as we have seen, he insists – against Heidegger's self-limitation to '"It" calls' – that we can be set free from ourselves for ourselves only by such action. Yet that action is real and effective only in the present moment of our existence if and when we find ourselves addressed by the word that is made concrete and specific in the act of communication. Rarely has such a burden of responsibility been placed upon the process of communication – but, for Bultmann, there is no prior, higher or more fundamental kind of truth by which the Word can be validated apart from its being received in life-transforming faith.

NOTES

1. Quoted in D. Fergusson, *Bultmann* (London: Geoffrey Chapman, 1992), p. 23.
2. On the theological sources studied by Heidegger, see T. Kisiel, *The Genesis of Heidegger's* Being and Time (Berkeley and Los Angeles: University of California Press, 1990).
3. It should, of course, be stated that in one important respect there was a profound dissimilarity between Heidegger and Bultmann. Heidegger was, notriously, to become the most seriously compromised of any major German intellectual figure in the Nazi period, on account of his Rectorship of Freiburg University in 1933, during which he sought to facilitate centralized state control over the life of the University. Although he subsequently claimed that he soon became disillusioned with Nazism and that his lectures during the Nazi years constituted a clear critique of Nazi principles, his reputation has continued to suffer from his stance at that time. Although not a highly political thinker, Bultmann was none the less a leading spokesman for the Theology Faculty of Marburg University in 1933 in its opposition to the imposition of the Aryan decree (banning the study of non-Aryan books). He was signatory to the Barmen declaration, opposing Nazi control of the Churches. His brother died in a concentration camp.
4. R. Bultmann, 'On the Question of Christology' (1927) in idem., *Faith and Understanding* (London: SCM, 1969).
5. Ibid., p.132.
6. Idem., *Jesus and the Word* (London: Collins, 1958), pp. 14–15.
7. Bultmann, *Faith and Understanding*, p. 132.
8. Ibid., pp. 139–40.
9. Idem., *History and Eschatology* (Edinburgh: The University Press, 1975), pp. 10–11.
10. Ibid., p. 149.
11. Ibid., p. 150.
12. Ibid., pp. 150–1.
13. Martin Heidegger, *Being and Time* (Oxford: Basil Blackwell, 1962), p. 320 (Heidegger's pagination p. 275).
14. Bultmann, *History and Eschatology*, pp. 151–2.
15. See James F. Kay, *Christus Praesens. A Reconsideration of Rudolf Bultmann's Christology* (Grand Rapids: Eerdmans, 1994).
16. Bultmann, *History and Eschatology*, p. 155.
17. Although Bultmann's views on gnosticism have been invalidated by subsequent research, this does not affect the basic point of demythologizing.
18. There has been extensive discussion concerning Bultmann's concept of 'myth' and various inconsistencies and other failings have been noted many times. Here, however, I am to some extent sidestepping

Bultmann's own definitions in 'New Testament and Mythology' by setting the problem of demythologizing in the wider context of historical interpretation. In other words, I do not regard the fundamental problem with myth as being that New Testament myths are objectively false in comparison with expressions of *Weltanschauung* from other times or places but that they belong to a historical horizon that, for many reasons, we no longer inhabit. The key element is not that 'Myth is an expression of man's conviction that the origin and purpose of the world in which he lives are to be sought not within it but beyond it…', but that 'The real purpose of myth is not to present an objective picture of the world as it is, but to express man's understanding of himself in the world in which he lives.' (Both from *K&M*, p.10.) For further discussion, see John Macquarrie, *The Scope of Demythologizing* (London: SCM, 1960); idem., *An Existentialist Theology* (London: SCM, 1955); Edwin M. Good, 'The Meaning of Demythologization', and Schubert M. Ogden, 'The Significance of Rudolf Bultmann for Contemporary Theology', both in Charles W. Kegley (ed.) *The Theology of Rudolf Bultmann* (London: SCM, 1966); Ronald W. Hepburn, 'Demythologizing and the Problem of Validity', in A. Flew and A. MacIntyre (eds.) *New Essays in Philosophical Theology* (London: SCM, 1955); also various contributions in *K&M*.

19.   R. Bultmann, *Existence and Faith* (London: Collins, 1964), p. 349.
20.   Ibid., p. 350.
21.   Ibid.
22.   M. Heidegger, *Phänomenologie und Theologie* (Frankfurt: V. Klostermann, 1970), p. 18.
23.   *Being and Time*, p. 494 (Division Two, section 45, n. vi).
24.   Thus Gareth Jones in his *Bultmann. Towards a Critical Theology* (Cambridge: Polity Press, 1991).
25.   R. Bultmann, 'Die geschichtlichkeit des Daseins und der Glaube', in *Zeitschrift für Theologie und Kirche*, 1933, Vol. 5 (New Series), p. 358. An English translation of the article under the title 'The Historicity of Man and Faith' is to be found in R. Bultmann, *Existence and Faith* (London: Collins, 1964). Note, however, that Bultmann uses the characteristically Heideggerian term 'Dasein' and not 'Mensch' (= 'Man') in the German text.

8

On the Boundary

Although Paul Tillich (1886–1965) was of the same generation as Gogarten, Barth and Bultmann, his life was significantly different from theirs in that, leaving Germany and the German-speaking world in 1933, he experienced something like an intellectual reincarnation in the New World of the United States, where, although his theology retained many of its pre-emigration features, the overall effect was significantly transformed. He was also unique amongst religious existentialists in the extent to which he held on to the nineteenth-century ambition to present his theology in and as a systematic whole. Furthermore, whereas Bultmann (and, despite the contemporary resonances of *The Letter to the Romans*, Barth) remained very much a theologians' theologian, addressing issues that were primarily (and often solely) of concern to theologians working within and for the Church, Tillich was from the very beginning of his career concerned to contextualize theological questions in relation to the social, political, cultural and intellectual situation of the day. One of the most significant figures in twentieth century theology to pay serious attention to the visual arts and, in doing so, laying the foundations for the current expansion of that field in theological study, he simultaneously played a key role in the dialogue between Christianity and Marxism, anticipating many of the themes of liberation theology in his writings from the 1920s and early 1930s. Nor did these areas exhaust his range of interests: psychoanalysis, metaphysics, the doctrine of nature and the dialogue between world religions all occupied him significantly at various times. In addition, his 'method of correlation', the redefinition of God as the 'Ground of Being', the concept of 'ultimate concern', the theory of symbolism and the idea of *kairos* were all original contributions that helped secure his place in the canon of twentieth-century theology, a place underpinned by his sermons through which, especially in the 1950s and 1960s, he reached a much wider audience than most theologians ever achieve! It is characteristic that he was once dubbed 'the apostle to the intellectuals'.

But how do Tillich's many and varied fields of interest relate to existentialism? Was this simply one more item in the long list of apologetic concerns? Or was it a continuing and defining aspect of his whole intellectual enterprise? And how can anyone who aligns himself with existentialism go on to devote himself to the writing of a systematic theology? Noting for now that Tillich himself regarded the existential dimension of his thought as central, let us briefly run through some of the main events of his life: if he is not a thinker whose life is palpably present in his work (like Kierkegaard or Dostoevsky), there are many points at which his intellectual stance was importantly shaped by the events and circumstances in which he participated: indeed, for one whose method of correlation demanded that theology relate itself to the questions being asked in the contemporary world, it could hardly be otherwise.

Tillich was born in East Prussia in 1886. He was a son of the manse, and he was to write of his home background,

> Quite obviously, no-one who grew up under these sociological conditions and under the influence of Lutheran theology could conceive of any revolutionary changing of reality. The only possible attitude is one of patient submission to the God-given authority.[1]

He was in his own person to disprove this dictum, drawing Barth's jibe that his whole theology was an incessant struggle against the Grand Inquisitor.

During his theological studies in Berlin, Tübingen and Halle he engaged extensively with the current movements of theological and philosophical thought, being influenced, like many others, by neo-Kantianism and the kind of theology represented by Troeltsch, the crisis of New Testament studies (above all by Schweitzer's *The Quest of the Historical Jesus*) and the beginnings of phenomenology. At the same time he came under the spell of Schelling, on whose work he wrote two higher degree dissertations, *Mysticism and Guilt-Consciousness* and *The Construction of the History of Religion in Schelling's Positive Philosophy*, also reading Kierkegaard and, later, Nietzsche. Schelling's influence was especially formative, and can be seen at many points throughout his work. Indeed, his fundamental project of producing an existential system of theology is in itself profoundly Schellingian. Other themes in his writing that can be closely correlated to Schelling's later philosophy are the insistence, against Hegel, on the openness of the dialectical process as the continuing process of world-creation/redemption and the primacy of the categories of possibility and actuality in this process, the continuing spur of an irrational ground of being that can never be exhausted in rational reflection, the acknowledgement of a mystical dimension of consciousness and the acceptance of the necessity of the Fall as an aspect of the process of creation. Of Kierkegaard he wrote that he

> was the first to break through the closed system of the idealist philosophy of essence... The importance of his work for post-war [i.e. First World War] German theology and philosophy can hardly be over-estimated. As early as my last student years (1905–1906), I came under the influence of his aggressive dialectics. (*BB*, p. 341)

The kind of reception of Kierkegaard current in that period is vividly portrayed in Thomas Mann's *Doktor Faustus*, when Mann describes the rural rambles of a student fellowship who pass their weekends in all-night discussions on the meaning of life, discussions in which Kierkegaard's concept of the demonic features strongly. Mann himself stated that he gathered much of the material for these chapters from conversations with Tillich. Nietzsche's influence came later, and it was, in Tillich's own expression, 'tremendous'. Yet, although he found in Nietzsche a powerful expression of 'the experience of the abyss' (*BB*, p. 322) that appealed to the ecstatic element in his own intellectual and personal make-up, his historical, social and political perspectives restrained him from becoming a full-blooded Nietzschean.

As a curate in a working-class district of Berlin in the years 1912–14, Tillich had his first encounter with the deprivation of the industrial proletariat, and although he did not at this point interpret that situation in the light of a socialist analysis, he became painfully aware of the inadequacies of the somewhat paternalist approach to social problems of the mainstream Church with its 'Inner Mission'. Married for the first time in the autumn of 1914, Tillich joined up a few days later as an army chaplain. He saw service throughout the war on the Western Front, being awarded the Iron Cross first class in 1918. It was during this period that he began to study art, in the first instance through poorly illustrated art books which he read off duty in the trenches and then, when on leave towards the end of the war, he had what he later described as a revelatory experience of the power of art before a Botticelli painting of the 'Madonna with Singing Angels' in Berlin.

The horror of the war itself and the social collapse of Germany in its aftermath impressed Tillich with a keen sense of the crisis of liberal culture and the conviction that the old pre-war order could not be restored. Unlike Barth, however, Tillich did not see a return to the simple clarity of Scripture as an adequate response to this situation. It was not only the authority of the contemporary Church and theological leadership that was being called into question, but the authority of all the historic resources of Christian theology. On the other hand, even in the most turbulent and chaotic aspects of contemporary reality there remained possibilities of experience and insight that pointed beyond the violence of the present to eternal truths and values. The contemporary task of theology was therefore to enter as deeply as possible into the heart of the contemporary crisis and prophetically to name those elements within it in which the power of renewal and transcendence was to be found.

For Tillich himself the artistic and cultural situation provided abundant material for such a venture. He was especially impressed by the prophetic force of expressionism in the visual arts and, albeit chiefly at a theoretical level, he was highly engaged politically, aligning himself with the Marxist Independent Social Democratic Party.

In these post-war years Tillich also experienced considerable personal turmoil, divorcing and then remarrying Hannah Gottschow with whom he remained for the rest of his life – even if their marriage was far from conventional in traditional Christian terms. What he came to experience as the legalism of Christian morality was, indeed, to be another area in which he would wage his ceaseless war against the spirit of the Grand Inquisitor.

After a brief period at Marburg and at Dresden, he was appointed to a Professorship in Philosophy at Frankfurt in 1929, where he remained until forced into emigration. It is characteristic that, during the inter-war years, he held positions in both philosophical and theological faculties and that, during the Frankfurt period, he was closely involved with what became known as the Frankfurt School, a group of left-wing social theorists who could not accept the stultifying constraints of communist domination but sought to apply

Marxist insights and methods in a more open and liberal manner. Key members of the group were Max Horkheimer, Theodor Adorno (whose 'habilitationsschrift' *Kierkegaard: The Construction of the Aesthetic* was written under Tillich's supervision), Karl Mannheim, Karl Mennicke and Friedrich Pollock.[2] Not only were all the members of this group on the left (although Tillich himself typically welcomed even Nazi students into discussion sessions, so long as they respected the spirit of dialogical exchange), many of them were also Jewish and it was inevitable that they would be amongst the early victims of Nazi Terror. As early as July 1932 stormtroopers and Nazi students rioted, physically assaulting left-wing and Jewish students and Tillich called for the expulsion of those responsible. At the end of 1932 his most substantial political work, *The Socialist Decision*, was published: as its title suggests, it was, in effect, an existentially argued summons to oppose Nazism in favour of the socialist alternative. When Hitler came to power it was rapidly banned. Ten days after the *Machtergreifung* (21 March 1933) stormtroopers occupied the university and, a fortnight later, Tillich and others of his circle were suspended from teaching duties. Later that year Tillich, Hannah and their daughter Erdmuthe left Germany for America, where, despite the enormous language problems he was to encounter (there was little motivation for pre-war German theologians to learn English!) he was to begin a new career, taking American citizenship in 1940 and teaching in New York, Harvard and Chicago. During the late 1950s and early 1960s he attained something like cult status on American campuses, preaching and lecturing with great intensity and was lionized wherever he went. During this period his political interest declined, but he remained occasionally outspoken, opposing nuclear deterrence and continuing to speak positively of Marx (a provocative move in 1950s America). He was one of a select group of leaders of intellectual life invited to the platform at President Kennedy's inauguration. He also continued to pursue his passionate interest in the visual arts, and to engage in dialogue with psychoanalysis – modernist art and psychoanalysis being defining preoccupations of the American intelligentsia in that period.

Tillich's influence on theology in the United States has been incalculable, greater than in Germany itself or elsewhere in Europe. Yet his thought was shaped by the European tradition, as is particularly clear with regard to his relation to existentialism. Tillich himself regarded existentialism as an almost inevitable development for someone of his intellectual and historical situation. This was not merely to do with the influence of such thinkers as Schelling, Kierkegaard and Nietzsche but with the fact that the tension between the visions of an integrated, all-embracing unitary culture offered by idealist philosophy and ecclesiastical and political conservatism were so profoundly shattered by the realities of industrial society, science and the social catastrophe unleashed in 1914. 'When with 31 July 1914, the nineteenth century came to an end, the Existentialist revolt ceased to be revolt. It became the mirror of an experienced reality' (*CB*, p. 136). Belief in harmony was one of the pillars of the bourgeois social order, but Marxist analysis shows this to have been always an illusion. The reality of bourgeois society was not harmony but the incessant conflict between classes, between capitalists and workers. The war, and the events it set in train, demonstrated this to be the case. In such a situation it is only naive idealism or political Romanticism to believe in the reinstatement of a unitary social order. Existentialism, on the other hand, situates itself precisely at the point where the impossibility of such harmony becomes manifest.

It should immediately be said that Tillich's use of the term 'existentialism' is very broad. He regarded expressionist art, Marxism and psychoanalysis as in some sense 'existential', because they all point to the concrete and problematic existence of human beings in historical actuality in such a way as to render impossible any harmonizing intellectual overview of the human situation. Heideggerian philosophy is simply one expression of this wider picture, even though it is an expression that Tillich regards as singularly important. Like other religious existentialists he sees the pre-history of modern existentialism stretching back through such figures as Pascal, Luther, Eckhart, Augustine and Plato.

Well aware of the charge of excessive broadness, Tillich distinguished between existentialism in the narrow sense of a particular philosophical movement and what he called the existential attitude. This is how he defined the existential attitude in *The Courage to Be*, perhaps the most widely read of all his English writings.

> The existential attitude is one of involvement in contrast to a merely theoretical or detached attitude. 'Existential' in this sense can be defined as participating in a situation, especially a cognitive situation, with the whole of one's existence. This includes temporal, spatial, historical, psychological, sociological, biological

conditions. And it includes the finite freedom which reacts to these conditions and changes them. An existential knowledge is a knowledge in which these elements, and therefore the whole existence of him who knows, participates. (*CB*, p. 124)

The more specific content of existential thought is definable in relation to a history of ideas that includes: Plato's insights into the distinction between the realm of ideal or essential truth and the vision of human life in a world subject to change and decay as a life of estrangement and alienation; the Christian and especially the Augustinian view of human existence being determined by the drama of fall, sin and salvation; the medieval experience of the demonic; and the contingency, anxiety and despair experienced in the wake of the nominalists' demolition of the medieval synthesis. The Protestant Reformation contained existentialist elements, but, after the initial moment of Luther's anguished quest for a gracious God, Protestantism soon came to understand itself in an objective way and to take an authoritarian attitude. Existential elements are also to be found in Kant, in his preservation of the distinction between human intellectual capacities and the reality of the thing-in-itself and his doctrine of radical evil. They are also present in Hegel's emphasis on the role of negation, his recognition of the importance of passion and the problematic status of the individual. Within the modern bourgeois period, however, the existentialist voice has, typically, been the voice of protest against an understanding of reality or a social practice that attempts to assert as fact the existence of a harmonious totality that stands in contradiction to the real situation of individuals and communities.

Elsewhere Tillich speaks of existentialism as 'a universal element in all thinking [that] is the attempt of man to describe his existence and its conflicts, the origin of these conflicts, and the anticipations of overcoming them.'[3] As the expression of revolt against ideologies of harmony, it is 'the protest of the existing man in his estrangement, his finitude, in his feeling of guilt and meaninglessness ... a protest against the world-view in which man was nothing but a piece of an all-embracing mechanical reality, be it in physical terms, be it in economic or sociological terms, or even be it in psychological terms.'[4] But whereas those who gave voice to this protest in the nineteenth century were lonely prophets on the margins of the cultural mainstream, 'In the twentieth century the outcry of existentialism became universal' – and Tillich cites such examples as Heidegger, Jaspers, Sartre and Marcel in philosophy and Eliot, Auden and Kafka in literature.[5]

Tillich's extensive essay 'Existential Philosophy: Its Historical Meaning' follows a similar line. He concludes that

> What all philosophers of Existence oppose is the 'rational' system of thought and life developed by Western industrial society and its philosophic representatives. During the last hundred years the implications of this system have become increasingly clear: a logical or naturalistic mechanism which seemed to destroy individual freedom, personal decision, and organic community; an analytic rationalism which saps the vital forces of life and transforms everything, including man himself, into an object of calculation and control; a secularized humanism which cuts man off from the world and from the creative Source and the ultimate mystery of existence. The Existential philosophers, supported by poets and artists in every European country, were consciously or subconsciously aware of the approach of this self-estranged form of life. They tried to resist it in a desperate struggle which drove them often to mental self-destruction and made their utterances extremely aggressive, passionate, paradoxical, fragmentary, revolutionary, prophetic and ecstatic ... [They] were trying to discover an ultimate meaning of life beyond the reach of reinterpretation, revived theologies or positivism ... They turned toward man's immediate experience, toward 'subjectivity' ... as ... living experience ... They turned toward Reality as men experience it immediately in their actual living, to ... inward experience ... If the experience of this level of living is 'mystical,' Existential philosophy can be called the attempt to reconquer the meaning of life in 'mystical' terms ... [But] in this context the term does not indicate a mystical union with the transcendent Absolute; it signifies rather a venture of faith toward union with the depths of life ...[6]

This survey of Tillich's understanding of existentialism has introduced many of the key terms of his thought. We now need to look at these in more detail.

II

The systematic nature of Tillich's mature thought means, as he himself acknowledged, that all the parts of the system are interconnected in an essentially circular manner. In one respect, therefore, it scarcely matters at what point one begins. The dialectic of autonomy, heteronomy and what Tillich calls theonomy does, however, connect with much that has already been said, and I shall therefore begin here.

Tillich sees the principle of autonomy as one of the defining features of the eighteenth-century Enlightenment. He accepts Kant's definition of autonomy as

> man's conquering the state of immaturity so far as he is responsible for it. Immaturity ... is the inability to use one's own reason without the guidance of somebody else. Immaturity of this kind is caused by ourselves. It is rooted in the lack of resoluteness and courage to use reason without the guidance of another person.[7]

Over against authoritarian attempts to constrain freedom of thought, Tillich takes an essentially positive view of autonomy. 'We could', he writes, 'define autonomy as the memory which man has of his own created goodness. Autonomy is man's living the law of reason in all realms of his spiritual activity.'[8] Not only the Enlightenment principle of freedom of thought but also the Protestant affirmation of individual faith show something of the principle of autonomy.

Heteronomy, as the subjection of the individual (person or community) to the will of another is the contrary of autonomy. Heteronomy is a particular temptation for religions when they seek to coerce the assent of the individual. Conspicuous examples of the clash between religious heteronomy and Enlightenment autonomy would be the Catholic Church's suppression of Galileo or fundamentalist attempts to ban the teaching of evolutionary theory in schools in the United States. Even in the midst of the German Church struggle, Tillich sees the danger of heteronomy emerging amongst Barthians, of whom he says that 'The extremely narrow position of the Barthians may save German Protestantism, but it also creates a new heteronomy, an anti-autonomous and anti-humanistic attitude that I must regard as a denial of the Protestant principle' (*BB*, p. 315).

Although autonomy is to be affirmed over against heteronomy, it is not of itself able to generate any content. Autonomy concerns the form or the appropriation of truth, not its substance. Left to itself the principle of autonomy drains the meaning out of the substantial powers of life, leaving us empty and uprooted. By way of contrast, heteronomous systems (religious traditionalism, for example) have content, but only at the price of ignoring the freedom of the individual in appropriating that content. It would seem that the antagonism between autonomy and heteronomy is irreconcilable and, indeed, much of modern history (and especially modern religious history) would suggest that that is so. Tillich, however, perceives a third power, theonomy, in which (in the religious sphere, for example), we have 'our own personal experience of the presence of the divine Spirit within us, witnessing to the Bible or to the church ... Where this inner witness is lacking ... obedience to authority would be mere external subjection and not inward personal experience.'[9]

But how can we distinguish such theonomy from heteronomy?

As Tillich sees it, theonomy cannot be reached by denying or turning back from the pursuit of autonomy. On the contrary, it is arrived at by entering into the deepest ground of autonomy itself. Doubt can only be overcome in a religious sense when the doubter discovers a principle of inner certainty that no one else can give him. This is possible because the doubter always has such a principle within him, because to question the meaning of life or to enquire after truth is already to presuppose that question and enquiry are worth pursuing. To approach the issue in this way is to see that the 'answer' to such ultimate questions can only be found in and through the courageous act of questioning itself.

The breakthrough to that which is presupposed in all questioning, is therefore not a mystical experience in the sense of a flight beyond the world into a dimension beyond words and beyond consciousness or an encounter with a transcendent object. Rather, it is the moment of rebirth, of a renewed grounding in that which renders language and consciousness possible. This is, in its essence, the argument of *The Courage to Be*: that, in face of the modern anxiety about the meaninglessness of life, an anxiety everywhere testified in existentialist art and literature, 'The act of accepting meaninglessness is in itself a meaningful act. It is an act of faith' (*CB*, p. 171).

However, the particular kind of anxiety that comes to expression in the typical modern crisis of doubt and faith is only one form of what is itself a still more fundamental dynamic. All such forms are culturally variable: we can, for instance, see that in Late Antiquity the dominant kind of anxiety was anxiety in face of fate, in the Middle Ages it was anxiety concerning death and damnation, in the

Reformation period anxiety concerning personal guilt. Each case is culturally specific and yet reveals the ontological dialectic of being and non-being that underlies them all.

Just as question and answer are essentially interdependent, so too are being and non-being. 'The question of being', says Tillich,

> is produced by the 'shock of non-being.' Only man can ask the ontological question [the question of being] because he alone is able to lok beyond the limits of his own being and of every other being ... He is not bound to 'beingness'; he can envisage nothingness; he can ask the ontological question. (*ST I*, p. 207)

To ask the ontological question is only possible in the light of the possibility of non-being, for it is to ask, 'Why is there something rather than nothing?' This possibility of non-being is disclosed both in relation to the origin of the world out of nothing and, most painfully, in face of the prospect of our own death and relapse into non-being. It is also theologically important from another perspective, for, if God were only to be thought of in terms of Being, He would be static and an object amongst objects. If we are to have a theology of the living God, we will require the concept of non-being.

Although each form of anxiety manifests this ontological dialectic in its own way, its ontological character is most sharply disclosed in the modern crisis of doubt and meaning,

> For the anxiety of meaninglessness undermines what is still unshaken in the anxiety of fate and death and guilt and condemnation ... Even in the despair of having to die and the despair of self-condemnation meaning is affirmed and certitude preserved. But in the despair of doubt and meaninglessness both are swallowed by non-being. (*CB*, pp. 68–9)

In the light of the dialectic of question and answer it follows that the way forward is through the acceptance of despair, for only then will we be able to discover that 'the power of being ... is present even in the face of the most radical manifestation of non-being' and that the experience of non-being is itself dependent on being.

> Meaninglessness, as long as it is experienced, includes an experience of the 'power of acceptance', [and] to accept this power of

acceptance consciously is the religious answer of absolute faith, of a faith which has been deprived by doubt of any concrete content, which nevertheless is faith and the source of the most paradoxical manifestation of the courage to be. (*CB*, p. 172)

Paradoxical – and yet, it seems, there is an important sense in which being and non-being are not merely synthesized in some sort of equal and complementary way, but that being overcomes non-being. Just as theonomy represents the shining through of divine immediacy in such a way as to relocate the strivings of the autonomous self on the ground of substantial truth (a ground that heteronomy, left to itself, reveals, but in a distorted manner), so too the descent into the abysses of non-being culminates in a renewed experience of being. It is thus axiomatic for Tillich that although the concept of non-being can help us to formulate a concept of God as living, none the less the statement that 'God is Being-Itself' is the one non-symbolic statement we can make about God. The 'being' of God represents that beyond which there can be no further appeal, the unconditional dimension that is secretly present in all conscious life. Thus, although he cannot accept the ontological argument in any of the forms in which it has been stated (and certainly not in the sense of providing any sort of proof for the existence of God) Tillich states that 'nothing is more important for philosophy and theology than the truth it contains, the acknowledgement of the unconditional element in the structure of reason and reality … A philosophy of religion which does not begin with something unconditional never reaches God' (*ST I*, pp. 230–1).

But this does not guarantee the validity of any objective theological system. Absolute faith is neither mysticism, nor the experience of an objective being 'out there'. The God who is revealed in absolute faith, the God who is Being-Itself, is not an object amongst objects or a being amongst beings. He is the God beyond the god of theism.

Moreover, the dialectical interrelationship of the elements means that, just as the experience of non-being in the anxiety of doubt and meaninglessness can lead us towards the revelation of God as Being-Itself, so too the understanding of God as Being-Itself leads us back to the question of creation and the manifestation of divine being in, with and under the conditions of created being – *including non-being*. If existence is inexplicable without essence, essence is what it is only in its manifestation in existence. Once more, we encounter the circularity of the system – a circularity that, Tillich insists, is virtuous, not vicious.

At this point, however, we are brought up against what, from the standpoint of Christian orthodoxy, is a highly problematic aspect of Tillich's theology. Traditionally, metaphysical theology has tended to identify God with being and being with goodness. The goodness of the created order that God approves in Genesis 1 is itself an aspect of the goodness that inheres in all being. For Tillich, however, the existence of creation, i.e. that a world *exists*, means that it exists in separation from the plenitude of divine being. It can only do this as a structurally complex whole in which nothing exists in simple self-identity. That anything *exists* therefore means that it exists in the mode of a fusion of being and non-being. To exist, as Tillich puts it, is to stand out from non-being, but it is also to enter into a state of estrangement from the self-identity of essential being and therefore is also tragic. He does not hesitate to spell out the implication that 'there is a point in which creation and the Fall coincide, in spite of their logical differences' (*ST II*, 50).

Within creation, Tillich sees human beings as having a special status. Human beings do not simply exist, they exist as freedom, or, in the traditional language of theology, as endowed by God with the gift of free will. But once again the dialectical structure of reality complicates the picture, because, just as there can be no being without non-being, so too freedom is a meaningless concept unless connected to its polar opposite, destiny. A free creature, therefore, is also a creature who has a destiny. Tillich's picture of the fall is therefore highly ambiguous. If, on the one hand, we say that the fall is necessary because non-being is implied in the very structure of a world coming into existence, we must not forget that the human subject, as finite freedom, can only fall to the extent that it does so freely. Its fall is always essentially its own act for which it must bear full responsibility. It is in the light of this that theology does not talk merely about estrangement but about sin. On the other hand, the fact that freedom can only exist within a world that is what it is by virtue of its estrangement from the eternal self-sameness of the divine essence corresponds to the dimension of destiny that determines it no less than that of freedom. Its fall, then, is not an external necessity. It is free, yet it is also its destiny, its tragic destiny to experience sin.

Being and non-being and freedom and destiny are only two of the pairs of ontological polarities by means of which Tillich expounds his metaphysical understanding of the human situation. Self and world, individualization and participation, dynamics and form are other important elements that help him to fill out the picture. In principle each and all of these polarities can coexist in a state of complex balance and harmonious complementarity. In existence, however, subsequent to the fall, these structures are transformed into what Tillich calls 'structures of destruction' and it is in this form that we typically encounter them in every level of our being. His explication of these structures of destruction constitutes one of the most insightful sections of his *Systematic Theology*. Take, for example, the account of the interrelationship between self-loss and world-loss:

> Self-loss is the loss of one's determining centre, the disintegration of the unity of the person. This is manifest in moral conflicts and in psychopathological disruptions ... The horrifying experience of 'falling to pieces' gets hold of the person. To the degree in which this happens, one's world also falls to pieces. It ceases to be a world, in the sense of a meaningful whole. Things no longer speak to man; they lose their power to enter into a meaningful encounter with man, because man himself has lost this power. In extreme cases the complete unreality of one's world is felt; nothing is left except this awareness of one's own empty self. (*ST II*, p. 71)

But if we then try to 'get a grip' on ourselves, without taking into account the whole actual context of our existence (our relationships and other external circumstances) we soon learn that

> There is no empty self, no pure subjectivity ... The attempt of the finite self to be the centre of everything gradually has the effect of its ceasing to be the centre of anything. Both self and world are threatened. Man becomes a limited self, in dependence on a limited environment. He has lost his world; he has only his environment. (*ST II*, p. 71)

A similar pattern is repeated whenever the ontological polarities turn against each other or become separated from each other: freedom becomes anarchic individualism and caprice, destiny turns into grim fate – whereas, ideally, 'having a destiny' is a precondition of free action. This is particularly clear in existentialism, which, Tillich says,

> described the dialectics of this situation in terms of the restlesness, emptiness, and meaninglessness connected with it. If no essential relation between a free agent and his objects exist[s], no choice is objectively preferable to any other; no commitment to a cause or a person is meaningful; no dominant purpose can be established ... If man's freedom is not directed by destiny or if it is a series of contingent acts or arbitrariness ... Man has used his freedom to waste his freedom; and it is his destiny to lose his destiny. (*ST II*, p. 73)

The same pattern is to be found in terms of the relationships between dynamics and form and between individualization and participation. In each case what belongs essentially together as part of the holistic structure of life becomes sundered and the polarities become mutually destructive, with the result that 'Estranged from the ultimate power of being man is determined by his finitude' (*ST II*, p. 77). The result is anxiety about death, suffering, loneliness, doubt and meaninglessness – in a word, despair, 'the final index of man's predicament ... the boundary line beyond which man cannot go' (*ST II*, p. 86).

At this point, however, the circle of the system turns once more. The point of maximum estrangement becomes the point at which the question about meaning reveals a dimension of depth in which the way to an answer is to be found.

This dialectic of the boundary situation is characteristic of Tillich's method: pushed to an extreme, each and every polarity discloses its inability to stand by itself and thus its dependence on what appears as its opposite, however paradoxical it may at first seem. The extremity of estrangement discloses our need for God, or, as Tillich puts it, the quest for the new being. New being, as Tillich defines it, 'is essential being under the conditions of existence, conquering the gap between essence and existence' (*ST II*, p. 136). 'The New Being is not something that simply takes the place of the Old Being. But it is a renewal of the Old which has been corrupted, distorted, split and almost destroyed. But not wholly destroyed. Salvation does not destroy creation; but it transforms the old creation into a new one' (*BB*, p. 166).

III

However, the fact that we feel a need for the renewal of our being does not of itself guarantee that such renewal can ever be actualized. The claim of Christian faith, though, is that in the personal life of Jesus as the Christ, in his words, deeds and sufferings, the new being *has* become actual and that it is thus actual in one existing personal life is, for Tillich, significant for the totality of existence. The possibility of fulfilled life is no longer merely abstract or theoretical but is realizable.

Fully realized as the once-for-all *kairos*, or moment of fulfilled time of which Jesus himself spoke when he preached that 'The time is fulfilled, repent for the kingdom of God is at hand', the new being is to be appropriated in those moments of decision to which our destiny brings us again and again, individually and collectively. Although the general shape of Tillich's thought at this point is broadly similar to that of Bultmann, he does not individualize the moment of decision as Bultmann does. There are moments of decision in the lives of communities no less than in the lives of individuals. This, indeed, is the premiss of Tillich's 1932 book, *The Socialist Decision*: that time was, for Tillich, a *kairos* in the life of Germany, a moment when, in the concreteness of its historical destiny, the nation was called to choose renewal. Instead, as we know, it chose a path that led to disaster on a massive scale – but this too is characteristic of historical choice: the moment of *kairos* comes to us as a destiny, but not as a necessity; how we respond is always a matter for freedom.

Again in contrast to Bultmann, Tillich explores quite extensively the cosmic dimensions of the new being. The theory of spirit set out in the third volume of his *Systematic Theology* depicts the life of human spirit as participating in and bringing to expression the totality of life in its multidimensional reality. Suggestive rather than definitive and, perhaps, revealing once more his affiliation to Schelling, Tillich makes clear that the mystery of redemption cannot exclude nature. Nature, he says, 'is subjected to the laws of finitude and destruction. It is suffering and sighing with us.'[10] And, somehow, the Christ event is also a revelation of salvation for nature: the earthquake that accompanied the crucifixion, Tillich asserts, shows that

the earth participated in the agony of the man on the Cross ... Trembling and shaking the earth pointed to another ground on which the earth itself rests: the self-surrendering love on which all earthly powers and values concentrate their hostility and which they cannot conquer ... [On Good Friday] the earth ceased to be the foundation of what we build on her. Only in so far as it has a deeper ground, can it stand; only insofar as it is rooted in the same foundation in which the Cross is rooted, can it last. (*BB*, pp. 283–4)

In the moment of *kairos,* the moment of concrete historical choice, whether that be individual, collective or cosmic, we are poised between two different powers. On the one side is *logos,* the sphere of reason. But the demands of reason itself (or, ontologically speaking, the demands of essential being) can only be experienced in the mode of *kairos,* that is, as matters of temporally conditioned existence. Yet this does not mean that *kairos* necessarily excludes *logos.* On the contrary, as the New Testament witnesses, the moment of the fullness of time, the coming of Jesus as the Christ, is also the revelation of the *logos.* None the less there is no timeless or extra-historical revelation of *logos* capable of resolving the discords of existence in its estrangement from essential being. The reunification of essential and existential being can only take place in, with and under the conditions of existence themselves, including the confrontation with death experienced by Jesus on the cross.

The moment of *kairos* is threatened from the other side by the demonic, by the violent power of the depths that threaten to reduce the ordered world to chaos. If Tillich seems to stand in the long Augustinian tradition that identifies the fall in some way with the principle of non-being, he does not want to say that evil is mere vacuity. The demonic reveals the sheer force and violent energy of evil. It is precisely this aspect of evil that forces us to confront the fact that evil will never be overcome by rationality alone. If evil is to be conquered, it can only be on the ground of those depths from which evil itself draws its greatest strength. The conquest of evil in the *kairos* does not, as we have just seen, deny rationality, but it does not come about by virtue of rationality itself.

Ultimately, the only power that is able to overcome evil definitively is the power of love. 'Death is given power over everything finite, especially in our period of history. But death is given no power over love. Love is stronger than death. It creates

something new out of the destruction caused by death ...'
(*BB*, pp. 280–1):

> This love is the ultimate power of union, the ultimate victory
> over separation. Being united with it enables us to stand above
> life in the midst of life. It enables us to accept the double-faced
> rulers of life, their fascination and their anxiety, their glory and
> their horror. It gives us the certainty that no moment is possible
> in which we can be prevented from reaching the fulfilment
> towards which all life is striving. This is the courage to accept
> life in the power of that in which life is rooted and grounded.
> (*BB*, pp. 195–6)

IV

The triumph of love over the demonic power of death and over the
despair of meaninglessness, a triumph evidenced in Jesus as the
Christ and as the bearer in historical time of the New Being, could
seem to be a fairly uncontroversial summary of Christian doctrine.
But even in such a summary statement it is possible to see how
Tillich's revision of Christianity was highly controversial. First, in
contrast to Barth's insistence on the sole authority of the Word of
God revealed in scripture, Tillich seems to see the gospels as exem-
plifying a pattern of redemptive action that is grounded in a more
general understanding of existence. As we saw in Chapter 6, he
regarded the Barthian view of scripture as inconsistent in the way it
made of scripture an exception to the otherwise universal ambiguity of existence. There can be no such exception according to Tillich.
Scripture itself, and the events revealed in it, participate fully in
the estrangement and ambiguity of all existence and, conversely,
scripture is not the sole testimony to the quest for the new being.
Because of the dialectical structuring of being in all its forms,
the separation of existential from essential being never entirely oblit-
erates the ultimate testimony of existence to essence. Anticipations
and analogues of the gospel are to be found throughout the domain
of human existence and experience. Thus, for Tillich, modern art,
even when atheistic, bore indirect testimony to the quest for the new
being – and the same could be said for Marxism, psychoanalysis
or existentialism.

The suspicion that, in Tillich's theology, the proclamation of Jesus as the Christ is in some sense 'merely' the localized occurrence of a more general experience could be further fuelled by his acknowledgement of what he regards as the symbolic nature of the gospel picture of Christ. The testimony of the gospels, he argues, is not primarily 'evidence' for historical facts. Instead, the gospels are to be read by analogy to the way in which we look at an expressionistic portrait. Such a portrait does not show us what its subject looked like in a realistic or photographic sense: instead it shows us the powers and passions that rule its subject, even if this means distorting its empirical appearance. As an expressionistic portrait the gospels reveal their symbolic nature. But, for Tillich, a 'symbol' is never 'only' a symbol. Whereas a sign is merely a conventional signifier without any intrinsic connection to that which it represents, a symbol is somehow charged with the presence or power of what it symbolizes. A royal symbol elicits the respect due to the person of the sovereign. A great work of art brings us into the very presence of its subject matter.

Tillich does not deny that to speak of religious doctrines or texts as symbolic is to weaken their claims to literal truth. Indeed there is only one non-symbolic statement we can make about God: that God is Being-Itself. Everything else, he says (and this clearly includes the whole Biblical drama of creation, fall and redemption), is symbolic. It is not the statement of a literal truth, but the communication of an understanding and a power. Moreover, as if to compound his errors in the eyes of traditionalists, he acknowledges that symbols are historically conditioned and have a life and death. The Roman Eagle may have aroused awe (or hatred) amongst citizens of the Ancient world: in us it evokes a merely historic or aesthetic admiration or interest. The image of Christ Pantocrator and the other symbols of glory no longer speak to a generation that has known two world wars, the Holocaust and the atomic bomb.

But none of this moves Tillich to want to reject symbols or to demythologize them. Whilst he fully acknowledges that symbols require interpretation, he rejects the idea that any propositional statement can adequately convey the truth of an important symbol. The symbol says more than the literal fact or statement. 'Symbols and myths cannot be criticized simply because they are symbols. They must be criticized on the basis of their power to express what they are supposed to express' (*ST II*, p. 176). Theology must learn to be sensitive to the power of symbols and to read the signs of the times, discerning which symbols and complexes of symbols have the power to transform the existence of contemporary humanity. He is clearly in no doubt that, for the twentieth century, it is the symbolism of the cross that has the most powerful appeal, a symbolism that he finds not only in avowedly religious art, but even in such secular works as Picasso's *Guernica*.[11]

Another aspect of the question as to whether Tillich's account of the gospel reduces it to being 'merely' the symbol of a universal pattern of human experience concerns his eschatology. We have already noted that he speaks of the interdependence between the once-for-all *kairos* of the new being revealed in historical time and a multitude of particular *kairoi* that engage particular individuals and communities at particular historical junctures. But is there really a once-for-all in Tillich's theology? Does history really have an end? To put it another way. The circularity of Tillich's system has been mentioned several times: if we begin with the modern experience of meaninglessness, we find ourselves being led back to an ultimate ground of meaning, yet, if we begin with the doctrine of divine being, we find ourselves led into the history of the world in its estrangement from the divine ground. Does the cycle of dialectically determined becoming simply continue forever, eternally oscillating between the polarities of being and non-being?

Like so many of his theological generation, Tillich himself draws a sharp distinction between the biblical concept of linear time, time directed towards the final vindication of God's purposes in history, and the kind of cyclical time characteristic of many other religious traditions that reflect their contextualization in the cycles of agricultural life. But to talk of the end of history is to talk symbolically and Tillich is quite clear in his assertion that, once this is understood, 'The eschatological problem ... ceases to be an imaginative matter about an indefinitely far (or near) catastrophe in time and space and becomes an expression of our standing in every moment in face of the eternal' (*ST III*, p. 421). 'The eternal' is not outside of time, nor is eternal life conceived by him as, in any sense, an 'after'-life. The eternal is not the opposite of time but is that which gives us time. In the experience of the eternal we no longer experience time as mere succession, moment following moment into extinction, but as meaningful time, time filled with presence. The concept of 'presence' (or 'the present') is thus a key to the whole question of time. For the present is the only dimension of time that we ever actually experience. The past no longer is, the future is not yet, only the present, a moving boundary between past and future, 'is'.

> The riddle of the present is the deepest of all the riddles of time ... Whenever we say 'now' or 'today', we stop the flux of time for us. We accept the present and do not care that it is gone in the moment that we accept it. We live in it and it is renewed for us in every new 'present'. This is possible because every moment of time reaches into the eternal. It is the eternal that stops the flux of time for us. It is the eternal 'now' which provides for us a temporal 'now'. We live so long as 'it is still today' – in the words of the letter to the Hebrews. Not everybody, and nobody all the time, is aware of this 'eternal now' in the temporal 'now'. But sometimes it breaks powerfully into our consciousness and gives us the certainty of the eternal, of a dimension of time which cuts into time and gives us our time. (*BB*, p. 107)

The eschaton, then, cannot be regarded as a future at which we may one day arrive in the course of historical time. The eschaton, like the answer that is presupposed in the asking of the question, is what always already indwells authentic historical time and what empowers us to historical action, *despite* the contradictions and ambiguities of our existential estrangement. It is what gives us not just the courage to be, but the courage to act.

In his Marxist years, Tillich found himself close to another independent Marxist thinker, Ernst Bloch, whose 'philosophy of hope' saw 'the principle of hope' rather than the necessary histori-cal laws proclaimed by orthodox Marxists as the true source of liberative historical action. Tillich agreed. He could not accept any kind of belief in an earthly utopia, but unconditionally affirmed what Bloch had called 'the spirit of utopia'. This, said Tillich, is 'the power which changes reality ... the spring of all great historical movements ... the tension which impels man beyond everything reassuring and safe to new uncertainty and unrest. Utopia is the power of renewal.'[12] The motivation and energy of effective histori-cal action is to be found only in the tension between anticipation and realization.

Tillich's theology, then, presents a succession of paradoxes. He addresses the crisis of modern culture to an extent and with a serious-ness that few theologians have matched. Yet he retains a confidence in the power of systematic thought to understand and to interpret that crisis that equally few have sought to emulate. Similarly, although he sets out to explicate Christian doctrine in a systematic and coherent way, his systematic theology could plausibly be read as a systematic and radical revision of virtually every major Christian doctrine, transforming faith in God and in Jesus Christ as His Son into a justification of existential choice within the horizons of a purely inner historical, this-worldly view of life. Is Tillich really a systematic *theologian*? Or is he an existentialist thinker, expressing himself through symbols drawn from religious tradition but interpreted and applied anew?

Could it be that it is in the very unanswerability of these questions that Tillich serves to focus the problematic of any existentialist theology? For, whether we look at it from the side of existentialism or from the side of theology, it would seem that religious belief necessarily foreshortens our perspective on the uncertainty, ambiguity and anxiety that existentialism sees as integral aspects of the human condition. Perhaps, therefore, we should not seek to understand Tillich as one who claimed to have squared this circle, but as one who found himself on the unstable boundary between the two worlds of faith and anxiety and as one for whom, answerable or not, the question as to how to hold together both faith and anxiety, both theology and existentialism, was a question he could not avoid. However problematic (and perhaps, often, contradictory) his 'answers' may have been, the question was (and, I suggest, is) not one he asked for himself alone. It is a question that must engage all who are concerned with religion in the contexts of modernity and postmodernity.

NOTES

1. P. Tillich, *Impressionen und Reflexionen* (*Gesammelte Werke*, Vol. XIII [Stuttgart: Evangelisches Verlagswerk, 1972]), p. 409.
2. For the early history of the Frankfurt School, see Martin Jay, *The Dialectical Imagination* (Boston MA: Little, Brown and Co., 1973).
3. P. Tillich, *On Art and Architecture* (New York: Crossroad, 1987), p. 90.
4. Ibid., p. 91.
5. Ibid.
6. Idem., *Theology of Culture* (New York and London: Oxford University Press, 1959), pp. 105–7.

7.   Idem., *Perspectives on Nineteenth and Twentieth Century Protestant Theology* (London: SCM, 1967), p. 24.
8.   Ibid., p. 25.
9.   Ibid.
10. Idem., *The Shaking of the Foundations* (Harmondsworth: Penguin, 1962), p. 87.
11. See my *Art, Modernity and Faith* (London: Macmillan, 1991), Chapter Four, 'Into the Abyss'.
12. P. Tillich, *Gesammelte Werke*, Vol. 13, p. 173.

9
The Russian Idea

Religious existentialism is sometimes portrayed as a phenomenon of the Protestant world: a reformulation in the context of modernity of Luther's passionate and individualistic doctrine of salvation by faith alone. Yet it was not only through Dostoevsky that Russia contributed to the development of religious existentialism in the twentieth century. This contribution was reflected chiefly in the writings of Nicholas Berdyaev (1874–1948) and Lev Shestov (1868–1938), whose work, although related in many ways to the kind of existentialism springing up in Protestant theology in the 1920s and 1930s, is also profoundly marked by its Russian origins, both with regard to the concerns and issues they address and with regard to their manner of argumentation.

Because Berdyaev's thought is intimately engaged with the interpretation of the historical events through which he lived – above all, the tragic course of Russian history in his lifetime – it is worth contextualizing his thought biographically.

Nicholas Alexandrovitch Berdyaev was born into an aristocratic family which had connections to the court and a tradition of military service. Something of the flavour of Berdyaev's background can be gleaned from a comment he makes relating to his maternal aunt: 'My aunt owned the town of Belaya Tserkov, about a hundred and fifty thousand acres of land in the district of Kiev, and palaces in Warsaw, Paris, Nice and Rome' – although his own home circumstances were considerably more modest.[1] He himself was destined for a military career and was educated at the Academy for the Kiev Cadet Corps. The only things he liked about military life, however, were riding and shooting, and at the age of 20 he abandoned the army to study philosophy in the University of Kiev. Like many other young Russian intellectuals he found himself attracted by the powerful revolutionary currents of the time and, with some reservations, came to regard himself as a Marxist and was sufficiently politically active to travel to Zürich for a meeting of European Trade Unionists, meeting G. V. Plekhanov, one of the leading Russian Marxist theorists of the time, then living in exile.

Another acquaintance of this period was A. V. Lunacharsky, later People's Commissar of Education in the Communist government. Berdyaev was active in meetings, participated in demonstrations and was involved in the dissemination of socialist propaganda. He also – perhaps reflecting his general inclination to side with outsiders – made many friends amongst Jewish intellectuals, to his mother's disgust. Amongst these was Lev Shestov. In 1898 he was (for the first, but by no means the last, time in his life) arrested in the wake of a police raid on an underground press. Although he was not held for long (in his autobiography he suggests that his father's friendship with the provincial governor helped him secure favourable treatment) he was eventually sentenced to three years' internal exile in Vologda, in northern Russia. Although he continued to associate with many of the other exiles and political activists (including Lunacharsky, who was also sent to Vologda during Berdyaev's time there) his own tendency was increasingly religious, and he attempted to forge a theoretical reconciliation between idealism and Marxism, or, as Lunacharsky put it, he began to enter 'into the dusk of mysticism, whence he plunged straight into the night of a philosophical Christianity'.[2]

In 1904, after his return from exile, Berdyaev (now married) moved to St Petersburg. This was a time of political and intellectual ferment and the year that followed was to see 'Bloody Sunday' (when unarmed demonstrators were massacred in front of the Winter Palace), the disastrous Russo-Japanese War and a general strike organized by the Soviets. Yet Berdyaev himself was now increasingly distanced from the hard edge of political life and involved himself with the brilliant philosophical, literary and artistic group at the heart of what was known as Russia's 'Cultural Renaissance'. Dmitri Merezhkovsky, his wife Zinaida Hippius, Vyatcheslav Ivanov, Andrey Bely, Vassily Rozanov and Sergei Bulgakov (another ex-Marxist from Kiev) were central figures of this group, which met for intense discussions about the meaning of life and the destiny of Russia in what became known as 'The Ivory Tower' of Ivanov's apartment. Berdyaev also renewed his friendship with Shestov, who was not, however, so closely identified with the Renaissance. Symbolism, Nietzscheanism, Dionysianism and Occultism contributed to a feverish atmosphere of artistic experimentation and, sometimes, it was rumoured, magical practices – with a strong orientation towards neo-paganism and a sexually charged mysticism.

Berdyaev was attracted by many of the magnetic personalities he came to know in St Petersburg, and he played an active role in a sequence of journals in which many of the new ideas were discussed. Increasingly, however, the Dionysian and irrationalist tendencies of many of the representatives of the cultural renaissance went against his increasingly clear Christian orientation and his characteristic emphasis on the values of Spirit and freedom – values for the sake of which he had already split with Marxism. Although Merezhkovsky himself often used the word 'freedom', Berdyaev regarded the kind of freedom that Merezhkovsky associated with the glorification of the flesh as a quite different sort of freedom from that which he himself was seeking. He was also irritated by the indifference of this circle to social issues.[3]

Moving to Moscow in 1907, Berdyaev quickly joined the Moscow Religious-Philosophical Group, a group that also debated the burning religious issues of the day but did so in a less esoteric manner than the St Petersburg circle, promoting many well-attended public lectures and discussions, and including issues of politics and economics, although these were looked at very much in the light of their spiritual significance. Once more Bulgakov was a member of the group which also included Pavel Florensky, who became one of the leading apologists of Orthodoxy and took holy orders. Like Ivan and Alyosha Karamazov the passion 'for asking ultimate questions and seeking ultimate solutions' was, in what Berdyaev regarded as a truly Russian trait, the only thing that mattered. 'Belinsky', he wrote, 'would say, after an argument had gone on all night: "We can't go home, we haven't yet decided the question of God." So it was with us, when Bulgakov, Gershenzon, Shestov, Ivanov, Bely and others foregathered.'[4]

Berdyaev himself read more and more Orthodox and other Christian literature. Sometimes he visited an inn called 'The Pit' to where the kind of religious wanderers and pilgrims occasionally mentioned in the pages of Dostoevsky, Tolstoy and other writers resorted and held meetings. Berdyaev regarded these people as

the epitome of Russia in search of God, truth and justice – courageous, untrammelled, spontaneous and boundless ... There was a vast variety of religious movements represented at the gatherings: *Bessmertniki* (Immortals), Baptists and various shades of Evangelicals, left-wing Dissenters, *Dukhobors*, secret *Khlysty*, Tolstoyans and others ... They were particularly remarkable for their language. The language of the intelligentsia seemed pale and abstract in comparison with their rich, vivid and powerful speech.[5]

He was particularly taken with the *Bessmertniki* who believed that they would never die and that only those who believed in death were subject to it. Although he found much fanaticism in these circles he believed that he had a natural sympathy for these representatives of 'the people' and understood their aspirations. He also visited the Zossimova Hermitage which was a fashionable site amongst converts to Orthodoxy, who were often attracted by the charismatic *starets* movement. Berdyaev was not himself personally moved, yet, whilst maintaining serious reservations about the reactionary and obscurantist stance of the Orthodox hierarchy and without ever identifying any particular conversion experience (although he does narrate a powerful dream, culminating in a vision of the crucified Christ that bears many characteristics of the kind of vision not untypical of a conversion process), he now came to see himself as a decidedly Christian and, indeed, Orthodox thinker. None the less, as he was to put it much later, 'I have never, or very seldom, experienced what are known as the joys and comforts of religious life. Not only did an irreducible element of the tragic remain with me, but tragedy had for me an eminently religious significance.'[6]

In 1909 Berdyaev contributed to a collection of essays, *Milestones* (or, as it is sometimes translated, *Landmarks*), which was so clear in its critique of a merely materialistic understanding of the Russian situation that *The Great Soviet Encyclopedia* of nearly 50 years later described it as 'the most complete expression of counter-revolutionary renegade opinion against which the Bolshevik-Leninists waged consistent and stubborn war'.[7] But Berdyaev had not simply joined the forces of reaction. Critical of the theocratic constitution of the Church in Russia he wrote that 'Only Jesus can command the unclean spirit to depart from the body of Russia! Only Christ can be the Redeemer! But for that it is necessary that there be an inner relation to Christ.' His hostility to the ecclesiastical polity of Russia led him to publish a number of polemical articles, the most serious of which criticized the Holy Synod of the Russian Church for requesting the government to send a gunboat to Mount Athos to deal with the mutinous behaviour of a new sect of monks.[8] So strong were Berdyaev's words that charges of blasphemy were brought against him – charges that could theoretically have led to life-long exile in Siberia if proved. However, the year was 1913, and before the case could come to court the First World War broke out.

The ambiguity of Berdyaev's position, critical both of the Bolsheviks and of the institutions of pre-revolutionary Russia, continued throughout the revolutionary period. On the one hand, he never ceased to criticize Bolshevik ideology and was arrested on several occasions, on one occasion being interrogated by Dzerzhinsky himself, one of the most feared leaders of the Cheka (as the secret police were called at that time). Referring to this event, Solzhenitsyn later cited Berdyaev as an outstanding example of how secret police methods were effective only against those who allowed themselves to fear or to be spiritually compromised by the regime.[9]

None the less, Berdyaev continued to hold the semi-official position of acting president of the All-Russian Union of Writers, held a chair of philosophy in Moscow University and initiated the Free Academy of Spiritual Culture, which was also tolerated by the authorities.

In 1922, however, he was arrested again and, with a number of others regarded as undesirable by the communists, was expelled to Germany. From there he and his wife moved on to Paris where, once more, Berdyaev found himself at the heart of a brilliant and varied talking society. This time his friends came to include Jacques Maritain, Étienne Gilson, André Malraux, Gabriel Marcel, Emmanuel Mounier and Paul Nizan – and once more he renewed his friendship with Shestov. In this period he became active in ecumenical affairs and in the international Christian youth movement, often speaking for Orthodoxy at a variety of gatherings.

Even here, however, his ambiguous stance towards the Church and towards his fellow exiles, most of whom were strongly tsarist, haunted him. On the one hand, When the Metropolitan Sergius, responding to the Soviet government's legalization of Orthodox practice, called on exiles to swear their loyalty to the Soviet government, Berdyaev incurred the extreme wrath of most of the exiles in Paris by supporting the Metropolitan's call. On the other hand, when Sergius later declared Bulgakov's teaching to be heretical, Berdyaev responded with an article entitled 'The Spirit of the Grand Inquisitor', the contents of which need little explanation!

Before 1914 Berdyaev's thought had been extremely optimistic, looking towards the dawning of a new era of spiritual life, but, unsurprisingly, the 1920s and 1930s saw him taking an ever-bleaker view as to the possibility of fulfilling human hopes within the limits of historical existence. Everywhere the values of personality and freedom seemed to be being subordinated to collectivisms of left and right, to dehumanizing ideologies (amongst which Berdyaev included Barthianism![10]) and to the combined hegemony of the machine and of mass culture. Yet the downfall of liberal humanism also opened the way to the rediscovery of passion, depth and titanic forces still latent in the human spirit. Bolshevism, for all its errors, was sometimes seen by Berdyaev in its very extremism as a manifestation of such dormant powers: the other side of totalitarianism is 'a thirst for the integral and an integral transfiguration of life'.[11] It could yet prove to be the harbinger of a new Middle Ages, in which the collective, society, was suffused with the values of personality.[12]

During the war years Berdyaev lived mostly in Paris. Having been arrested by the secret police of the Tsar and of the Soviet government he now experienced detention at the hands of the Gestapo. However, he was for the most part free to write (though not to publish) and to maintain domestic and social relationships. After the war the Soviet government sought to persuade him to return to Russia, although he declined, until such time as his books should be published there. Achieving substantial international recognition, he was honoured with an honorary doctorate from Cambridge University in 1947 – the only other Russians to have been thus honoured in the past having been Tchaikovsky and Turgenev. In 1948 he died.

In his lifetime, Berdyaev achieved a guru-like status amongst some admirers. M.-M. Davy wrote of him:

All of [his] experiences belonged to his religious life and took the form of a personal revelation occurring at an innermost depth. External events were echoed on a mysterious plane, indescribable but real, and all the more real for being incommunicable to anyone who has never known a revelation of that kind resounding through his inner universe. It could never become a subject for teaching or even for relating as a fact or an incident. It can be discovered and put to the test by the change in the subject who benefits from it, or by his approach, but it can only be described with images borrowed from the language of symbolism.[13]

Certainly, his works are often aphoristic, imaginative, sometimes polemical, frequently repetitive and rarely argued or referenced.

Unlike many of the other religious existentialist writers he was not, essentially, an academic thinker and academic writers are, in their turn, inclined to find his style of writing intensely irritating. Yet, however difficult the precise application of many of his ideas may be, the general shape of his thought was consistent over his long literary career and his main ideas and themes are readily grasped. Many of them are already contained in one of his earliest books, *The Meaning of the Creative Act* (1912), and I shall therefore begin this brief summary of his thought with this work.

Berdyaev referred to the idea of freedom as the *leitmotif* of his life's work and, indeed, there is scarcely a page in any of his many books that does not deal with the question of freedom directly or indirectly. In contrast to many other religious existentialists, Berdyaev seems to affirm the Romantic conception of the self as essentially self-creating. Whereas, for example, Kierkegaard carefully qualified what he read as Schlegel's idea of the self-creating self in terms of his own concept of self-choice, Dostoevsky critiqued the posture of those who sought to make themselves the self-creating man-God and Bultmann insisted on the need for God's act to intervene if the self is to become capable of self-commitment, Berdyaev insists on the creative freedom of the self. Creativity is, as he sees it, a primordial aspect of human selfhood.

> *Creativeness is neither permitted nor justified by religion – creativeness is itself religion*...The creative experience is unique and self-sufficient – it is not something derivative; its roots go into the deepest depths. At its best, Christianity justified creativeness but it never rose to the consciousness that what matters is not to justify creativeness *but by creativeness to justify life*. In its religious-cosmic sense, creativeness is equal in power and value with redemption. Creativeness is the final revelation of the Holy Trinity – its anthropological revelation...Love is not only grace but the activity of man himself. (*MCA*, p. 110)

Such words could easily be read in an anti-Christian sense, but that is not Berdyaev's intention. On the contrary, it is God's will for humanity that it realizes its own creativeness. Furthermore, 'Human nature is creative because it is the image and likeness of God the Creator' (*MCA*, p. 110). In contrast to nineteenth-century Prometheanism, Berdyaev does not seek to play off human freedom against humanity's creaturely status vis-à-vis God. Rather, he attempts to combine a high evaluation of divine freedom with a no less high evaluation of human freedom.

> The being of the world is creature; being which has been and continues to be created. And the stamp of the creative act lies on all created being. A thing created, createdness, speaks of the creator. Createdness is creativity. The creation of the world is creative development in God, His emergence from divine solitude; it is the call of divine love. (*MCA*, p. 128)

This creaturely creativity is also linked by Berdyaev to another of his key concepts: personality. 'The creative act', he says, 'is a free and independent force, immanently inherent only in a person, a personality' (*MCA*, p. 135). It is as creative *personality* that the human subject is the true image of God.

The mystery of creativeness is not only founded on the creaturely reflection of divine creativeness, it is also bound up with the divine act of revelation and redemption in Christ.

> Christ ... redeems and restores *human* nature to its likeness unto God ... Human nature finally justifies itself before the Creator not by extinguishing itself but by its own creative expression. Man must absolutely *be* ... Repentance or purification is only one of the moments of religious experience, one of the acts of the mystery of Christ. We must not stop at this moment: we must go on to positive spiritual living. (*MCA*, p. 111)

Such 'positive spiritual living' is, in fact, nothing less than the continuance of creation. Creation, for Berdyaev, is not what happened once, 'in the beginning', but a process that continues and that is decisively revealed in its implications for humanity in God the Son. 'Christology', he says, 'is the doctrine of continuing creation' (*MCA*, p. 138). The redemption won in Christ is not directed towards 'returning' humanity to some primitive state of universal harmony. In Berdyaev's eyes that would be 'a process without gain or increment' (*MCA*, p. 138). Instead, the continuing world-process is to be regarded as 'the eighth day of creation', in which the creativity revealed in Christ is carried forward towards completion 'by man's creativity in the Spirit' (*MCA*, p. 138). The influence of Jacob

Boehme can be sensed in such speculations: for Berdyaev, as for Schelling, Boehme opened up a vision of the world as being itself the realization, in time, of the eternal self-realization of God.[14] In this realization the relations between the three persons of the Trinity are projected onto the plane of temporality, such that history becomes the history of the divine life in time as, successively, the age of the Father, of the Son and of the Spirit. This is not, however, to be understood as if history were merely the reflection, in time, of a pre-determined divine plan. On the contrary, the role of human creativity, revealed in Christ but to be enacted by us now, in the Spirit, is decisive. The completion of the process is dependent on human freedom. 'God expects from man the highest freedom, the freedom of the eighth day of creation ... *The final, ultimate freedom, the daring of freedom and the burden of freedom, is the virtue of religious maturity*' (*MCA*, p. 158).

Berdyaev, of course, realizes that his high estimation of freedom stands in a certain tension to conventional versions of Christianity but this is because, he believes, the institutionalized Church has objectified the Christian message. The Churches have failed to realize the radicality of what happened in Christ. Instead of being an agent of freedom, 'Christianity has always been a training, a guardianship of the immature' (*MCA*, p. 158). Since, in Berdyaev's sense, love is possible only on the basis of freedom, it follows that, in one of his most extreme statements, 'In the whole life of the Church, there is no love: there is no love in the typical Christian hierarch; no love in clerical care or lay obedience ...' (*MCA*, p. 334). In the new epoch of the Spirit, 'Not only Christian priesthood, but Christian prophecy must become life' (*MCA*, p. 335). We shall return to Berdyaev's understanding of Dostoevsky, but we can see here how the poem of the Grand Inquisitor, in its depiction of the Church as 'correcting' Christ's offer of freedom in favour of a paternalistic 'care of souls', must have appealed to him – although, naturally, he does not accept the Grand Inquisitor's own claim that he does it all out of love.

If his conception of freedom leads him to criticize the authoritarian structures of Church life, Berdyaev categorically denies that the kind of freedom he wishes to promote is individualistic or the freedom of moral or sexual licence. It is freedom working within and for the overall context of the creative process, freedom working with and for the freedom of God. Already Berdyaev is appealing to the Russian idea of *sobornost*, an idea popularized by the nineteenth-century philosopher A. S. Khomiakov. This is the idea of community as a community of persons in the sense of a whole that is greater than its parts but that, none the less, does not violently subordinate those parts to the good of the whole: 'fellowship' rather than 'society'. Another way in which Berdyaev contextual-izes human freedom is by reference to the Renaissance idea of the interrelationship between micro- and macrocosm. What happens in the human sphere never happens in isolation from the whole cos-mic scheme: we live in an unceasing process of mutual influence. Yet this should not be taken in such a way as to diminish the role of human freedom. On the contrary, humanity itself is the point at which the different worlds or dimensions of the cosmic whole meet and it is in the mystery of human freedom that the whole meaning and history of the cosmos is decided. As the meeting-point between two worlds, the human situation is, perhaps para-doxically, inescapably dualistic, for it is in the exercise of our freedom that it gets decided whether the deterministic life of nature or the freedom of the divine will prevail. 'Man', says Berdyaev, 'knows himself as the image and likeness of God and as a drop in the ocean of the necessities of nature' (*MCA*, p. 60) and we exist in and as the struggle to determine what the relationship between these will be. He regards this dualism as coming powerfully to expression in the Russian psyche. It is characteristic of Russia, he writes, that its essence is expressed both in St Seraphim of Sarov and in Pushkin.

Berdyaev's philosophy is therefore crucially a philosophy of his-tory – not in the sense that he believed it possible to attain some kind of overview of historical events or to discover the laws of his-torical development (although, obviously, such claims were very much discussed in the Marxist circles amongst which he at one point moved), but in the sense that what happens in the dimension of history is determinative for the whole complex of relationships between creature and creator, God, humanity and world. But, of course, if we speak of Berdyaev's 'philosophy', we have to do so in a very particular sense. As he himself put it in *The Meaning of the Creative Act*, 'Philosophy is in no sense at all a science and in no way should it be scientific ... The "scientific" ... is bondage of the spirit to the lower spheres of being' (*MCA*, pp. 23, 25).

If virtually all of the major themes and positions of Berdyaev's subsequent writings are to be found already in *The Meaning of the Creative Act*, there was one major respect in which he later changed, rather than merely amplified, the views set out there. Whereas *The Meaning of the Creative Act*, written in 1912, was essentially optimistic in its view of a coming age of the Spirit in which humanity would realize its vocation to creative love, the experiences of war and revolution that followed led him to take a more sombre view of historical possibility and, indeed, to question whether spiritual life could ever be unambiguously manifested within the historical process. This also leads to a more sharply dualistic understanding of freedom in its tensile relation to the other dimensions of human life.

Because it is the single most characteristic concept of his whole philosophy, we shall amplify the picture of Berdyaev's thought as set out in *The Meaning of the Creative Act* by focusing on his concept of freedom and on how freedom stands in relation to Being, nature, society and history.

For Berdyaev freedom is, as we have seen, virtually synonymous with the religious aspect of human existence. As he puts it in *Freedom and the Spirit*: 'Spirit is freedom unconstrained by the outward and the objective, where what is deep and inward determines all. To be in the spirit is to be in oneself ... to win true freedom is to enter into the spiritual world.'[15]

We can regard freedom either as a desirable goal to be achieved – as in the pursuit of various kinds of individual or communal freedoms – or, and this, in Berdyaev's view, is the more significant understanding of freedom, as 'the mysterious source of life, the basic and original experience, the abyss which is deeper than being itself and by which being is determined'.[16] This freedom is absolute, not least because it is what God himself 'expects' from us. 'True liberty is that which God demands from us and not that which we demand from God.'[17]

If, therefore, freedom is the most primordial dimension of humanity, and conceals within itself the defining mystery of the God-relationship, it is by definition prior to Being and it follows that any philosophy that seeks to understand human existence in the light of a primary concern for Being is going to miss what is most important in human life. This orientation towards Being, rather than towards freedom, was, for Berdyaev, characteristic of Aristotelianism and of Western European religious philosophy, with its great exemplar in St Thomas Aquinas, whose thought was being reappropriated in a contemporary mode by neo-Thomists such as Maritain and Gilson, with whom, as we have seen, Berdyaev came into close contact after his arrival in Paris. Fundamentally, he insists, we have to choose between a philosophy of Being and a philosophy of Freedom. There is no middle way.

> A philosophy which lays the concept of being as its foundation stone, is naturalistic metaphysics. Being is nature (*ousia*), it belongs to the objectivized world which is brought into being by rationalization. To think of spirit as being means to think of it in the naturalistic way as nature, as an object. But spirit is not an object, it is not nature, it is not being in the sense of substance. Spirit is subject, it is an act, it is freedom. (*SF*, p. 75)

In a sense akin to that of Kierkegaard (although he himself refers to the earlier Russian philosopher, Vladimir Soloviev), Berdyaev states that 'Being is a product of abstract thought ... Being has no existence' (*SF*, p. 75). 'In mediaeval terminology *essentia* has no *existentia*' (*SF*, p. 78).

In Berdyaev's view the pursuit of ontology is potentially enslaving, since the very project of ontology is to determine the nature, the essence, of the human subject in terms of its relation to a prior understanding of Being even if this understanding is itself based on some kind of primordial mystical experience (as in the ontology of Maritain). For being is static and freedom dynamic, 'being is only the congealed or indurated part of life, life which has been cast out into objectivity' (*SF*, p. 81).

The same logic runs through Berdyaev's critique of the subjection of freedom and of Spirit to nature – an issue that was of immense significance to him both in the context of his relation to the Merezhkovsky circle with its cult of neo-paganism and to the naturalistic, pseudo-biologistic interpretation of history found in some forms of slavophilism as well as in fascism.

At one level the possibility of the subjection of spirit to nature is universal. It is part of the human condition and the human task is, as we have seen, precisely to assert and to maintain the values of spiritual freedom in a never-ending struggle with the laws of nature within us. Technology is one sign of the human attempt to create a space for the exercise of freedom in the midst of nature – although Berdyaev does not believe that technology itself can fully reflect the urge to express our primordial freedom, since the realm of technology is itself objective and comes to stand over against the human subject as an external constraint upon our freedom. We become dependent on our own creations. Science and technology offer liberation from nature, but put in its place a second nature.

But if science reifies our relation to nature in the sense of defining us (practically as well as intellectually) in relation to necessary objective laws, the Romantic revolt against science is no less likely to succumb to what Berdyaev calls 'the lure of the cosmos and slavery to it' (*SF*, p. 97). This lure may take various forms. 'It may take the form of an erotic sexual lure (Rozanov, Lawrence) or of the mass of the nation (the mysticism of *narodnitchestvo*) or of the earthly lure of the soil, and the lure of blood, race and family (the return to the land, racialism) or the lure of the collective-social (the mysticism of collectivism and communism)' (*SF*, p. 97).

If the scientific-technological view of nature seems at first glance to stand in complete opposition to the Romantic-Dionysian view, there is none the less, as Berdyaev sees it, a kind of antipathetic symmetry between them that is characteristic of the modern situation. 'From slavery to the mechanism of nature [science] he [man] returns to slavery to the pandemonism of nature [Romanticism].' But 'Fusion with cosmic life does not emancipate personality, it brings about its dissolution and annihilation' (*SF*, p. 101). This becomes particularly clear in its manifestation in reactionary politics.

Indeed, the sphere of politics and society is one that is crucial to Berdyaev, because it is here, above all, that the implications of human decision-making reveal their true character. 'Of all the forms of slavery to which man is liable,' he writes, 'the greatest importance attaches to the slavery of man to society' (*SF*, p. 102). Berdyaev sees temptations to such a slavery in virtually every kind of social theory or political practice. Whether society is construed in terms of organic growth or in terms of the intellectual and cultural values of 'civilization' or in terms of socialist collectivism it is the same story: the original freedom of the person is put at risk in the cause of the collective. Nor does Berdyaev regard modern individualism as a significant alternative. He rejects as an illusion 'the conviction that individualism is the resistance of the individual man and his freedom to the surrounding world which is always bent on doing violence to him' (*SF*, p. 135). For individualism itself has an objectified view of human existence. Just as there is an unholy symbiosis between scientific and romantic views of nature, so too individualism is simply the obverse of collectivism. Individualism is a stance taken in the sphere of objectivity, whereas personalism, Berdyaev asserts, is located 'in the sphere of the subject world, that is to say of existentiality' (*SF*, p. 135). Personalism is not opposed to common life as such, only to its objectification and its tendency to obscure the values of personality and freedom. Berdyaev's ideal, as has already been touched on, is comprised in the Russian term *sobornost*, which one of his translators renders 'altogetherness' and of which Berdyaev himself wrote that it was 'the organic union of freedom and love, community'.[18]

Of all the forms of slavery to society, slavery to the state was, in Berdyaev's view, the most pernicious – and yet almost universal, in one form or another, in human history. It is 'the inclination to deify Caesar' that 'is always present, it is revealed in monarchy, but may also appear in democracy or in communism'.[19] But, he believes,

> Christianity cannot be reconciled to the sovereignty of any kind of earthly authority – not the sovereignty of a monarch, not that of a people or of a class. The only principle reconcilable with Christianity is the assertion of man's inalienable rights. But the state recognizes these unwillingly. And even the principle of the rights of man has been deformed: instead of implying the rights of the spirit against the wilfulness of Caesar, it was included in Caesar's realm and came to mean not so much the rights of man as a spiritual being, as it did the rights of a citizen, that is of a partial being.[20]

Any form of authority is suspect. Indeed, Berdyaev says, 'Every authority, openly or in disguise, has poison within itself. True liberation will come only with the elimination of the idea of sovereignty, regardless of the subject to which this sovereignty applies.'[21] Yet although Christianity charges us to defend the values of the person against every authority and power that would demean them, Christianity itself does not seem to have given any clear vision of how to bring about a better social order. Berdyaev admits that, as he understands it, 'in Christianity there has been no revelation about society. This revelation ... must come in the epoch of the Holy Spirit.'[22] But – as we have seen – the advent of this epoch was increasingly obscure and problematic for Berdyaev, even if his writing never ceased to show signs of what the independent Marxist thinker Ernst Bloch called 'the spirit of utopia'.

The question as to the nature of the age of the Spirit and the manner of its coming go straight to the heart of Berdyaev's philosophy of history.

Here Berdyaev distinguishes between three levels of time. First of all there is what he calls cosmic time, the cycles of nature that determine human life *qua* biological entity. Then there is historical time, time that 'is symbolized not by the circle but by the straight line stretching out forwards' (*SF*, p. 259). Although historical time, as the field of action of human history, adumbrates a vision of human freedom as that towards which history progresses, it none the less remains under the sway of objectivity and is always likely to succumb to understanding the person in the light of the collective. But, in addition to cosmic and historical time, there is also what Berdyaev calls existential time, the time of meta-history. Just as historical time does not mean the cessation of cosmic or biological time – the human being who acts in history is still a biological entity who must eat, sleep, reproduce and die – so too, meta-history does not mean the cessation of history. Rather, it is the sphere of the creative act, the dimension of freedom in which each of us always already exists in the very deepest levels of our existence. 'Within history there is meta-history, which is not a product of historical evolution. There is the miraculous in history … the break-through of events which belong to existential time into historical time.' Such events include the revelation of God in Christ, a revelation that like all such irruptions of existential time 'in historical time … only shines through the burdensome environment of objectivization' (*SF*, p. 262). Therefore, at the level of history itself, the question as to the meaning of history is always unanswered and is in fact unanswerable: 'History is the failure of spirit, the Kingdom of God is not realized or expressed in it' (*SF*, p. 263). But that failure is interpreted by Berdyaev as itself summoning us to renew the attempt to realize meaning by the exercise of our freedom in which, and in which alone, God acts.

The emergence of meta-history in, with and under the conditions of history as the emergence of authentic *sobornost*-like community is clearly never going to be an objective event. Yet that does not mean that it leaves no trace at all in history. In some beautiful and powerful words on memory, Berdyaev indicates how spiritual community might exist within history and how the history of the spiritual community itself is sustained:

Memory of the past is spiritual; it conquers historical time. This … [is] a creatively transfiguring memory. It carries forward into eternal life not that which is dead in the past but what is alive, not that which is static in the past but what is dynamic. This spiritual memory reminds man, engulfed in his historical time, that in the past there have been great creative movements of the spirit and that they ought to inherit eternity. It reminds him also of the fact that in the past there lived concrete beings, living personalities, with whom we ought in existential time to have a link no less than with those who are living now. Society is always a society not only of the living but also of the dead; and this memory of the dead ... is a creative dynamic memory. The last word belongs not to death but to resurrection. But resurrection is not a restoration of the past in its evil and untruth, but transfiguration. (*SF*, p. 111)

History never comes to an end on the plane of history itself. It only achieves its end when we act freely and creatively in it, creating an order of personal community that, in its communal memory, overcomes the entropy of historical becoming and establishes a realm of spiritual existence that is, in an important sense, transtemporal or meta-historical. We shall see that Berdyaev's position here is very close to Tillich's concept of the *kairos*, which is in turn influenced by Kierkegaard's reflections on 'the moment' – and Berdyaev himself acknowledges his affinity to both of these conceptions (*SF*, p. 260). Thus far we might also say that Berdyaev's eschatology is a form of demythologization – albeit a form whose rhetorical richness does not immediately attract the suspicion of reductionism in the way that the language of demythologization does.[23]

A further consequence of Berdyaev's view of history is the persistence of a tragic element in his thought. If history has no end in historical time, we certainly cannot believe in any kind of naive 'happy ending'. For Berdyaev tragedy and the possibility of freedom are intertwined. 'A final elimination of the tragic element from life would mean the suppression of freedom,' he writes.[24]

But if meta-history is not the 'end' of history in what would generally be thought of as a literal sense, it marks a genuine *novum* within the historical process. 'Eternity is eternal newness, eternal creative ecstasy, the dissolving of being in divine freedom',[25] which also suggests that it is somewhat misleading to speak of meta-history simply as eternity 'breaking in' to history. For that which 'breaks in' is not itself a timeless eternity, but an eternity that is what it is as creative and dynamic and that requires a 'history' in which to exist. Eternity is not founded on static being but, on the contrary, the novelty of the eternal issues 'from freedom, from what we think of as "non-being"...'[26]

Berdyaev was a profoundly Russian thinker, but he drew heavily on a number of Western sources. Jacob Boehme, Angelus Silesius, Kant, Fichte, Schelling and Nietzsche (as well as Marx!) were all important in the original development of his thought and he later came to acknowledge kinship with such Western thinkers as Kierkegaard. None the less his most important inspirations are from Russian sources and, above all, from his reading of Dostoevsky, of whom he wrote, 'I personally know no more profoundly Christian writer than Dostoevsky' (*D*, p. 209). Not only does he regard him as a great Christian writer. He also sees him as 'a great thinker and a great visionary ... a dialectician of genius and Russia's greatest metaphysician' (*D*, p. 11). Dostoevsky's novels are novels of ideas, but not ideas in the sense of Plato: 'For Dostoevsky ideas are fiery billows, never frozen categories; they are bound up with the destiny of man, of the world, of God himself ... Ideas are not prototypes of being, primary entities, much less norms; they are the destiny of living being, its burning motive-power' (*D*, p. 12). A Christian, a metaphysician – and a Russian: 'So great is the worth of Dostoievsky that to have produced him is by itself sufficient justification for the existence of the Russian people in the world; and he will bear witness for his countrymen at the last judgement of the nations' (*D*, p. 227).

Dostoevsky's central vision, according to Berdyaev, is of man 'as a self-contradictory creature, in the highest degree unhappy, not only suffering but in love with suffering'.[27] However, this emphasis on suffering is not masochistic. Suffering is important because it is tied up with freedom, an idea that is most clearly developed in the poem of the Grand Inquisitor. As Berdyaev puts it, 'A refusal of freedom would mitigate suffering.'[28] This, we can see, relates closely to Berdyaev's own eschatology, since freedom is possible only in a situation of conflict and struggle and for which there can be no guarantee of a happy ending. As he understands Dostoevsky,

[he] arrive[s] at the existence of God through a consideration of the freedom of the human spirit: those of his characters who deny this freedom deny God, and inversely. A world in which goodness and righteousness reign by compulsion, whose harmony is ensured by undeniable necessity, is a godless world,

a rationalised mechanism, and to reject God and human liberty is to push the world in that direction. (*D*, p. 87)

According to Berdyaev such tortured and divided characters as the underground man, Raskolnikov and Ivan Karamazov do, in an important sense, speak for Dostoevsky himself. Their descent into the depths is simultaneously a revelation of the freedom that is a precondition of a true God-relationship.

Yet, if freedom is absolutely integral to Dostoevsky's religious vision in such a way as to rule out any falsely optimistic anticipations of the Kingdom of God, Dostoevsky's thought is also profoundly Russian and profoundly Christian in its eschatological orientation. The riddle of human freedom is bound up with the deep longing for a better order of things. But this better order cannot come about through natural or historical progress. It is, ultimately, a question of resurrection, not evolution. This gives Russian thought in general and Dostoevsky's thought in particular a passionately messianic character. For Dostoevsky the Russian people have a God-bearing mission to the world, 'he believed that the Russians as a people were bound to say their own word to the world, a new word, at the end of time.'[29]

Dostoevsky is also of central importance in the work of Lev Shestov. Shestov was born (in 1866) Leib Isaakovich Schvartsman, the son of a wealthy Jewish businessman in Kiev. He finished his high school education in Moscow, having had to leave his Kiev school on account of political involvements. After graduating in law from Moscow University in 1889 he went into the family business, dividing his time between Kiev and Europe whilst at the same time pursuing literary and musical interests. After a period of travel, during which he completed two books of literary studies, *Shakespeare and his Critic Brandes* (1898) and *Good in the Teaching of Tolstoy and Nietzsche: Philosophy and Preaching* (1899), as well as acquiring a 'secret' wife in Switzerland (whom he did not acknowledge to his family till after his father's death), he became acquainted with Berdyaev and Bulgakov and their associates. His reputation as an original thinker was confirmed by two further books, *Dostoevsky and Nietzsche: The Philosophy of Tragedy* (1903) and *The Apotheosis of Groundlessness* (1905). Living variously in Russia, Switzerland and Germany, Shestov first settled in Russia in 1914, fleeing to Paris in 1919, to spend most of the remainder of his life in France.

Shestov's writing, like that of Berdyaev, does not fit within the parameters of what is normally regarded as philosophical writing in the West. Assertive, aphoristic and hyperbolic in the extreme, Shestov's entire career is, in effect, a sustained attack on reason and ethics in their claim to provide insight into the human situation. If he is in any sense a philosopher he is, essentially, an *anti*-philosopher. But if we are to be denied the resource of reason in our attempt at self-understanding, what can we turn to? The answer, according to Shestov, is the Bible. In the line of Tertullian he asserts that 'what is said in [the Bible] directly contradicts what men have found out through their intellectual vision.'[30] Indeed, the source of all philosophy is the forbidden fruit of the knowledge of good and evil. The Fall is not rooted in moral disobedience but in the desire for knowledge, knowledge that promises freedom but in fact subjects the freedom of the human subject to the necessity of universal laws. 'Reason eagerly strives to hand man over to the power of necessity ... rather than trust in its Creator.'[31] 'Knowledge has not brought us freedom ... knowledge has enslaved us, has put us utterly at the mercy of eternal truths.'[32] The appeal to necessity, an appeal that is always implicit in the pursuit of knowledge, is, ultimately, rooted in the fear of freedom: 'The fear of freedom is undoubtedly the basic characteristic of our perhaps distorted but nonetheless real human nature.'[33] But, in contrast to philosophy, the Bible, as the Word of God, is centrally concerned with human freedom and 'God never uses coercion, but then, truth is not God: it coerces.'[34] We must, then, choose between, on the one hand, Abraham and Job and, on the other, Aristotle and Hegel.

It is the achievement of Kierkegaard, Dostoevsky and Nietzsche to have called into question the rule of reason and its relevance to faith and to have made clear the choice we must make. When, on the other hand, the Neo-Thomists seek to re-establish the medieval synthesis between faith and reason, they are simply rehearsing the triumph of Athens over Jerusalem. When a Catholic philosopher such as Gilson states that 'the substitution of knowledge for faith is always a positive gain for the mind,' Shestov disagrees utterly. Since all philosophy ultimately relies on the idea of necessity, an idea that, in the last resort, is equivalent to the coercion of the thinking subject, Christianity must sever all links with philosophy and reason. Thus, 'for Kierkegaard coercive knowledge is an abomination of desolation'[35] – a view with which Shestov concurs. In Kierkegaard, to whom he devoted his important *Kierkegaard and*

Existential Philosophy (1936),[36] Shestov found an important antidote to the philosophical or metaphysical approach to Christianity. Kierkegaard's emphasis on possibility, for instance, pointed to a better way than that of coercive knowledge: 'for God all things are possible. This constitutes *the struggle of faith: a mad struggle for possibility*. For only possibility reveals the way to salvation.'[37] Similarly,

> Faith is a new dimension of thought, unknown and foreign to speculative philosophy, which opens the way to the Creator of all earthly things, to the source of all possibilities, to the One for whom there are no boundaries between the possible and the impossible.[38]

Kierkegaard's route to this insight not only involved taking on the absolutization of reason that he found in Hegel, it also meant confronting ethics, since ethics, in its various forms, is fundamentally concerned with understanding and legislating for human behaviour in terms of universal norms or criteria. Ethics, no less than speculative philosophy, appeals to necessity and coercion.

What Shestov found in Kierkegaard, he had already found in Dostoevsky. In a famous phrase he asserts that, so close is the bond between these two thinkers, 'Dostoevsky is Kierkegaard's double.'[39] He speaks of Dostoevsky as one to whom the Angel of Death gave powers of vision inaccessible to the everyday consciousness. 'What attracts Dostoevsky?' he asks, 'The "perhaps", the unexpected, the suddenness, the darkness, the caprice, all those things which from the point of view of science and common sense either do not or should not exist.'[40] Dostoevsky's singular double vision makes him, not Kant, the true critic of metaphysics, for Dostoevsky asks whether in fact 'reason has any right to judge between the possible and the impossible'.[41]

> He to whom the Angel of Death has given the mysterious gift, does not and cannot any longer possess the certainty which accompanies our ordinary judgements and confers a beautiful solidity on the truths of our common consciousness ... that is why, in his 'theory of knowledge', Dostoevsky renounces all certainty, and opposes to it as his supreme goal – uncertainty. That is why he simply puts out his tongue at evidence, why he lauds caprice, unconditional, unforseen, always irrational, and makes mock of all the human virtues.[42]

For Shestov it is axiomatic that the decision as to whether we allow ourselves to be guided by reason or by the irrational is not a decision that reason itself can make. It is prior both to reason and to the irrational. The most fundamental question of philosophy is the question concerning 'what matters most', *to timiotaton*, and the decision as to what matters most is not one that philosophy (in the sense of the rational justification of knowledge) is any better equipped to resolve than religion or art. Indeed, in the face of this question all the conventional lines of demarcation between religion, art and philosophy break down.

In the line of thinkers who have understood this, Shestov names not only Kierkegaard and Dostoevsky but Pascal, Luther (to whom he also devoted a book, *Sola Fide*) and Plotinus. Amongst those who have insisted on the absoluteness of reason he lists (in addition to Hegel) Kant, Spinoza, Aristotle, Plato and Socrates – as well as the whole 'Christian philosophy' of the Middle Ages. Throughout the history of ideas, the same conflict is repeated over and over again in various forms. Just as Dostoevsky is Kierkegaard's 'double', so too, Shestov says, Spinoza is the second incarnation of Socrates.[43] Spinoza, indeed, is a supremely consistent advocate of reason and, as such, the mirror image of Luther: like Luther he insists on the separation between faith and reason, but whereas Luther, faced with this antinomy, chooses faith, Spinoza chooses reason – but is unable to recognize that this is precisely a choice. This failure means that what Spinoza regards as freedom, happiness and the good is in fact the renunciation of everything that really makes for freedom, happiness and the good. Why *must* we choose *acquiescentia* – 'Why not prefer anxiety?' asks Shestov.[44] 'It is', he says, 'in the "must" that the meaning of Spinoza's geometrical method and Socrates' dialectical method lies.'[45] Once more we see Shestov's view that to assert of the priority of reason is not itself reasonable. Rather, it is the result of a choice and to impose that choice on others is to practise coercion. The hegemony of reason is, in the last resort, always violent, always coercive. But we do not *need* to accept it. We can learn – from Nietzsche amongst others – that the conviction of the philosopher precedes the truth of his philosophy.

Such is our anxiety in face of the immense nothingness in which we must freely choose the fundamental values and truths that are to direct our lives, that even thinkers such as Dostoevsky, Nietzsche and Kierkegaard find it difficult to sustain their deepest insights into this situation. Dostoevsky's attempt to play the part of propagandist for Orthodoxy and for the government is untrue to the deepest insights of his own writing. 'All that he had to tell, Dostoevsky told us in his novels ... and the title of prophet, which he sought so diligently ... did not suit him at all.'[46] By allowing himself to be cast in this role, Dostoevsky put himself 'in tow of others who, compared with him, are utter nonentities, and he goes'.[47] Nietzsche also fails to carry his repudiation of objective truth through to its ultimate conclusion. In his doctrine of eternal recurrence, says Shestov, 'the important thing ... is not the word being defined, but the word doing the defining, i.e. not recurrence, but eternity.'[48] Even Nietzsche is finally compelled to claim for his thought an eternal quality that transcends any act of will. Kierkegaard similarly draws back from the full implications of his assault on Hegel and on universal ethics, and fails to eliminate a dimension of coercion from his depiction of the God-relationship. Kierkegaard's late thought sets out criteria for authentic Christianity such as martyrdom, but, Shestov states, 'Faith is not proved by martyrdom or sacrifices. Faith is not proved at all.'[49] Even Kierkegaard's account of the fall suggests that there is some power external to human freedom at work. But, for Shestov, the 'knowledge' that lures us into subjection to necessity does not really exist at all: it is a fiction of our own devising. We fall by our own choice. Kierkegaard, however, saw man as powerless before necessity.[50]

Despite his friendship with Berdyaev and despite their common insistence on the freedom of the human subject, Shestov is critical of Berdyaev's attempt to reconcile existential and speculative philosophy. Where Berdyaev maintains that revelation cannot overrule reason or conscience, Shestov asserts that the content of revelation is, by all human standards, an impossibility and that reason and conscience are unable to pass judgement on it.[51] Yet, paradoxically, it is Shestov who maintains that humanity can, in defiance of all reason, find perfect freedom, overcoming nothingness through the act of faith. Berdyaev, however, sees even God as constrained by the nothingness of His own darkness, and vulnerable to tragedy.[52]

Yet Shestov's faith is won at a cost that few are willing to pay, intertwined as it is with the vision of a universe in which, it seems, anything can happen at any time. Perhaps Shestov is the most consistent of all existential thinkers, religious or secular: but perhaps it is not just difficult but impossible for anyone to follow him in his unique path.

NOTES

1.   N. Berdyaev, *Dream and Reality* (London: Geoffrey Bles, 1950), p. 9.
2.   Quoted in D. Lowrie, *Rebellious Prophet* (London: Gollancz, 1960), p. 59.
3.   A useful anthology of Renaissance writings in English is Bernice Glatzer Rosenthal and Martha Bohachevsky-Comiak (eds.), *A Revolution of the Spirit: Crisis of Value in Russia 1980–1924* (New York: Fordham University Press, 1984). See also B. Rosenthal (ed.), *Nietzsche in Russia* (Princeton University Press, 1986); A. Pyman, *A History of Russian Symbolism* (Cambridge: Cambridge University Press, 1994).
4.   *Dream and Reality*, p. 165.
5.   Ibid., pp. 196–7.
6.   Ibid., p. 182.
7.   Lowrie, p. 13. An English translation of these essays is available in B. Shragin and A. Todd (eds.), *Landmarks*: a *Collection of Essays on the Russian Intelligentsia – 1909* (New York: Karz Howard, 1977).
8.   It should be said, however, that the Holy Synod was a lay governmental body and not necessarily representative of the episcopal hierarchy.
9.   A. Solzhenitsyn, *The Gulag Archipelago* (London: Collins/Fontana, 1974), p. 130.
10.   See N. Berdyaev, 'Die Krisis des Protestantismus und die Russische Orthodoxie. Eine Auseinandersetzung mit der dialectischen [*sic*] Theologie', in *Orient und Occident*, Nr. 1, Bern-Leipzig (1929).
11.   N. Berdyaev, *Towards a New Epoch* (London: Geoffrey Bles, 1949), p. 109.
12.   See E. Lampert, *Nicholas Berdyaev and the New Middle Ages* (London: James Clarke, n.d.).
13.   M.-M. Davy, *Nicholas Berdiaev. Man of the Eighth Day* (London: G. Bles, 1967), p. 43.
14.   See Chapter 1, above.
15.   N. Berdyaev, *Freedom and the Spirit* (London: Geoffrey Bles, 1935), p. 117.
16.   Ibid., p. 126.
17.   Ibid., pp. 126–7.
18.   N. Berdyaev, *The Russian Idea* (London: G. Bles, 1947), p. 162.
19.   N. Berdyaev, *The Realm of Spirit and the Realm of Caesar* (London: V. Gollancz, 1952), p. 72.
20.   Ibid., pp. 72–3.
21.   Ibid., p. 85.
22.   Ibid., p. 84.
23.   For a contrary interpretation, see C. S. Callan, *The Significance of Eschatology in the Thoughts of Nicolas Berdyaev* (Leiden: E. J. Brill, 1965).
24.   N. Berdyaev, *Spirit And Reality* (London: G. Bles, 1939), p. 126.
25.   N. Berdyaev, *The Beginning and the End* (London: G. Bles, 1952), p. 170.

26. Ibid.
27. *The Russian Idea*, p. 179.
28. Ibid., p. 180.
29. *The Russian Idea*, p. 202.
30. L. Shestov, *Kierkegaard and the Existential Philosophy* (Athens: Ohio University Press, 1969), p. 4.
31. Ibid., p. 16.
32. Ibid., p. 25.
33. Idem., *Athens and Jerusalem* (Athens: Ohio University Press, 1966), p. 125.
34. *Kierkegaard*, p. 236.
35. Ibid., p. 20.
36. Shestov was, curiously enough, directed to Kierkegaard by Edmund Husserl, with whom he developed a surprisingly warm friendship. For the relationship between Shestov and Husserl, see A. Valevicias, *Lev Shestov and His Times* (New York: Peter Lang, 1993). For Shestov's reading of Kierkegaard, see J. M. McLachlan, 'Shestov's Reading and Misreading of Kierkegaard', in *Canadian Slavonic Papers* Vol. XVIII, No. 2, pp. 174–86.
37. Ibid., p. 21.
38. Ibid., pp. 26–7.
39. Ibid., p. 21.
40. L. Chestov [sic], *In Job's Balances* (London: J. M. Dent, 1932), p. 20.
41. Ibid., p. 28.
42. Ibid., pp. 42–3.
43. *Athens and Jerusalem*, pp. 184ff.
44. Ibid., p. 194.
45. Ibid., p. 196.
46. L. Shestov, *Anton Tchekov and Other Essays* (Dublin and London: Maunsel and Co., 1916), p. 82.
47. Ibid., p. 71.
48. L. Shestov, *Dostoievsky, Tolstoy and Nietzsche* (Athens: Ohio University Press, 1966), p. 292.
49. Ibid., p. 223.
50. Ibid., p. 209.
51. See James C. S. Wernham, *Two Russian Thinkers* (Toronto: University of Toronto Press, 1968), especially Chapter 11.
52. For this distinction I am indebted to I. I. Evlampiev, 'Kierkegor i problema nichto v russkom ekzistentsializm', in T. V. Shitsova (ed.), *Kierkegor i Sovremennost* (Minsk: Rivshugo, 1996).

10

Paradox and Mystery:
Catholic Existentialism

I

The distinctively Russian visions of Berdyaev and Shestov show that religious existentialism was never a narrowly Protestant (and still less a narrowly German) phenomenon. Roman Catholicism also produced several outstanding thinkers who could be described as existentialist, despite the hostility of the official hierarchy to the spirit of existentialism. This hostility was due partly to the anti-authoritarian and individualistic style of existentialist thought and partly to its supposed denial of reason, since the kind of Thomist theology dominant in the Catholic Church in the first half of the twentieth century laid great emphasis on the continuity between reason and faith and insisted that a rational empiricism modelled on Aristotelian principles could provide an adequate basis for justifying fundamental theological truths.

In turning to Miguel de Unamuno and Gabriel Marcel as the two most outstanding existentialist thinkers within the Catholic tradition we will not therefore be surprised to find that both were lay-men, unconstrained by the kind of discipline imposed on clergy in this period.[1] Unamuno was indeed profoundly ambivalent towards the official teaching and discipline of the Church. He defended the Church's spontaneous resistance to humanist rationalism, arguing that it was the merit of Catholicism to recognize the primacy of will and life (*TSL*, p. 78). Protestantism, on the other hand, is imprisoned in 'the tyranny of the letter'.[2] Whereas Catholicism doesn't lose sight of the single most decisively religious question of all, the question of immortality, Protestantism's emphasis on justification easily degenerates into mere ethics (*TSL*, p. 67). Because of the priority it gives to the Word, Protestant doctrine mutates into conceptuality, whilst Catholicism stays close to the passionate, suffering reality of actual life. Unamuno is even prepared to commend the Church's condemnation of Galileo, its resistance to Darwinism and the declaration by Pius IX that Catholicism and modern civilization are irreconcilable (*TSL*, p. 72). However, Unamuno was not a Catholic polemicist *à la* Belloc. No less than Shestov, he saw the Aristotelianism of Catholic theology as a cuckoo in the theological nest. Scholasticism is fundamentally committed to the belief 'that we must of necessity find a solution to every problem' (*TSL*, p. 93) and that what is good for us – happiness – must coincide with what is the case – truth. Such a belief, however, 'is but a pious wish' (*TSL*, p. 93). We have no guarantee that life on earth must have a happy outcome. The basic impulse of human life, as of all life, is to perpetuate itself, to strive to maintain itself in being, to live and not to die. But we can never *know* whether this impulse is realizable. When the Church, buttressed by Aristotelian reason, attempts to offer just such knowledge, Unamuno is brutally dismissive. He says of a standard Thomist textbook of philosophy (written by the Cardinal Primate of Spain) that 'it is totally lacking in any originality and faithfully mirrors the abyss of vulgarity, imbecility and dotage into which the doctrine we call Thomism has fallen.'[3] It is little wonder that in 1953 he was denounced by a leading Catholic bishop as the greatest heretic of modern times and that in 1957 both *The Tragic View of Life* and *The Agony of Christianity*, his two most directly theological works, were placed on the Index of proscribed books.

Unamuno's ambivalence towards the Catholic Church is, significantly, mirrored in many other aspects of his thought. Indeed, ambivalence and paradox characterize the very lineaments of his intellectual style and are also reflected in his passionate involvement in Spanish political life.

Unamuno was born in Bilbao in 1864. He pursued an academic career, becoming Professor of Greek at the University of Salamanca in 1891. Later he was appointed rector of the university, a public and politically sensitive post from which he was dismissed and in which he was reinstated several times subsequently. He rejected the secular and anti-religious elements in the socialism he had espoused at an early age, declaring that the only freedom for which he struggled was the freedom to be himself. None the less, he remained anti-monarchist and, later, anti-dictatorial. This stance led to his exile in 1924 and, although the dictator Primo de Rivera pardoned him after a few months, he chose to remain in exile (mostly in Paris) until after de Rivera's fall in 1930. Returning to

Spain he was elected to the Cortes in 1931, where he criticized both Republicans and Monarchists, also disappointing many of his fellow Basques by advocating the cause of Spanish unity, a cause seen by many Basques as, effectively, Castilian hegemony. The last year of his life, 1936, encapsulated many of the paradoxes of his public career. Having been nominated rector for life of Salamanca University, he was dismissed by the Republican government. Reinstated by Franco, he was once more dismissed after publicly denouncing fascism. He was placed under house arrest and was a potential target for liquidation when he died suddenly on 31 December 1936.

The ambivalences and paradoxes of his own life made Unamuno naturally sympathetic to Kierkegaard. He learned Danish in order to be able to read Kierkegaard's works in the original and he referred to him as 'our brother Kierkegaard' (*TSL*, p. 109). Like Kierkegaard he regarded passion as a guide to truth, and argued that the individual's passionate concern for their own life, although irrational, is the generative ground of faith. The beginning of wisdom is to be found in the experience of what he called 'the man of flesh and bone', whom he described as 'The man who is born, suffers and dies – above all, who dies; the man who eats and drinks and plays and sleeps and thinks and wills; the man who is seen and heard; the brother, the real brother ... I, you, reader mine, the other man yonder, all of us who work socially on the earth' (*TSL*, p. 1). Against this, the 'man' studied by philosophers in the line of Aristotle is 'merely an idea ... a no-man' (*TSL*, p. 1).

As his description of 'the man of flesh and bone' indicates, suffering and the encounter with death provide vital clues to the meaning of the human condition. 'Suffering is the substance of life and the root of personality,' writes Unamuno, 'for it is only suffering that makes us persons' (*TSL*, p. 205). Suffering is also 'the most immediate revelation of consciousness, and it may be that our body was given us simply in order that suffering might be enabled to manifest itself' (*TSL*, p. 211). But if it is indeed the body, as a brute, unconscious reality that makes consciousness aware of itself and simultaneously reveals the limitations of consciousness, this is not intended by Unamuno in a reductionist sense. The body, by virtue of its resistance to mind, may be the immediate cause of self-consciousness and of suffering, but there are degrees of consciousness and of suffering that are not merely reflexes of physiological conditions. Even bodily suffering, Unamuno says, is already spiritually charged. How much more the kind of suffering that, following Kierkegaard, he calls anguish. Anguish brings existence itself into question, compelling me to ask about the reality of the life and the suffering I am experiencing. It is in anguish, and only in anguish, that we are led to grasp the reality of existence in the most profound sense. This applies not only to the reality of human existence and of the existence of the world. It also applies to the existence of God: 'suffering tells us that God exists and suffers, but it is the suffering of anguish, the anguish of surviving and being eternal. Anguish discovers God to us and makes us love Him' (*TSL*, p. 207).

At this point it becomes clear that the faith recommended by Unamuno does not mitigate his 'tragic view of life'. The leap of faith does not carry us out of a desolate universe devoid of consolation into a haven of bliss secured against all the changes and chances of life and death. Indeed, in a formulation that Unamuno admits may sound blasphemous to some, God Himself suffers and needs our pity.

> God, the Consciousness of the Universe, is limited by the brute matter in which He lives, by the unconscious, from which He seeks to liberate Himself and to liberate us. And we, in our turn, must seek to liberate Him. God suffers in each and all of us ... and we all suffer in Him. religious anguish is but the divine suffering, the feeling that God suffers in me and that I suffer in Him. (*TSL*, p. 207)

In this vision of a limited, suffering, emergent God, striving to realize a future immortality in and through the travails of nature and of history, Unamuno may remind us of Schelling's dynamic theogony. If it is objected that this vision breaks away from the ground rules of Christian orthodoxy (and certainly talk of the suffering of God was far less acceptable in the first half of the twentieth century than it is perhaps today), Unamuno would reply that, none the less, something like this is what we must say if faith is really to be faith, since faith means, precisely, not having the kind of guarantees that rational theism claims to provide.

As well as writing works of a directly theological or philosophical nature, Unamuno was also a poet and novelist, and his novels offer important insights into his understanding of the relationship between God and his creatures. In *Mist* (1914) he calls conventional assumptions about the relationship between a writer and his 'fictional' characters into question. The Prologue is written by Víctor Goti, one of the minor characters in the novel, and, in the course of the narrative, Augusto Pérez, the 'hero', visits his creator, Unamuno. Augusto has decided that, faced with the meaningless-ness of his existence, he will take his life into his own hands and vindicate his freedom by means of the one absurd gesture left to him: suicide. Unamuno, however, has determined to kill him off by natural causes. Unamuno tells him that what he, Augusto, wants is, in the last resort, neither here nor there, as he is merely a fiction. "'I'll be damned if I let you die that way,"' expostulates the author, "'I simply will not have it. And that's that!"'[4] However, Augusto is reluctant to accept this. He puts it to Unamuno that he himself doesn't exist apart from his characters, that is, apart from the image or role he creates for himself through the characters of his novels and, by extension, through the various roles he adopts in his social and public life. He also reminds Unamuno that he too is subject to death no less than his creatures. Either way, of course, Augusto must die. The issue, however, is whether death is mere fate, befalling him as an external power, or whether he is able to be free in face of it.

It seems that it is, finally, the author who kills him and that Augusto's attempts to become 'real' end in failure. However, his friend Víctor Goti claims in the prologue that Unamuno is mistaken and that Augusto really did commit suicide. Moreover, after Augusto's death Unamuno begins to wonder whether he has done the right thing, and considers resuscitating him. In the course of his musings he falls asleep and, in his dream, Augusto appears to him and together they discuss whether such a resuscitation is possible. Augusto argues that it isn't.

> '[I]t is the same for a creature out of fiction as it is for a man of flesh and blood, which you specify is a man of flesh and blood and not fictional flesh and fictional blood. You can bring him to life and you can kill him, but once you've killed him, you cannot … no, no, you cannot resuscitate him.'[5]

And he goes on to ask rhetorically, "'Do you think it's possible to resuscitate Don Quixote?"'

Much of Unamuno's exploration of the complexities of fact and fiction, of role and reality, recall the kind of issues raised by Kierkegaard in connection with his pseudonymous writings (as well as anticipating L. Pirandello). Many of these issues are taken further in *How to Make a Novel* (1926/7), which itself straddles the frontier between fiction and criticism, and in which Unamuno articulates how his own life is inseparable from the roles he creates for himself through his writing and his political stance. The same applies by extension to his political opponents, who become what they are in history, he claims, by virtue of the role that he, Unamuno, assigns to them in his personal drama. Social reality is thus itself constituted by the complex interaction of role projection and role interpretation.

Although Augusto compelled Unamuno to admit that Don Quixote could not be resuscitated, there is a sense in which the unifying thread of Unamuno's writing is precisely the passionate and paradoxical attempt to do just that.

In Unamuno's eyes, Don Quixote is no mere character from a sixteenth-century novel. He is more 'real' than his creator Cervantes. He is the embodiment of essential Spanishness and, for Unamuno, of Christianity. He is 'Our Lord Don Quixote', 'a living and eternal man ... worth all theories and all philosophies' (*TSL*, p. 323) and Cervantes is his evangelist. This 'real' Don Quixote 'lives amongst us, animating us with his spirit ... this Don Quixote continues to incite us to make ourselves ridiculous, this Don Quixote must never die' (*TSL*, p. 323).

If life is a dream, an illusion in which we are mere dream-creatures, fictions, of an author-deity, the example of Don Quixote shows us how, none the less, we may stake our all, our meaning and our existence, on what we believe ourselves to be and on the values that we will to will into existence. This is what Don Quixote did in his attempt to live out the illusory values of knight-errantry, and no matter what absurd errors of fact he was led into by his quest, Unamuno believes that his story is a profound vindication of such a will to believe. Indeed, according to Unamuno, the apparent wrong-headedness of many of the Hidalgo's adventures is merely apparent. Take, for example, the adventure of the windmills, which Don Quixote attacked believing them to be giants.

> The knight was right: fear and fear alone, made Sancho and makes all of us poor mortals see windmills in the monstrous giants that sow evil through the world. Those mills ground flour for bread, and men confirmed in blindness ate of that bread. Today they do not seem to be windmills, but locomotives,

dynamos, turbines, steamships, automobiles, telegraphy with and without wires, bombs, instruments of ovariotomy; but they conspire to the same damage. Fear, sanchopanchesque fear, alone makes us fall on our knees and cry mercy before the monstrous giants of mechanics and chemistry. And, at last, at the base of some colossal factory of an elixir of long life, the human race, exhausted by weariness and surfeit, will give up the ghost. But the battered Don Quixote will live, because he sought health within himself, and dared to charge at windmills.[6]

The Don's vision is true because, by enacting it, he comes to know the one thing needful, a knowledge summed up in his own words: "'I know who I am,'"[7] and, comments Unamuno,

therein lies both his power and his misfortune. His power, because, as he knows who he is, he has no reason to fear anyone but God, who made him be what he is; and his misfortune, because he alone knows, here on earth, who he is; and, as the world knows it not, all he does or says will appear to them as if done or said by one that does not know himself, by an insane person.[8]

Like Kierkegaard's Abraham, Don Quixote (that is, each of us as Don Quixote) can only justify transgressing the laws of universal reason and morality by being ready to suffer for that transgression in his own person. However, unlike (some interpretations of) Kierkegaard's Abraham, his action is not purely inward: it is a direct challenge to the world in its prevailing complacency and questions the legitimacy of what the world holds to be universal. Does this, then, collapse the distinction between a knight of faith in Kierkegaard's sense and a Nietzschean 'superman'?

On one occasion Unamuno did speak of a 'really Christian doctrine ... hidden under the superficial paradox of the superman'.[9] But, despite his own combative and polemical character, he rejected Nietzsche's rhetoric of domination and repudiation of pity. For Unamuno it is precisely pity or compassion that draws us into the common task of constructing the immortality of an emergent divine community. Pity, and a belief in ultimate pardon, are also, he argues, essential characteristics of Don Quixote himself, exemplified in his freeing of the galley-slaves. This proves Don Quixote's belief that 'the ultimate and definitive justice is pardon', and,

Unamuno adds, 'God, nature, and Don Quixote chastise only to pardon ... [Don Quixote] could not have believed, however orthodox he may have been, in eternal punishment, and he did not believe in it.'[10]

Unamuno's legacy is as ambiguous as his own thought. A Catholic thinker, denounced as a heretic; an existentialist *avant la lettre* who can be read as offering an important corrective to Sartre[11] – or, alternatively, as one who mystifies the this-worldly paradoxes of early twentieth-century culture by a religious rhetoric that defies all logic.[12] Despite his opposition to successive Spanish dictatorships he remains suspect to those on the left because of his support for conservative Castilian values. Determined to uphold 'classical' traditions in Spanish literature, his own novels contribute to the modernist subversion of 'classical' conceptions of fiction.

Such a mixed reception would obviously not have displeased Unamuno himself. Misunderstanding, conflict and even confusion must necessarily surround all who take upon themselves the burden of our Lord Don Quixote. The hunger for immortality may be the most visceral of all our desires, yet it is a hunger that, as Unamuno understood it, common opinion is collectively determined to ignore. To know and to affirm who I am will always involve the risk of becoming a Quixote: 'And Christ came', wrote Unamuno in *The Agony of Christianity*, 'to bring us agony: struggle and not peace.'[13]

II

The problems of establishing any clear-cut definition of religious existentialism are well brought out if we simply consider the different attitudes taken by various religious existentialists towards the question of Being. Whereas Bultmann insisted that the whole question of fundamental ontology lay outside the sphere of interest of the theologian, Tillich regarded the courageous affirmation of meaning by the individual as disclosing an ontological structure that can and should be systematically explained. But whilst Tillich can claim to speak non-symbolically of God as 'Being-Itself', Berdyaev and Shestov saw ontology as a temptation that religious thought should resist. As we turn to Gabriel Marcel we find ourselves dealing once more with an existential thinker[14] who, like Tillich, was strongly committed to understanding the human condition in terms of its orientation towards Being. Yet, as we shall see, Marcel never claimed the status of theoretical or speculative knowledge for his ontology, and insisted that the question of Being could not be detached from the struggle of existing individuals to maintain the values of freedom, faithfulness and love in the concreteness of their actual situatedness in life. It is in connection with this that his many dramatic works are an important complement to his more formally philosophical writings, because they set out the complexity of the life situations in which and through which alone human beings are able to relate to Being. Their dramatic form draws attention to the limits of any purely theoretical understanding of existence. Paul Ricoeur (one of the most significant philosophers influenced by Marcel) said of them that 'the tragedy consists in the fact that nothing is solved for the characters. And nothing is resolved because the bearers of meaning or hope are always challengeable, or even suspect, sometimes even unbearable.'[15] Marcel responded by suggesting that there may even be an affinity between the role of drama in his thought and Kierkegaard's strategy of indirect communication. He also composed music and these extra-philosophical interests are not irrelevant to the style and tenor of his thought, which, for the most part, is set out in a series of occasional articles and journals (such as the *Metaphysical Journal* of 1914–23 and *A Metaphysical Diary* of 1928–33) and is of a more occasional, allusive, suggestive and imaginative nature than most academic philosophy or theology. Indeed, Marcel did not primarily work as an academic but as a dramatist, critic and editor.

Marcel was born in 1889 into a family background that was, as he himself notes, strongly agnostic. Of his father he wrote,

> imbued with the ideas of Taine, Spencer and Renan, his position was that of the late nineteenth-century agnostics; acutely and gratefully aware of all that which art owes to Catholicism, he regarded Catholic thought itself as obsolete and tainted with absurd superstitions.[16]

His mother died when he was very young, and the chief female influence in the household was his aunt, whom he described as having

> an acute and implacable sense of the absurdity of existence. Nature, if not utterly evil, [was] at least indifferent to right and

wrong ... [in this] essentially uninhabitable world ... there was only one resource: to forget oneself, to strive to lighten the burden of one's fellow sufferers, and to submit to the most severe self-discipline ...[17]

Not surprisingly, Marcel spoke of his home and school background as having 'an unstable and arid climate in which ... I found it difficult to breathe';[18] it was, he said, 'a desert universe'[19] and the school system he endured was 'abstract and inhuman'[20] – a set of reactions that culminated in a profound rebellion against 'a world hedged with moral restrictions and ravaged by despair'.[21]

III

The philosophical influences on Marcel's formative years are seen in the precocious undergraduate dissertation he wrote on the relationship between Coleridge and Schelling (written in 1909, when he was 20), in which he broached issues that were to be of continuing importance for the rest of his religious and philosophical quest.

Marcel describes how Coleridge attempts to move beyond the associationism of Hartley, a philosophy that reduced the human subject to being a mere reflex of material processes, towards a kind of personalism that does not, in turn, reduce the reality of the world to a mere appearance of a world of ideas. Crucial to this development is Coleridge's religious pilgrimage, in the course of which he discovered the failure of any purely moralistic programme of self-betterment and the need for faith and grace. Even though Marcel doubts the extent of Coleridge's acquaintance with Schelling's later thought, it becomes clear that both thinkers shared a number of concerns that, quite apart from the question of Coleridge having plagiarised various passages from Schelling, inevitably led to certain similarities in their conclusions. Both were strongly attracted by the idealist project of thinking the world in its essential unity – and yet both were also aware that the dynamism of life and the ineradicability of moral evil made any closed system impossible. Finding the Fichtean concept of a moral world-order inadequate, both sought to ground moral thought in the religious conception of God as transcendent and personal. In attempting to formulate a philosophical position that would allow both for a concept of God as the *living* God and for the reality of the struggle against evil, both also had a common point of reference in Jacob Boehme. Although Coleridge came to believe that Schelling remained too idealistic (and therefore incapable of allowing for the personal character of God), Marcel concludes that both Coleridge and Schelling were attempting to take into account a concept of freedom quite different from that to be found in Spinoza or in Hegel, where 'freedom' is simply the name given to the act of comprehending the necessary laws that make the world what it is. The radical concept of freedom to be found in Coleridge and Schelling is, simply, the consequence of taking seriously the religious affirmation that God created the world freely. This affirmation, says Marcel, is

> the ultimate term, perhaps inaccessible to philosophical develop-
> ment, that imposes itself on Schelling and Coleridge as being
> uniquely compatible with the sovereign aspirations of religious
> thought. And it is easy to see how the terrain of immanence is
> thereby definitively left behind in favour of superior domains
> where even Being no longer 'is'. And does not this exigency of
> liberty itself appear to us as essential to a conscious and coherent
> dynamism, that is, to a philosophy that, simultaneously refusing
> to look on the world either as an ensemble of abstract relations or
> as subjected to a process of blind development, affirms that that
> in us which is better and superior cannot be absolutely without
> relation to what lies at the basis of things and some profound
> analogy must subsist between the inner principle that animates
> our actions and the energy at work in them.[22]

This 'exigency of liberty', beyond empirically and rationalistically determined forms of reason and determined solely by its relation to a quite other order or level of Being, is to be a recurrent motif in Marcel's own thought.

The opening pages of his *Metaphysical Journal* show Marcel, at the beginning of 1914, still wrestling with the problematics of idealist philosophy posed by contemporary neo-Hegelianism. Also visible in the background of Marcel's argument is Descartes and, indeed, Marcel's approach to the question of God in these pages can be read as a reworking of Descartes argument for the existence of God. Setting out to secure the foundations of knowledge, Descartes had begun by attempting to doubt everything it was possible to doubt. 'Is anything at all indubitable?' he asked himself. 'Why should the exter- nal world revealed by the senses be taken more seriously than a dream? Perhaps I myself do not exist?' At this point, however, doubt contradicts itself, because, even in the moment when I doubt my existence I know that my doubt itself is real. 'I think, therefore I am' – *Cogito ergo sum*. But this does not solve all Descartes' problems since, although I can no longer doubt my own existence in so far as I am a thinking being, it is still possible for me to doubt the reality of the external world. Perhaps the whole world of appearances is a deception and not at all what it seems. It is at this point in his argument that Descartes raises the question of God. For, in a reworking of Anselm's ontological argument, he argues that God cannot be thought of as not existing any more than a triangle can be thought of as anything other than a figure the angles of which add up to 180°. Moreover, since it is possible for me to have a clear and distinct idea of God, it therefore follows that God does indeed exist. The concept of God thus serves to ground the existence of a reality external to my thought and is at one and the same time the guarantee both of the reality of the external world and of my own reality as thinking subject.

The fundamental structure of Marcel's argument is essentially similar to that of Descartes, although his manner of arguing is, in an expression he himself used of his philosophical style, 'sinuous' rather than linear, twisting and turning through several months' journal entries – and his final resolution of the question points in a very different direction from that taken by Descartes himself.

Marcel begins by asking how thought can truthfully represent being, given that the process of reflection spontaneously abstracts from the immediate experience of being. Marcel early on flags what he calls a landmark of which his thought never loses sight:

> My actual state of consciousness, which is bound up with the position of the organic body that it expresses, is the landmark in relation to which the infinite multiplicity of what can be thought by myself as existing is ordained. All existence can be traced back to the landmark, and outside all relation to it, it is only by a contradiction that we can think existence. (*MJ*, p. 14)

Marcel distinguishes between judgements of existence, in which existence is treated as a predicate attached to an objectively defined entity, and what he calls the 'positing of an existent' or an 'experience-limit' that is entirely spontaneous and is prior to the processes of rational thought. Indeed all judgements concerning existence presuppose the experience-limit that, Marcel says, 'is reduced to a contact between a body bound up with a perceiving consciousness, and an external datum' (*MJ*, p. 25). It is therefore meaningless to talk about the problem of the existence of the external world (as some philosophers do), because all judgements concerning existence or non-existence are only possible on the basis of an imagined relation to the experience-limit, i.e. to the experience of an embodied consciousness: therefore the external world is always already implicitly posited as existing in each and every judgement of existence. All explicit ratiocination is made against the background of an assumed relation to the world that reflection itself can never get behind.

But, if Marcel seems to be rejecting the premises of Descartes' argument, it soon becomes clear that he continues to be troubled by the possibility that, for spiritual beings such as we are, it remains unclear whether we can be sure of the reality of our ideas. In the last resort Marcel's concerns in the *Metaphysical Journal* are not narrowly epistemological and he leaves the question as to the reality of everyday experience hanging in mid-air in favour of the question as to the reality of our spiritual identity. The question of epistemology, he claims, can only be resolved when we know who we are in our innermost depths.

Marcel asks, 'Is truth possible regarding what is not manifested in space?' (*MJ*, p. 26). His own argument would seem to imply that, since all affirmations of existence are tied, however indirectly, to a spatially located experience and since 'to speak of truth regarding what is outside existence is a contradiction in terms' (*MJ*, p. 29), there is nothing outside the conditionality of spatially limited experience. Whatever is, is verifiable in relation to bodily experience.

Yet if Marcel has sought to reconnect an over-intellectual model of the self – as self exclusively identified as a *thinking* self – to its basis in corporeal existence, he has not wanted to reduce thought to physiology. To speak of truth is only possible when one speaks of thought. So, although 'Truth only regards what is in space and time', it is also the case that 'a truth is only *for* thought which is defined non-spatially and non-temporally' (*MJ*, p. 30). By virtue of its character as *thought*, truth therefore belongs to the domain of what is 'beyond' existence, what Marcel calls 'the realm of mind which is the realm of freedom' (*MJ*, p. 30) and which is also the domain of 'the absolutely unverifiable'.

It is in this realm, the realm of mind, freedom and the absolutely unverifiable, beyond existence, that it becomes proper to speak of God. If we forget this, we will speak of God as an existent being.

But God cannot be a datum given to the subject in an external way. Yet, in asserting this, Marcel has not forgotten the need to ground all human thought in bodily existence and because we are ourselves inextricably bound up with a world of space, time and immediate experience, 'God' will always appear to us and be debated by us as if he were an object amongst objects, whether the focus be on 'experiences' of God or on historical or other evidences of God. But God is beyond all this, beyond all essence. This is why it is appropriate, in relation to God, to speak of faith rather than knowledge.

But then, if God is so completely unknowable and so indeterminable in terms of the normal categories of experience, doesn't all talk about God become completely arbitrary, for how can any one thing we say of God be considered truer than any other?

To answer such questions we need to be clearer regarding the kind of affirmation that faith in God is. Marcel begins by returning to the *cogito*. Here, he suggests, in the self-evident truth that whatever else I may or may not be, I am a *thinking* being, we have another example of a statement that cannot be verified in relation to any particular experience or set of experiences because it is always already implied in all experience. The justification of the *cogito* cannot be made in terms of evidence but only on the basis of a free act, for 'Thought creates itself when it thinks itself; it does not discover itself, it constitutes itself' (*MJ*, p. 31). But then what of the danger that the freedom of the *cogito* will absolutize itself in such a way that we end up with the god of the philosophers, the god who is thought thinking itself, free but solitary? Marcel's response to this is that, first, to speak of the affirmation of an absolute freedom is to imply a relationship, albeit not (in this case) a relation of one existent being to other existent beings: the ego cannot affirm absolute freedom of itself alone, but only of an other; and, second, since 'The subject of faith is not thought in general ... [but] must be concrete' (*MJ*, pp. 40–1), that is, an individuality that is not reducible to the abstract universality of the *cogito*. Thus 'Faith is only possible on condition that from the *cogito* there springs forth that which is individual' (*MJ*, p. 40).

None of this, Marcel hastens to add, has the character of proof. We are, after all, in the realm of freedom. We cannot prove the necessity of faith or that faith is implied in the nature of consciousness. None the less, the nature of consciousness does establish the possibility of faith. Moreover, since 'to think faith is to think faith in God'

(*MJ*, p. 39), it is also to establish the possibility of God. For what is faith? Faith is that act in which '*the mind posits God as the positer*' (*MJ*, p. 46), the act, that is, in which the individual understands himself not as the freely self-positing act of thought but as this concrete individual who owes his existence to the free creative act of God.

We are now close to seeing why, for Marcel, the act of faith is not simply arbitrary. For, to understand oneself as a concrete individuality created by God, is to secure the unity of consciousness that is otherwise so problematic. Whereas a philosophy based solely on the *cogito* confronts the object-world as something essentially alien, something it can never fully understand or get behind, faith affirms that both object-world and thinking-self are 'linked transcendentally', joined together by virtue of the affirmation of God as creator of all reality. This God is no longer the god of the philosophers, the god who is nothing but thought thinking itself. He is the God who can be the God of the concrete person, engaging both corporeal and intellectual dimensions of human reality.

If Marcel thus finds in God a guarantee for the reality both of the thinking subject and of its world, it is no less clear that it is a 'guarantee' of a quite different kind from that offered by Descartes. Whereas Descartes' argument did claim the status of proof, ensuring the objective reality of my experiences and judgements regarding the world and thus laid the foundations of my knowledge of the world, Marcel's argument finishes with an act of faith that can never be objectified. This act of faith is itself only possible on the basis of a conversion that is in turn only thinkable 'by the intervention of grace' (*MJ*, p. 50). Grace, as the category *par eminence* by which God is revealed to me, is untranslatable into terms of knowledge. 'Grace implies the absolute irreducibility of the strictly religious mode of intelligibility in relation to all objective intelligibility' (*MJ*, p. 53), Marcel states. Indeed, even to ask about the 'reality' of grace is to commit a categorial error, since 'grace lies outside the categories of modality', of which 'reality' is one (*MJ*, p. 54). 'Grace … must be thought as unthinkable' (*MJ*, p. 59) and the same unthinkability adheres to all the manifestations of grace in experience. Religion, in the concrete form of personal sanctity, 'can only be the object of a cult,' Marcel asserts. On the one hand, this means that

> A cult some humble person devotes to a saint of whom he knows nothing and of whom, doubtless, he forms an image which is gross and inexact historically, has more *being* than the volumes

piled up by men of learning so as to reduce the saint to normal proportions or even to establish that he never existed. (*MJ*, p. 47)

And yet, on the other hand, it is far from justifying any claim made on behalf of religion since many such claims are based precisely on a confusion between what can and what cannot be regarded as a legitimate object of knowledge. Thus, if the Church insists on the reality of a miracle as an historical fact, Marcel replies that 'As long as devotion still implies objective affirmations we have a failure to realise absolute religion – the religion of the saint for whom all is pure actuality, all is revelation...' (*MJ*, p. 48). The application of historical method to religious belief misses the point because of its own prior assumptions as to what can or cannot count as fact. Similarly Marcel asserts that 'theodicy is atheism' (*MJ*, p. 64), since to attempt to justify God in the face of suffering is inevitably to quantify and objectify God, something that is alien to faith. Finally 'Religion *is* only for the person who surrenders himself to it' (*MJ*, p. 84).

Descartes' enquiry began with doubt but ended with metaphysical certainty regarding the reality and knowability of the world. Because Marcel can only arrive at such certainty on the basis of faith, his position is necessarily inconclusive with regard to metaphysics. 'From the standpoint of metaphysical knowledge the world remains the site of uncertainty, the reign of the possible, it remains contingent in relation to religious thought' (*MJ*, p. 97).

Marcel is therefore willing to surrender a considerable swathe of debated territory to the claims of historical and scientific knowledge – and yet he does not want to concede that religion is thereby reduced to something completely irrational or arbitrary. Because faith arises as a self-transcendence of the *cogito*, 'at least a distant communication seems possible' between the interests of the thinking self and the believing self (*MJ*, p. 57). Perhaps more importantly, faith is in its own inner character a transcending of solipsism, a movement of the 'I' towards an 'other' and a breaking out of the circle of reflection reflecting itself. In its affirmation of God as other and, particularly, as an irreducibly other freedom, God becomes 'the real foundation of communication between individualities' (*MJ*, p. 62). In being open to the freedom of God, I am therewith also opened to the freedom of others.

Here we see the emergence of a number of interconnected themes that are characteristic of Marcel's mature thought. God, as the ground of relationship, is ultimately only 'knowable' in and through love; God is never knowable impersonally, as an object, a 'he' or third party, but only as a 'thou': the question concerning God cannot be posed in terms of a 'what' or a 'that' (as in such questions as 'what is the nature of God?' or 'does God exist?') but only in terms of 'who' and, as such, is also a question concerning the person 'who' asks it. Personality alone is the seal that guarantees the truth of religious affirmations. If life is to be regarded as a trial, 'To triumph in the trial is to maintain oneself as soul, to save one's soul' (*MJ*, p. 202), i.e. to attain and to maintain oneself as personality, as the 'thou' that I always am for God, held in a bond of mutual recognition. In terms of this personal relationship between the soul and God, Marcel states that to think of God is to think of Him 'as absolute appeal' or 'absolute witness'. By this difficult but important concept Marcel wants to say, continuing the metaphor of juridical process, that I appeal to the existence of God (or, as he would prefer to put it, to the *presence* of God) as to one who can witness to my existence as person, as 'thou'. Conversely, because of the mutuality of the personal, I–thou relationship, God's existence (or presence) can only be affirmed on the basis of the testimony of the one for whom that presence is a real presence in love. Just as the personal life can only be thought of in terms of the 'thou' who can never become a 'he' or a 'she', so too it is only to be thought of in terms of 'being' rather than 'having'. All profoundly personal feelings cannot be spoken of as things we 'have', because we are who we are in those very feelings.

By the conclusion of the *Journal*, Marcel tells us, he reached the view that it was impossible for him to set out his thought in the conventional philosophical manner and, indeed, with the major exception of his Gifford lectures (published as *The Mystery of Being*) most of his subsequent work was in the form of occasional pieces, supplemented, of course, by his plays and music. In attempting to set out the main aspects of his thought in a consistent way, guided to a considerable extent by *The Mystery of Being*, we must therefore be wary of believing ourselves to have achieved a definitive structuring of them. In doing so we shall also meet again concepts and arguments familiar from the pages of the *Journal*.

IV

The question of Being lies at the heart of Marcel's thought. This question arises for Marcel on the basis of what he calls 'the ontological exigence'. Noting that some of his translators have used the word 'need' for the French *exigence*, Marcel warns against being misled into thinking that he is speaking of something necessary. Being does not confront us as the term of a necessary deduction or as a necessary condition of our existence. Nor, on the other hand, is this *exigence* a 'need' in the sense of something I 'want'. It is, Marcel says, 'not a simple desire or a vague aspiration. It is, rather, a deep-seated interior urge, and it might equally well be interpreted as an appeal' (*MB II*, p. 37). It is also, he adds, something that is demanded of us.

Looking around at the modern experience of life, we can see countless examples of individuals being reduced to mere functionaries, cogs in the machine and consumers of mass-produced goods. The division of labour and the social fragmentation consequent upon it, the mechanization of production, the spirit of abstraction and the degradation of human ideals in ideologies of left and right (including, Marcel believes, Sartrean existentialism) all contribute to a situation that some experience as the 'lack of something … impoverishment … aridity' (*MB II*, p. 40). Here the ontological *exigence* makes itself felt. Our destiny as human beings, as persons in the fullest sense of the word, cannot be fulfilled merely by virtue of the fact that we exist. Something more is required of us. Undeterred by the charge that he is indulging in mere sentimentality, a pointless nostalgia for a lost paradise that never was, Marcel affirms the feeling that we need a 'fullness which is the contradiction at once of the hollowness of a functionalized world and of the overpowering monotony of a society in which beings take on more and more the appearance of specimens which it is increasingly difficult to differentiate' (*MB II*, p. 42). This feeling, he says, is metaphysically significant, and its ultimate referent is 'being' – but, of course, not 'being' in the sense of a genus, a substratum or an object of possible knowledge, that is, not 'being' as a topic within philosophical metaphysics in any conventional sense, but 'being' as given in, to and for faith.

An important aspect of what Marcel says about Being is the distinction which he popularized between 'having' and 'being'. 'Having' characterizes the kind of relationship I have to external things, to my body *qua* instrument or even to my thoughts and ideas in so far as I think of them as things that somehow belong to me. The self that is determined by the mode of having is, Marcel says, 'a thickening, a sclerosis … of the body … in so far as my body is something I have' (*BH*, p. 181). Having lies at the root of desire (as distinct from love) in which I want to have for myself what I see others enjoying. It is also profoundly implicated in the problematics of contemporary technology.

To see the world in terms of having is, Marcel says, to see it by analogy to the management of an estate and the debate between autonomy and heteronomy is a typical example of the kind of insoluble dilemmas that arise on the basis of this analogy. For if heteronomy means having my affairs managed by another, autonomy means managing my affairs for myself – but none the less 'still administration' (*BH*, p. 142), still a mode of 'having' rather than of 'being':

> 'I want to run my own life' – that is the radical formula of autonomy. It refers essentially to *action* and implies ... the notion of a certain province of activity circumscribed in space and time. Everything belonging to the order of interests, whatever they are, can be treated with relative ease as a province, a district marked off in this manner. Furthermore, I can administer, or treat as something to be administered ... everything that can be compared ... to a *possession* – something *I have*. But where this category of *having* becomes inapplicable, I can no longer in any sense talk about administration, whether by another or myself, and therefore I cannot talk about autonomy either. (*BH*, p. 143)

The domain of being, in which the category of having becomes inapplicable, is also – importantly – the domain of love, of the 'thou' and of true creativity. 'A man *is* a genius, but *has* talent,' says Marcel (*BH*, p. 188).

Naturally, because Being is not something to be approached in the mode of having, we cannot 'know' it by defining its essence or listing its attributes. In another famous distinction, Marcel suggests that Being cannot be looked at as a problem, but as a mystery. 'A problem', he says,

> is something which I meet, which I find complete before me, but which I can therefore lay siege to and reduce. But a mystery is something in which I am myself involved, and it can therefore only be thought of as *a sphere where the distinction between what is in me and what is before me loses its meaning and its initial validity.* A genuine problem is subject to an appropriate technique by the

exercise of which it is defined: whereas a mystery, by definition, transcends every conceivable technique. (*BH*, p. 127)

A mystery can be degraded into a problem, as when the mystery of evil is turned into 'the problem' of evil, as if it were something that could be 'solved' by finding a verbal formula, instead of being taken to heart as a matter of personal responsibility. Similarly, because 'mystery' belongs to what is only accessible on the plane of concerned inwardness, it is never going to be possible to make a 'mystery' the matter of public discourse. As such it is always susceptible of being transformed from what it really is into the faith of others, something I hear talked about which does not essentially concern me.

Corresponding closely to the distinction between mystery and problem is the further distinction between presence and object.

> We can, for instance, have a very strong feeling that somebody who is sitting in the same room as ourselves, sitting quite near us, someone whom we can look at and listen to and whom we could touch if we wanted to make a final test of his reality, is nevertheless far further away from us than some loved one who is perhaps thousands of miles away or perhaps, even, no longer among the living. We could say that the man sitting beside us was in the same room as ourselves, but that he was not really *present* there, that his *presence* did not make itself felt. (*MB I*, p. 205)

Such a situation is 'communication without communion.' Someone to whom I am talking but whom I do not feel to be present 'understands what I say to him, but he does not understand *me*' (*MB I*, p. 205). 'Presence' in this sense partakes of the quality of mystery. For when it is a question of dealing with or using an object, then there are procedures that can be taught objectively. Presence, however (of which, for Marcel, charm is one commonly encountered aspect), cannot be taught. There is no such things as the art of making one's presence felt or of being charming.

Being only comes into view in relation to the self and the question of Being can never be detached from the self as it experiences the demand of the ontological exigency. The question of Being is inseparable from the question 'Who am I?'[23] As Marcel had concluded by the end of his *Metaphysical Journal*, the 'I' which is at stake in this question is always the concrete, particular 'I' and, as such, quite distinct from the 'I' implied in the Cartesian *cogito*, the rational, universalizable, thinking self – although there is none the less some distant communication between them. In distinction from the thinking self the 'I' with which Marcel is concerned is first and foremost characterized by 'incarnation' (*BH*, p. 16). Incarnation, Marcel states, is

> the central 'given' of metaphysic … the situation of a being who appears to himself to be *bound* to a body. This 'given' is opaque to itself … The opposition between subject and object is found to be transcended from the start … [This is] A fundamental predicament which cannot be in a strict sense mastered or analysed. (*BH*, p. 16)

Whereas discourse about the self based on the *cogito* invariably summons up those metaphors 'which depict consciousness as a luminous circle around which there is nothing, to its own eyes, but darkness', Marcel's view suggests that 'On the contrary, the shadow is at the centre' (*BH*, p. 18). What this means is that, by virtue of my being incarnate, 'bound to a body', I can never penetrate myself totally with the light of consciousness. At my very centre as a conscious and incarnated being I am a riddle and a mystery to myself and it is out of this situation of profound questionableness, in which I am a question to myself, that the question or exigence of Being makes its presence felt.

This is not, however, radical subjectivism, because the self envisaged by Marcel is never alone in its world. Indeed, by virtue of its embodiedness 'the world' is always already present at the very centre of the self. Most importantly, the world is present to me in and as the other. Receptivity in the sense of openness to the other is a fundamental aspect of the self.

This points to one of the key elements in Marcel's opposition to Sartre's existentialism. As Marcel reads Sartre, the view expressed in Sartre's *Huis Clos* that 'hell is other people' is simply the summation of the view of the other worked out at length in *Being and Nothingness*. The 'whole tendency' of Sartre's understanding of the other, Marcel says, 'is to assert that human communication is doomed to failure; that the sense of community – forming part of a *we*-subject – is only experienced on such occasions as when a regiment is marching in step or a gang of workmen is pulling together ...'[24] In Sartre's view community will always end up by crushing individuality. In the same spirit, Sartre's analyses of love all tend to show love as manipulative and appropriative, either wresting my self away from the grasp of the other or imposing my will on the other. Even generosity, the giving of a gift, will invariably turn out to be 'a means of enslaving others'.[25] The 'metaphysical pride' at the root of Sartre's anthropology is his belief that 'to receive is incompatible with being free', but Marcel responds by affirming that there is a kind of receptivity that is quite distinct from the mere passivity of wax receiving the imprint of a seal and that, on the contrary, belongs to the constitution of freedom itself. As we have seen, both in the context of his Coleridge study and in the context of the *Metaphysical Journal*, the possibility of human freedom is intimately bound up with the existence of the self as a being freely created by God.

It is also fundamentally oriented towards the human other. As an embodied being I am always – in the very centre of my self – related to the world, 'in a situation' as Marcel puts it. I am never cut off from other human beings, but share with them in a common participation in Being. The self-defeating nature of the ego's attempts to sustain itself in isolation from others is teased out by Marcel in a number of concrete descriptions. Take the example of a 'shy young man who is making his first appearance at some fashionable dance or cocktail party' who is much too self-conscious of himself, i.e. of how he will look in the eyes of the others, to relax and have a good time, who feels

> that he has been literally thrown (as Christians were thrown to the lions) to the malevolent lucidity of other people's glances. Thus he is at once preoccupied with himself to the highest possible degree and hypnotized at the same time to a quite supreme degree by others, by what he imagines other people think of him. It is this paradoxical tension which your [he is speaking to a Scottish audience] excellent word *self-consciousness* so compactly expresses. (*MB I*, pp. 176–7)

In such a situation the young man will be unable to be present, in Marcel's sense of the term, nor will he be able to be present to others. He is not in any deep sense 'with' the other party guests. His state is, Marcel says, 'quite at the opposite [pole from] ... intersubjectivity'.

But now events take a turn for the better. Someone comes up to the young man and is welcoming to him.

> 'I am glad to meet you,' says the stranger, 'I once knew your parents', and all at once a bond is created and, what specially matters, there is a relaxation of tension. The attention of the young man ceases to be concentrated on himself, it is as if something gripped tight inside him were able to loosen up. He is lifted out of that stifling here-and-nowness in which, if I may be allowed a homely comparison, his ego was sticking to him as an adhesive plaster sticks to a small cut. (*MB I*, pp. 177–8)

This is perhaps a banal example of intersubjectivity and Marcel is well aware that he could seek more profound or elevated examples from the spheres of artistic or religious experience. But its very banality helps to indicate the essential point all the more clearly: that a dimension of 'withness', of 'being together', of participation in a shared situation is integral to the human condition and that possibilities of genuine communication are always being opened before us. The world is no mere ensemble of 'other minds' but meets us, concretely, in the person of a 'thou'.

A further key term in Marcel's philosophical vocabulary is fidelity or creative fidelity. Fidelity, he states, is really

> the exact opposite of inert conformism. It is the active recognition of something permanent ... ontologically ... it refers to a presence, or to something which can be maintained within us and before us as a presence, but which *ipso facto*, can be just as well ignored, forgotten and obliterated; and this reminds us of the menace of betrayal which, to my mind, overshadows our whole world.[26]

Fidelity, in other words, is not merely a matter of being faithful to a principle or faithfully obeying a rule, but is always related to the disclosure of Being in the meeting with the 'thou': it is the active, creative effort of maintaining oneself in an openness or receptivity towards that disclosure and towards its meaning and implications for the rest of my life. Being shows what is perhaps its most significant aspect when regarded 'as the place of fidelity' (*BH*, p. 47).

Love and marriage provide particularly significant examples of the conflicts between faithfulness and betrayal, and these conflicts are made more complex by the question as to whether the faithfulness concerned is really directed towards the other or is mere adherence to a heteronomous moral code or is simply a matter of personal pride. It is therefore hardly surprising that this is a territory frequently visited by Marcel in his plays, as in *A Man of God*. The play concerns Claude Lemoyne, a Protestant pastor, and his wife Edmée. Some years previously Edmée had had an affair, and their daughter Osmonde is in fact the child of this relationship, although she does not know it. Claude has 'forgiven' Edmée, but, whilst promising her that he would not tell anyone else about it, he has in fact confided in his mother who lets slip that she knows. The situation is complicated by the fact that prior to the affair Claude had been experiencing intense doubts about his vocation and faith but, in the very depths of feeling himself abandoned by Edmée, he had received a reassurance of God's presence, which brought him peace of mind and in the power of which he was able to forgive Edmée. Claude's account of events is couched in characteristically Marcellian terms. In an 'absolute void' a light gradually dawned on him: 'What happened then was like an appeal to the very depths of my being. It had to be understood ... For the first time I was present to myself and was going to discover with whom I had to deal ...'[27] God transformed his suffering that he might help Edmée out of her despair and self-hatred. Yet it has become clear that the promise of silence he made to Edmée, a promise that was an integral part of her being able to accept the forgiveness he offered, was not kept. Nor did his willingness to make that offer of forgiveness really spring out of their relationship. It was not a response to her need but to his self-invented role as a Christian minister. All these tensions are brought to breaking-point when they are contacted by Edmée's former lover, who is terminally ill and wants to see his daughter. As Claude tries to play a magnanimous role and assures Edmée that he will be beside her to help bear her cross in this time of trial, she retorts that he is her husband, not her priest. Claude, she says, talks of 'trials', but really the whole thing is a comedy he is acting out for his own and not for her benefit – in short, it is a pose. Claude himself gradually comes to see the falsity of his own past. When Edmée recalls how she first fell in love with Claude's glowing eyes and brilliant talk, he says,

> You committed your life on the basis of a look or the intonation of a voice. A look which promised ... What? This mysterious

promise wasn't kept, and there you have the story of our life together … And when I think of God, it's the same. Sometimes I've thought that he was speaking to me, but it was only nervous excitement. Who am I? When I try to grasp myself, I slip through my own hands.[28]

By the end of the play, as Marcel himself was to put it, 'they both stand shivering in a kind of moral nakedness, having stripped themselves of all self-deception.'[29]

Fidelity to being, the being disclosed in the loving revelation of the other 'thou', cannot be lived on the basis of a formula and those who understand their lives in the light of formulae – even if they are formulae involving such terms as fidelity, mystery, love and hope – risk transforming life into a play. Not, of course, that Marcel wants to belittle drama – indeed, he criticizes Sartre for implying that all role-playing is somehow morally suspect, a case of 'bad faith' in Sartre's own sense. But the kind of self-dramatization of a character like Claude is precisely what inhibits him from fully engaging with the needs of those around him.

To discover and to speak of truth in the concrete complexity of such situations can never be a matter of objective knowledge or observation from the outside. Only the person who is actually engaged in the situation and speaks out of it can speak truth to it. Truth here is a matter of witness and testimony. A witness, Marcel argues, is quite different from a mere observer. Observation is detached and impersonal, but 'Every testimony is based on a commitment and to be incapable of committing oneself is to be incapable of bearing witness.'[30] It might seem as if a witness in a law court was contributing primarily to verifying an objective representation of disputed events but, Marcel insists, it is of the very essence of even legal testimony that the witness stakes himself and his own credibility in giving testimony – that is why such testimony is given under oath. Moreover, a further characteristic of legal testimony that is profoundly relevant is that it is always testimony 'to': 'the witness always conceives of himself as standing in the presence of someone … he is essentially a-monadic.'[31] Still more fundamentally, although a witness in legal proceedings speaks *to* the court, his primary concern is not with gaining a good reception for what he says. What matters above all is that he speaks according to his conscience. Although testimony bears on circumstances that are independent of the witness and have an objective aspect, it can only be given by one who is engaged and feels his responsibility towards conscience and truth: 'testimony is given before a transcendence, perhaps even before transcendence itself ...'[32]

If personal commitment is characteristic of giving testimony in the context of a case in law, it is pre-eminently true that these characteristics belong to (or *should* belong to) witnessing to the truth of God, an implication that is strengthened for Marcel because of the metaphysical significance of the concept of 'trial': 'for the philosopher,' he says, 'everything is in some way a trial' (*MB II*, p. 143) in the sense of a struggle for truth. It is also true that wherever in life we give testimony for the sake of a truth to which we pledge our personal commitment, we are in a sense bearing testimony for God since 'every approach to justice, for example, or to charity, in the person of my neighbour, is at the same time an approach to this [i.e. the living] God Himself ...' (*MB II*, p. 132).

A final, yet essential, dimension of Marcel's thought is that of hope. Much of what has been said might seem to represent the religious life as remaining true to and bearing witness on behalf of an experience or an epiphany that is always somehow envisaged as lying in the past. To relate to an other, in love, as a 'thou', however, is to be called to a commitment that always implies a future. Fidelity is never just fidelity to a grace received (though it is that) but also commitment to a common future in the light of that grace. Marcel affirms a line spoken by one of his fictional characters: '"to love a being is to say, 'Thou, thou shalt not die'"'(*MB II*, p. 153). What is the meaning of this obscure remark? It is, Marcel suggests, quite different from the mere utterance of a wish. It should have about it the ring of prophetic assurance. But, of course, the future towards which the remark points should not be conceived of as some sort of objective state of affairs, a state we might one day come to enjoy in the mode of having. That would be to make hope the equivalent of desire. But 'to hope is not essentially *to hope that* ... whereas to desire is always to *desire something*' (*MB II*, p. 162). Hope, he goes on to suggest, might be 'another name for the exigence of transcendence, or ... that exigence itself, in as much as it is the driving force behind man the wayfarer'.[33] If despair is the experience of time as closed or contracted, hope is 'an *open time*', that is, the experience of time as open to the projection and fulfilment of new tasks. Such hope, Marcel believes, is quite different from the hope that motivates historical materialism, willing as it is to sacrifice millions of lives in the present for the sake of a better future. Christian hope of resurrection confers a sacredness on life now, seeing in all life a promise of resurrection.

Marcel's thought, like that of many other religious existentialists, leaves open many fundamental philosophical or theoretical questions. Nor does it justify the reassertion of any kind of unreconstructed traditionalism. He himself acknowledged at the close of his Gifford lectures that nothing he had said establishes a basis for revelation or dogma. At best it could only serve as an approach to that. The human situation is not that of standing at the end of history and looking back on it in a single, all-encompassing gaze, but of being still underway, a pilgrim, following 'a difficult road ... strewn with obstacles' (*MB II*, p. 188).

Many of the themes broached by Marcel can, of course, be paralleled amongst other anxious angels – the protest against a depersonalized view of humanity, the rejection of scientific objectivity as a measure of religious truth, the insistence on involvement and engagement, a heightened awareness of the futural dimension of existence and (although this runs against the popular wisdom concerning existentialism) a concern for the interpersonal or dialogical aspect of truth, together with a sense for the importance of *how* truth is communicated. It is therefore not always easy to judge how far the recurrence of many of these themes in the generations since Marcel can be ascribed to his influence. Perhaps the most striking analogies are with Karl Rahner, who reproduces many characteristically Marcellian themes in a more technically rigorous and dogmatically precise form, and with Paul Ricoeur, perhaps the most significant contemporary figure to have been directly influenced by Marcel, an influence that can be detected in such themes as testimony, dialogue and hope in Ricoeur's own thought.

But Marcel's place in the history of ideas is not perhaps the key issue. For whatever place he is assigned in that history, he remains a thinker in whose writings many of the common assumptions and assertions of the liberal Christian conscience of the middle of the twentieth century are brought together and worked into a whole that, if not logically consistent, is humanly coherent and that seeks to ground the possibility of religious values of faith, hope and love in such a way as to make them once more accessible to those living in the heart of what Marcel himself had experienced as the desert universe of modern secularism.

Unamuno and Marcel by no means exhaust Catholic existentialism. The novels of Georges Bernanos provide many explorations of themes to be found amongst the anxious angels from Kierkegaard onwards: the hiddenness of faith in the world, its paradoxical relation to reason and ethics, the necessary misunderstanding that surrounds those who live by faith and the contradiction between faith and the structures of modern mass society. Theodore Haecker, an early German translator of Kierkegaard, could also be described as a Catholic existentialist and Romano Guardini might also be listed here. Between them, however, Unamuno and Marcel show the potential range of interests and concerns that link the superficially incompatible worlds of pre-Vatican II Catholicism and religious existentialism.

NOTES

1. Whereas many of the Protestant existentialists, such as Tillich and Bultmann, were ordained ministers.
2. M. de Unamuno, *The Agony of Christianity and Essays on Faith* (Princeton: Bollingen Series, Princeton University Press), p. 20.
3. Ibid., p. 165.
4. Unamuno, *Novela/Nivola. Selected Works of Miguel de Unamuno*, Vol. 6 (London: Bollingen Series LXXXV, Routledge and Kegan Paul, 1976), p. 221.
5. Ibid., p. 239.
6. Unamuno, *The Life of Don Quixote and Sancho according to Miguel de Cervantes Saavedra* (London: Alfred A. Knopf, 1927), p. 40.
7. Ibid., pp. 31–4.
8. Ibid., pp. 31–2.
9. See P. Ilie, *Unamuno: an Existential View of Self and Society* (Madison, Milwaukee and London: Wisconsin University Press, 1967), p. 127.
10. *Don Quixote*, pp. 88–9.
11. Thus R. R. Ellis, *The Tragic Pursuit of Being. Unamuno and Sartre* (Tuscaloosa: University of Alabama Press, 1988).
12. Thus Frances Wyers, *Miguel de Unamuno: the Contrary Self* (London: Tamesis, 1976).
13. *The Agony of Christianity*, p. 9.
14. Indeed, Marcel has been credited with coining the term 'existentialism'. German writers of the 1920s and early 1930s had tended to speak of 'the philosophy of existence'. Sartre singles him out in *Existentialism and Humanism* as a pre-eminent representative of Christian existentialism (although he goes on to argue that such an expression is a contradiction in terms).
15. In G. Marcel, *Tragic Wisdom and Beyond* (Evanston: Northwestern University Press, 1973), p. 232.
16. Idem., *The Philosophy of Existence* (London: Harvill, 1948), p. 81.
17. Ibid.

18. Ibid., p. 82.
19. Ibid., p. 83.
20. Ibid., p. 85.
21. Ibid., p. 83.
22. Idem., *Coleridge et Schelling* (Paris: Aubier-Montaigne, 1971), p. 242.
23. See *The Philosophy of Existence*, pp. 2ff.
24. Ibid., p. 53.
25. Ibid., p. 60.
26. Ibid., pp. 21–2.
27. G. Marcel, *Un Homme de Dieu* (Paris: Grasset, 1936), pp. 54–5.
28. Ibid., p. 191.
29. *Tragic Wisdom and Beyond*, p. 94.
30. *The Philosophy of Existence*, p. 68.
31. Ibid., p. 69.
32. Ibid.
33. 'Homo Viator' is also the title Marcel gave to a collection of his essays and reviews (London: Victor Gollancz, 1951).

11

The Life of Dialogue

Shestov, Berdyaev, Unamuno and Marcel collectively give the lie to the view that religious existentialism was exclusively a Lutheran-Protestant phenomenon. When we also take into account the cases of Martin Buber and Franz Rosenzweig we have to make the further acknowledgement that it was not exclusively Christian either, since their Jewish inheritance was central to virtually everything either of them wrote.[1] Focusing in the first instance on Buber, we have to add that, despite a resolute acceptance of the world in its fearful contingency and a powerful sense of the need for 'holy insecurity', there is a confidence and an optimism in his thought that many regard as far removed from the mind-set of the typical existentialist. Moreover, Buber was a thoroughly social thinker, for whom not only the relation to the Other but life in community was an ineluctable dimension of the human condition.[2] Like Unamuno, Shestov and Berdyaev, Buber was also somewhat older than many of the twentieth-century anxious angels, having been born (in Vienna) in 1878, and he came to intellectual maturity well before the First World War, even though *I and Thou*, the book for which he is best, and sometimes solely, remembered was not published until 1923. As a young man he rose to prominence in Jewish intellectual circles in the early 1900s and was involved in important debates with such leaders of the Zionist movement as Theodore Herzl and Chaim Weizmann. As editor of a sequence of journals he had contacts with many of the most brilliant figures of a particularly brilliant epoch in Central European life, including George Simmel, Franz Kafka, Hugo von Hoffmannstal, Max Brod, George Lukács and the anarchistic thinker Gustav Landauer, who was briefly a member of the revolutionary socialist government of Münich in 1918–19 before his murder by the Reichswehrtruppen who suppressed the uprising.

The kind of intellectual influences on Buber's young life are by now in part familiar but there are also differences from the typical existentialist curriculum. His first philosophical breakthrough came in his teens through reading Kant. This was followed, more profoundly, by the impact of Nietzsche. Kierkegaard (especially) and Dostoevsky also played a formative role. Jacob Boehme, whose mystical writings had helped shape Schelling's late philosophy, was one of the focuses of his academic research, but Boehme was only one of a number of mystical sources he studied: Nicholas of Cusa, Meister Eckhart (who was just coming into vogue in the early years of this century) and Angelus Silesius also feature, as do Hindu, Buddhist and Taoist writings and, most importantly, the mysticism of Jewish Hasidism, exemplified in the eighteenth-century figure of Israel Baal Shem, the founding Zaddik (or Teacher) of modern Hasidism. It was the teaching and, perhaps more importantly, what he perceived as the spirit of the Baalshem that was to be the most constant point of reference in Buber's intellectual life, from the time when he discovered it in 1905.[3] Hasidism, as Buber saw it, was unique in the extent to which it both affirmed the individual's experience *and simultaneously* affirmed the value of life in the community.

But it is not only Buber's interest in mysticism that differentiates him from some other existentialist writers: it is also the fact that it is perhaps Goethe rather than Hegel who stands for the humanistic ideal of a unitary world-view that can no longer be held together against the centripetal tendencies of modernity, although – like many of Hegel's critics – Buber's comments on Goethe often articulate both critique and respect. It is not by chance that the motto on the first page of the first edition of *I and Thou* was a couplet from Goethe's *West-östlicher Divan*: 'So I have finally won from you/ the presence of God in all elements.' The omission of these lines in late editions seems to have reflected Buber's concern to distance himself from what could be perceived as a pantheistic tendency in his thought: for if Buber is one of the great philosophers of duality, above all of the irreducible duality of the personal I and Thou, the principle of duality is always worked out in a complex dynamic in which the drive towards unification is no less significant than the impulse of duality. However, in critiquing the self-sufficiency of Goethean humanity, Buber rarely indulges the polemical spirit that Hegel provoked in so many of his critics. The longing for a unitary, all-inclusive vision is one that Buber felt powerfully in himself and although he found it inadequate, he could never reject it out of hand, not least when it came tinged with the aura of mysticism.

Outside the Jewish world, Buber's thought is almost exclusively associated with a single book, *I and Thou*, and, indeed, for many readers, with one part of that book, in which he sets out the basic contrapuntal relationship between the 'two basic words' of 'I–Thou' and 'I–It'. This is, naturally, to do a grave injustice to such a many-sided thinker in whom so many of the strands of German humanistic culture are woven together with such a rich and varied reading of religious sources – no matter how important those two words 'I-and-Thou' have proved in modern theology. We shall, of course, return to *I and Thou*, but let us first pause on the path to this decisive expression of dialogical philosophy, and take note of an important early work, *Daniel*. Following a brief exposition of *Daniel* and a somewhat fuller treatment of *I and Thou* we shall then look at Buber's attitude towards other philosophies of existence, notably those of Kierkegaard and Heidegger, and at how the insights of *I and Thou* relate to his interpretation of Hasidism. Other than recording the fact, we shall not here go in any depth into Buber's distinctive place within Jewish life and thought, nor develop further the previous comments about the importance of the social and political dimensions in his writing.

Daniel, published in 1913, pulls together many of the influences and interests of Buber's early intellectual development in a sequence of imagined dialogues that do not so much argue out a position as articulate a vision. Its subtitle, 'Dialogues on Realization', points both forwards towards the more clearly expressed dialogicality of *I and Thou* and subsequent works, and backwards towards the requirement of realization or actualization that he found not only in Kierkegaard and the late nineteenth-century philosophies of life but also in the vitality of Hasidism. Moreover, they also allude to what is an important element linking Buber's mystical thought to his later more world-affirming writings: that it is through humanity's realization (in the sense of making-real) of ultimate truth *and never apart from that* that God himself becomes 'real' in the world. The titles of the dialogues, though enigmatic, suggest the parameters of the problematic with which Buber is wrestling here: 'On Direction', 'On Reality', 'On Meaning', 'On Polarity' and 'On Unity'.

'Direction' is defined in a way that recalls Kierkegaard: 'Direction is that primal tension of a human soul which moves it to choose and realize this and no other out of the infinity of possibilities' (*Dan*, p. 55). It is exclusively characteristic of an existing being, facing a particular choice on the horizontal plane of earthly life.

An eternal being would not know and would never require direction. The next dialogue, 'On Reality', emphasizes the actual realization of the particular direction that has been chosen: 'power is drawn from the depths and collected and moved to action and renewed in work' (*Dan*, p. 69). 'Realization' is a unifying force: 'The creative hours, acting and beholding, forming and thinking, are the unifying hours. The hero and the wise man, the priest and the prophet are unifying men' (*Dan*, p. 72). But such men are rare in the modern world. For the modern world is given over to 'producers', to the spirit of what Buber calls 'orientation', 'crafty economy' or 'shrewdness'. Our age, he laments, 'is the age that does not realize' (*Dan*, p. 74). Again, echoes of the kind of *Zeitkritik* contained in Kierkegaard's *Two Ages*, in Dostoevsky and in Nietzsche, are plainly audible.

The third dialogue, 'On Meaning', contains a vivid account of an uncanny experience, told by Daniel's friend Reinold, who describes how, one night in his youth, he was out at sea in a small rowing boat when, suddenly, he became aware of an imminent storm. The searchlight of a nearby cruiser sweeps across the shore, and although the illumination it provides is only momentary, it none the less helps him to orient himself: 'for a moment I could compose myself and *knew* all' (*Dan*, p. 86). But then the storm arrives, and the lightning flashes that also illuminate the land, but in a random, chaotic way:

Spectral stretches of earth detached themselves from one another before me in a senseless service; not like parts of a shore, but like spectral shrieks. I 'knew' that they were connected ... but I *felt* no connection, rather shriek, shriek, and in between them the abyss. (*Dan*, p. 86)

Since that experience Reinold has lost the sense of security, the feeling for the orderedness and coherence of the world that had previously sustained him. 'The abyss' revealed between the fragments of landscape illuminated arbitrarily by the lightning insinuated itself into every relationship 'between thing and thing, between image and reality, between the world and me ...' (*Dan*, p. 86).

Daniel advises him to abandon the quest for security and to take the anxiety of his experience into himself.

All security which is promised, all security which is longed for and acquired, means to protect oneself. It is that which is promised to the believers of all old and new churches. But he who loves danger and practices realization does not want to protect himself but to realize himself. (*Dan*, p. 92)

And, even more forcibly, he tells Reinold:

your motto will be: God and danger. For danger is the door of deep reality, and reality is the highest price of life and God's eternal birth ... All creation stands on the edge of being; all creation is risk ... You must descend ever anew into the transforming abyss, risk your soul ever anew, ever anew vowed to the holy insecurity. (*Dan*, pp. 98–9)

The next dialogue, 'On Polarity', is significantly subtitled 'After the Theatre', and finds Daniel in deep discussion with another friend.[4] Daniel is trying to explain an almost revelatory experience that had befallen him as he watched the play and the interaction between the main characters.

[W]hat I saw was the spectacle of duality. But not good and evil; all valuation was only external dress. Rather the primal duality itself, being and counterbeing, opposed to each other and bound to each other as pole with pole, polar opposed and polar bound – the free polarity of the human spirit ... What they did only unfolded what they were ... and what truly stood in the center between them was not something mediating but the I of the spirit whose primal secret duality they revealed. (*Dan*, pp. 104–5)

This revelation, however, concerns more than the physical or spatial situation of the actors standing over against one another. It also concerns the way in which they relate to each other in language. 'The drama is pure dialogue; all feeling and all happening has in it become dialogue' (*Dan*, p. 120).

None the less, the over-againstness of the polarized figures whose interaction and dialogue constitute the drama is still envisaged as bound together by some principle of unity, and it is to the theme of unity that the final dialogue of the book is devoted. Here Buber makes it plain that the holy insecurity embraced by the one who risks the terrors of the abyss is not to be endured in the spirit of a Sisyphean labour, i.e. as an eternally repeated acceptance of meaninglessness. The experience of duality (and even of fragmentation) may seem to militate against the final triumph of a unifying horizon of meaning, but Buber proclaims the paradox that 'he who genuinely experiences the world experiences it as a duality … And to overcome this tension is his task' (*Dan*, p. 136). The experience of the divided self is resolved in the courageous act of one who truly realizes his direction: 'I had torn down the eternal wall, *the wall within me*. From life to death – from the living to the dead flowed the deep union' (*Dan*, p. 135). In the closing lines of the dialogue Daniel intimates to his friend that death has been the true subject of the dialogue all along – 'we have all the time spoken of nothing else' (*Dan*, p. 144). But precisely because 'the deep union' flows only for the one who has become open to his death, the ultimate symbol of the fruitlessness of all human endeavour, that which we cannot in any way manage, master or control, Buber insists that 'True unity cannot be found, it can only be created' (*Dan*, p. 141). Unity, in other words, cannot be construed as a 'given', as something inhering in the 'true nature of things'. It is something that becomes actual only in, through and for the exercise of human freedom, a freedom that is fully and unflinchingly conscious of the abyss of meaningless chaos with which a merely naturalistic conception of the world confronts us, i.e. the abyssal vision that we are chance products of a random evolutionary process.

Yet although *Daniel* lays the foundations for much of Buber's later work, he was to write of himself as still being too taken up with the fantasy of a mystical God-relationship separable from a committed and resolute involvement with the world. In *Dialogue*, a short work published in 1929, which expanded on the themes of *I and Thou*, he gives an anecdotal form to his repudiation of such mysticism. In the section entitled *Conversion* he describes how 'after a morning of "religious" enthusiasm' (*BMM*, p. 31) he received a visit from a young man, previously unknown to him. Although Buber describes himself as having been suitably polite and attentive he also recognizes that in a deeper sense he was not really 'there' for the young man. 'I omitted to guess the questions which he did not put,' he wrote. Later he learnt that the young man is no longer alive and that the questions he did not put were in fact questions that could have decided his destiny.[5] 'Since then,' he comments,

> I have given up the 'religious' which is nothing but the exception, extraction, exaltation, ecstasy; or it has given me up. I possess

nothing but the everyday out of which I am never taken. The mystery is no longer disclosed, it has escaped or it has made its dwelling here where everything happens as it happens. I know no fullness but each mortal hour's fulness of claims and responsibilities. (*BMM*, pp. 31–2)

From here on Buber was to proclaim only a 'worldly' religiosity, not unlike that which Bonhoeffer was to project from his prison cell a generation later – and yet, it is almost unmistakable that for Buber 'the world' is not the world as represented by secular reason or scientific rationality: even in its concrete contingency it is still a world coloured by the aura of an eclipsed transcendence. It is still a world in relation to which the word 'God' cannot be abandoned.[6]

Between 1916 and 1922 Buber worked on what was to become the book with which he is sometimes almost exclusively identified, *I and Thou*. Cryptic, enigmatic, sometimes almost impenetrably uni-idiomatic, replete with neologisms and, in some cases, torturing rare or even new meanings out of old words, *I and Thou* is not an easy book. None the less, the basic principle it is devoted to expounding resounds on every page with astonishing boldness and clarity and has entered into the stock-in-trade of twentieth-century intellectual life – even if in so doing it has, almost inevitably, been somewhat trivialized.

Like the opening bars of a great symphonic work, the opening paragraph sets out the theme of the book in declaratory phrases. 'The world is twofold for man in accordance with his twofold attitude' (*I&T*, p. 53). But this 'twofold attitude', we immediately learn, is not an 'attitude' in the sense of a psychological orientation, but is crystallized 'in accordance with the two basic words [man] can speak'. However, we must not think of these 'words' as simple 'words' but as 'word pairs', the word pairs 'I–You' and 'I–It'.[7]

Next, Buber establishes that although 'I' recurs in each word pair, it is in each case a distinct 'I', and is ontologically determined by the word it speaks. In speaking the basic word I–You, the 'I' commits its whole being or essence, but in speaking the basic word I–It is only ever able to give itself partially. To say I–You is to stand in relation; to say I–It is to 'have something for [one's] object' (*I&T*, p. 55) or to comport oneself towards the world in the mode of experience – and here, Buber insists, inner or mystical experiences are no less manifestations of the spirit of I–It than are other kinds of experience.

It can easily be seen, with a glance back towards *Daniel*, that I–You articulates the principle of holy insecurity, for the 'I' that is involved here is one that exists only in relation, that does not own or possess itself apart from what it is in relation to the other, with the consequence that it is always put at risk, always exposed to the new, always open-ended and incomplete. In the mode of experience, on the other hand, the 'I' always exists with a certain detachment in the face of the 'experiences' it 'has'. It is never fundamentally challenged or brought into question by experience. There is no real *relation* to the world in experience or, to put it differently, the relation assumed by experience is never such as to require us to qualify either term of that relation.[8]

Buber's basically dichotomous division is importantly qualified by a threefold distinction of the spheres in which, as he puts it, 'the world of relation [that is, the world of I–You] arises' (*I&T*, p. 56). These are the spheres of nature, humanity and God. In contradistinction to Kierkegaard and some of the other anxious angels, Buber's vision of the world is never exclusively anthropocentric. In Part I of *I and Thou* he brilliantly describes how a relation can arise in the encounter between the self and a tree, and later he speaks of an encounter occurring as he looks into the eyes of a cat. But whether with regard to plants, animals, other human beings or God, the same duality of I–You and I–It recurs. The movement of I–It reduces the world to the object of experience, whether it be experience in the mode of ecstasy or scientific observation (as when the 'object' becomes the individual example of a general law or species):

> But it can also happen, if will and grace are joined, that as I contemplate the tree I am drawn into a relation, and the tree ceases to be an It. The power of exclusiveness has seized me ... [And] when I confront a human being as my You ... then he is no thing among things nor does he consist of things. He is no longer He or She, limited by other hes and shes, a dot in the world grid of space and time ... neighbourless and seamless, he is You and fills the firmament. (*I&T*, pp. 98–9)

The conjunction of grace and will alluded to in this quotation is of the essence of the matter for Buber. An I–You mode of being in the world is not something one can train oneself for or discipline oneself in. It is not something that can be learned and there is no technique for acquiring it. Therefore it must be by grace. But not by 'grace alone'. The 'I' is not passive, and although there is a necessarily passive dimension in being open to grace, 'I' must speak the word and by my act, an act engaging my whole being, enter into the relation made possible by grace. Only so can I–You be spoken of as an 'encounter'. It is already a sign of the advent of I–It when either the subject or object is prioritized within the relation, for 'Relation is reciprocity' (*I&T*, p. 67) and 'In the beginning is the relation' (*I&T*, p. 69). What matters is 'the between'.

Buber none the less recognizes that I–It represents a dimension of life that cannot simply be denied. We cannot live in the fullness of I–You without respite. Even love must return to the It world and endure periods of latency. The It world is not to be renounced, but is to be seen as the chrysalis from which the You ever again emerges. What is troubling is that both in individual and in collective life, history demonstrates a seemingly ineluctable increase in the dominion of the It-world. The increase of knowledge, the institutionalization of religious and political movements, the development of the economy and of the state – all these reveal the hegemony of the principle of causality as it holds sway in the It-world. None of this is simply to be rejected, but nor can it ever be regarded as adequate. Indeed, Buber believes that the social and political crisis of the time reveals what happens when the It-world is removed from the direction that only the world of the personal, of I–You, can bestow:

> the state is no longer led: the stokers still pile up coal, but the leaders merely *seem* to rule the racing engines … They tell you that they have adjusted the apparatus to modern conditions; but you notice that henceforth they can only adjust themselves to the apparatus … (*I&T*, p. 97)

In an especially dark paragraph Buber declares that

> in sick ages it happens that the It-world, no longer irrigated and fertilized by the living currents of the You-world, severed and stagnant, becomes a gigantic swamp phantom and overpowers man. As he accommodates himself to a world of objects that no longer achieve any presence for him, he succumbs to it. The common causality grows into an oppressive and crushing doom. (*I&T*, pp. 102–3)

Buber is not calling us to renounce such a world. He is recalling us to the realization that every culture is based upon or is inspired by an original encounter. When, however, that encounter relapses into the mode of I–It both 'I' and 'It' become detached. In this situation the 'It' itself can grow into a terrifying and oppressive 'dehumanizing' power. But the 'I' is also distorted. Compare the I-saying of Socrates, or Jesus or Goethe, says Buber, with that of Napoleon, 'this master of the age evidently did not know the dimension of the You... He was the demonic You for the millions and did not respond; to "You" he responded by saying: It ...' (*I&T*, p. 117). In the domain of I–It, the 'I' no less than the 'It' can become the source of oppression.

Buber concludes the Second Part of *I and Thou* with the parable of 'One and All'. He pictures a man 'overcome by the horror of the alienation between I and world ...' (*I&T*, p. 120). Such a man may find security in constructing a grandiose vision of the origin of life, the history of the world and of himself as a part of this. Or he may turn instead to the world of inner feelings or vital experiences. He may intellectualize, or opt for 'life'. But in each case he overcomes his anxiety by a world-view that subverts the proper distinction between self and world. In the one case he makes himself into a mere part of the world, in the other, he internalizes the world into a mere aspect of himself. In each case he incapacitates in advance the possibility of genuine relation, of reciprocity, of I–You, since this depends on keeping both polarities apart – but, precisely, in relation, not collapsing either one into the other.

When Buber turns to the working out of the meaning of I–You in relation to God he does so in the conviction that the word God is itself indispensable, no matter how abused and misused in the course of history, but he is no less convinced that 'God' cannot (or should not) be conceived of as an entity existing somehow apart from the world. 'God' is thus not the object of a certain kind of I–You relation (as if the I–You relation was something that could be applied indifferently to trees, cats, society or God), but, in Buber's own words, 'Extended, the lines of relationships intersect in the eternal You. Every single You is a glimpse of that. Through every single You the basic word addresses the eternal You' (*I&T*, p. 123). The paradox of religion is that, although God is to be addressed and addresses us in each and every singular, unique contingent situation that we genuinely encounter, He is none the less not reducible to an inner-worldly happening or psychological mood. Buber does not try to hide this paradox. 'In the relation to God, unconditional exclusiveness and unconditional inclusiveness are one,' he writes; and 'One does not find God if one remains in the world; one does not find God if one leaves the world'; and again, 'Of course, God is "the wholly other"; but he is also the wholly same: the wholly present... the mystery of the obvious that is closer to me than my own I' (all quotes *I&T*, p. 127).

It is perhaps in attempting to describe this paradox that Buber rises to his most impassioned and poetic moments, whilst never losing sight of the intellectual finesse required to stay on the knife-edge between mere immanence and a kind of transcendence that denies the reality or significance of inner-worldly experience. Neither identity nor duality will do – but nor will any integration or synthesis constructed on the basis of reason or with the other tools of I–It. What matters is not arriving at a formula, but communicating a lived event, a spoken word, that is realized in the life of the individual, that is not given to us as a 'content' to be explained, interpreted or acted upon but as 'a presence as strength' (*I&T*, p. 158). In the face of the difficulty of this task Buber is clearly tempted by the silence of the Buddha, but he is able to resist this temptation by identifying the fundamental difference in goals between Buddhism and his own relational thought. Acknowledging that the Buddha can indeed teach the unification of the self and shows by the depths of his silence that he knows 'the You-saying to the primal ground' (*I&T*, p. 140), Buber finds in this silence a clue as to the Buddha's refusal to take seriously the world in its complex and concrete actuality. The Buddha's personal capacity for You-saying is falsified by a teaching that, in annulling the world, also annuls the very condition for articulating I–You in its fullest meaning. Once again Buber insists, 'I know nothing of a "world" and of "worldly life" that separate us from God' (*I&T*, p. 143).

As relational reciprocity our God-relationship is properly manifested in a movement of constant flow: God needs and seeks us, just as we seek Him, and if in sacrifice we relate ourselves to God, so, in revelation, God relates himself to us. But the movement between the polarities is not merely circular. As it develops there is real history and real novelty – and the real and repeated experience of failure. For 'the path is not a circle. It is the way' (*I&T*, p. 168).[9]

II

We have already noted that in his way towards *I and Thou*, Buber was significantly affected by his reading of Kierkegaard. At first this may seem strange: what can the prophet of encounter have found in the apostle of the individual? This is a question that Buber himself addressed in his 1936 essay 'The Question to the Single One', an essay which serves to sharpen our sense of Buber's intentions in *I and Thou* and also his relation to the wider existentialist tradition.

Much of Buber's Kierkegaard-reception is surprisingly affirmative. Kierkegaard's individualism is, for example, said to be more than just a religious version of the philosophical individualism represented by a thinker like Max Stirner. In such individualism there can be no responsibility and no truth. Both responsibility and truth are, Buber asserts, inseparable from openness to the reality of the other, and he adds that Kierkegaard went beyond Stirner's critique of 'the truth which is only noetic' (*BMM*, p. 69) by expressing a sense of truth as infinite subjective passion, inspiring a sense of absolute responsibility. Moreover, unlike Stirner's individual who 'owns' his own essence as a kind of metaphysical possession, the Kierkegaardian self is a self that each *must become*. It is not a datum but a duty, not a given but a task. Kierkegaard's way is, Buber acknowledges, 'a way' – 'And yet it is not the way' (*BMM*, p. 71).

What is lacking in Kierkegaard? The question is focused for Buber by the best-known of all of Kierkegaard's actions: the decision to renounce Regine out of a sense of religious obligation. For Buber this signals a false dichotomizing of the relationship between God and world.

> God is not an object beside objects and hence cannot be reached by renunciation of objects. God, indeed, is not the cosmos, but far less is he Being *minus* cosmos. he is not to be found by subtraction and not to be loved by reduction. (*BMM*, p. 80)

In a similar vein Kierkegaard's critique of politics is marred by a confusion between the debased form of the body politic that he correctly denounces under the figure of 'the crowd' and the real possibilities inherent in our common life. Buber accepts that in an age of dissolution, 'the Single One' must have the courage to step out from the crowd, not in order to be alone with God nor even (as Kierkegaard claims with regard to his own authorship) to detach other individuals from the herd-life of the crowd: it is instead 'to bring out from the crowd and set on the way of creation which leads to the Kingdom' (*BMM*, p. 88). Such a 'Single One' would not have

> to do with God essentially, and only inessentially with others ... [or be] unconditionally concerned with God and conditionally with the body politic. The Single One is the man for whom the reality of relation with God as an exclusive relation includes and encompasses the possibility of relation with all otherness ... (*BMM*, p. 88)

Such a Single One

> must face the hour which approaches him, the biographical and historical hour, just as it is, in its whole world content and apparently senseless contradiction, without weakening the impact of otherness in it. He must hear the message, stark and untransfigured, which is delivered to him out of this hour, presented by this situation as it arrives ... he must recognize that the question put to him, with which the speech of the situation is fraught – whether it sounds with angels' or with devils' tongues – remains God's question to him ... And he, the Single One, must answer, by what he does and does not do, he must accept and answer for the hour, the hour of the world, all of the world, as that which is given to him, entrusted to him. Reduction is forbidden ... (*BMM*, p. 89)

Buber seems prepared to recognize Kierkegaard as such a One, but Kierkegaard's message none the less falls short of taking fully seriously the responsibility that accrues to us from our situation in a social world for which, along with ourselves, we also have responsibility towards God.[10]

Buber also enters into dialogue with other contemporary philosophers of existence, especially Heidegger, in order to clarify further his own understanding of the religious situation. In his 1938 article *What is Man?* Buber turned to Heidegger's attempt to construct an existentialist ontology in *Being and Time*. Of Heidegger's relation to Kierkegaard Buber wrote that he had 'broken off its decisive presupposition, without which Kierkegaard's thoughts, especially those on the connexion between truth and existence, change their colour and meaning... [and] have been almost converted into their opposite' (*BMM*, p. 197). So, in discussing Heidegger's concept of guilt, and his interpretation of guilt as an ontological category to which we are awakened by the call of conscience, Buber picks up on Heidegger's remark that what we hear in the voice of conscience is nothing other than 'existence' itself. Now Buber accepts the case for tracing the structures of everyday experience back to their primal forms, in this case a primal guilt, but he finds Heidegger's discussion of conscience incoherent. Talk of conscience only makes sense if I accept into my understanding of life the presence of others before whom or in relation to whom I become guilty.

> Life is not lived by my playing the enigmatic game on a board by myself, but by my being placed in the presence of a being with whom I have agreed on no rules for the game and with whom no rules can be agreed on... Original guilt consists in remaining with oneself. If a form and appearance of present being move past me, and I was not really there, then out of the distance, out of its disappearance, comes a ... cry, as soft and secret as though it came from myself: 'Where were you?' *That* is the cry of conscience. It is not my existence which calls to me, but the being which is not I. (*BMM*, p. 203)

If Kierkegaard's Single One does not take seriously the claim of the human or social other upon him, he none the less acknowledges that with regard to God he exists in a defining relationship from which he can never escape and that bestows essential meaning on his life.

> Kierkegaard's Single One is an open system, even if open solely to God. Heidegger knows no such relation; and since he does not know any other essential relation his 'to become a self' means something quite different from Kierkegaard's 'to become a Single One.' Kierkegaard's man becomes a Single One *for* something, namely for the entry into a relation with the absolute; Heidegger's man does not become a self for something, since he cannot breach his barriers... this self itself to which he becomes opened is by nature closedness and reserve. (*BMM*, p. 209)

It is well known that in Heidegger's later thought there seems to be a turning – *away* from a purely 'existentialist' account of the human subject and *towards* an epiphany of the holy in new forms. Heidegger thus moves beyond a despairing acceptance of the death of God as the precondition of the human subject itself becoming the sole creator of values (as in Sartre) and interprets the present as the time between the gods who have fled and the God who is to come. Heidegger states that we cannot conjure such an advent or epiphany and here Buber agrees.

In all tongues since men first found names for the eternally nameless, those who have been named by this word [God] have been transcendent beings. They have been beings who by their nature were not given to us as knowable objects, yet beings whom we none the less became aware of as entering into relation with us. They stepped into relation with us, form-changing, form-preserving, formless, and allowed us to enter into relation with them. Being turned toward us, descended to us, showed itself to us, spoke to us in the immanence. The Coming One came of his own will out of the mystery of his withdrawnness; we did not cause him to come. That has always distinguished religion from magic ...[11]

However, whilst Heidegger seems to acknowledge the necessity of grace and – in his interpretation of Hölderlin – what Buber regards as implied in any doctrine of grace, that the gods need mortals no less than mortals need gods, there is an emphasis on passivity in Heidegger that Buber cannot accept.

In no sphere or time in the history of the relations between the divine and the human, however, has that proved true which Heidegger further asserts, namely, that 'neither men nor the gods can ever of themselves bring about the direct relation to the holy.' Always, again and again, men are accosted by One who of Himself disconcerts and enraptures them, and although over-come, the worshipper prays of himself to Him. God does not let Himself be conjured, but He also will not compel ... It may not be, indeed, unimportant to God whether man gives himself or denies himself to Him. Through this giving or denying, man, the whole man with the decision of his whole being, may have an immeasurable part in the actual revelation or hiddenness of the divine.[12]

In failing to allow for the positive role that falls to human beings in the encounter with God, Heidegger subjects the human subject to the fate imposed by history. No less than the anguished subject of *Being and Time*, the one who awaits the advent of the Coming One in the later Heidegger is numb in the face of the demand to take responsibility for the meaning that his life is to acquire in the encounter with the ultimate Other.[13]

III

For a positive representation of what he regards as an exemplary living out of the values of relation in the full concretion of actual life, Buber famously turned to the Hasidic sources of modern Judaism, to the eighteenth-century founder of modern Hasidism, Israel Baal Shem Tov, and his successors. It is not to our purpose here to investigate how far Buber's depiction of the Hasidim is historically accurate, but simply to see what he saw in them and how this related to his understanding of the contemporary crisis of religion.

The Baal Shem's own birth and origins are obscure and there are no authenticated writings attributable to him. Many of the stories told about him and many of the stories ascribed to him contain supernatural elements that do not assist biographical reconstruction in any normal sense. This, however, is unimportant to Buber, for it is not the historical facts that matter but the meaning of the life and the message communicated in the legend: 'the soaring up of a genuine vision of unity and a passionate demand for wholeness'.[14]

This fundamental vision is shaped by ideas taken over from Kabbalistic doctrines of creation and redemption. One key idea is that of sparks of light from the primordial creation having fallen into the lower world and becoming trapped in the world. It is the specific task of human beings to release these sparks and raise them through the gradations of created being until they are returned to their origin. An extension of this teaching concerning the holy sparks is that the Shekinah, the radiant Glory of God Himself, is likewise exiled into the world.

If the doctrine is mystical, the practice that flows from it is essentially simple and direct. It is in our everyday duties and encounters that the work of liberating the divine light must take place. 'In the clothes that you wear, in the tools that you use, in the food that you eat, in the domestic animal that toils for you, in all are hidden sparks that are anxious for redemption, and if you have to do with the things and beings with carefulness, with good will, and faithfulness, you redeem them.'[15]

> The disciples frequently quote the Baal-Shem-Tov's interpretation of the wonderful Aggadic saying that tells of the patriarch Enoch that he was a cobbler, and with every stitch of his awl, as it sewed together the upper leather and the sole, he joined together God and His Shekina.[16]

As the Baal Shem interpreted the legend, Buber goes on, it taught us that whatever we do we do with our whole being, with our bodies as well as our 'spiritual' self and that, indeed, there is no place for talk of any purely 'spiritual' God-relationship. Further to this, the legend points to the need for intention, and to perform every work we undertake as directed towards the unification of God and His Shekina. Buber sums up:

> Only on the path of true intercourse with the things and beings does man attain to true life, but only on this path can he take an active part in the redemption of the world. The Baal-Shem-Tov … saw even in the power of imagination a kind of meeting for which there are special tasks; more than ever, existence in reality is recognizable as an unbroken chain of meetings, each of which demands the person for what can be fulfilled by him, just by him and just in this hour.[17]

The Hasidic life thereby becomes a sacramental life, for it is a life that finds the holy in things, people and situations in their actuality and uniqueness. In working to transform the world in the direction of redemption the Hasid understands his role as that of service. This, Buber, believes, distinguishes him from the gnostic. 'The gnostic', he says, 'cannot serve and does not want to be able to', for the gnostic knows no higher right than the right of the knowledge he seeks.[18] '*Devotio*', on the other hand, 'means the unreduced service, practised with the life of mortal hours, to the divine made present … to whom, in the language of the *vita humana* wholly turned toward Him in the everyday, one can say Thou (Du) …'[19]

Buber was well aware that the history of Hasidic Judaism contained many examples of human failure and folly, jealousy and
rivalry. Indeed, these were themes at the heart of his most ambi-
tious work on Hasidism, *For the Sake of Heaven*, a kind of novel in
which various Hasidic tales are woven loosely into a narrative that
turns on the complex relationship between the Seer of Lublin and
his disciple and subsequent rival, Jacob Yitzchak, known as 'the
Yehudi' ('the Jew') – a conflict that Buber likens to that of Saul and
David. Written during the Second World War and set in the time
of the Napoleonic Wars, the novel broaches themes of messianism,
redemption and the religious life in dark times. The two protago-
nists, the Seer and the Yehudi, represent two diverse paths. The
Seer, who identifies Napoleon with the Gog of biblical prophecy,
believes it possible to hasten the coming of the Messiah by an
appropriately fervent fulfilment of ritual law. In conversation with
one of the Seer's supporters, Rabbi Mendel, the Yehudi warns that
their attitude fans the flames of the approaching conflagration, and
that there can be no assurance that it is a fire of purification preceding the final triumph of God over the powers of darkness.
Supposing, he asks, '"that this fire is nothing but a fire of destruction? God can kindle such a fire … But we? What gives us the right
to wish the evil an increase of power … Who tells us whom we
serve thereby, the Redeemer or the adversary?"'[20] He reminds
Rabbi Mendel of how many Israelite souls might perish in such an
inferno, and when Mendel ripostes that it is too late to think of
individual souls the Yehudi replies, '"Never will a work of man
have a good issue if we do not think of the souls whom it is given
us to help, and of the life between soul and soul, and of our life
with them and of their lives with each other. We cannot help the
coming of redemption if life does not redeem life."'[21]

The Yehudi's way is clearly endorsed by Buber himself, although
not to the exclusion of other ways – at one point in the narrative the
Yehudi, who, despite the rivalry of their respective pupils, retains a
deep respect for the Seer and for the teaching of Lublin, insists that
the heart of this teaching is that 'each has his own way of serving'.
In a parable which he calls 'How I Apprenticed Myself to a
Peasant', he sums up his own way by telling how he came across a
peasant who needed help in lifting his overturned wagon. Despite
the fact that he is himself a powerful man, the task seems beyond
him. He tells the peasant he can't do it. The peasant doesn't accept
his refusal and tells him that he can but isn't willing. Struck by the

force of these words the Yehudi realizes that if they use some boards they will be able to gain leverage and shift the wagon, and so it happened. Afterwards the Yehudi asks the peasant why he thought he was unwilling to help and, after some prompting, the peasant replies that he thought the Yehudi had been sent down that road simply for the purpose of helping him and, indeed, that the wagon itself was upset *in order that the help would be given*. In the language of the Kabbalah, the Yehudi spells out the implications of his story: '"You may meet the *Shechinah* upon the very roads of the earth. And what do you do when this meeting takes place? Do you stretch out your hands? Do you help raise up the *Shechinah* from the very dust of the road?"'[22]

Buber acknowledged an affinity between the Yehudi and Jesus of Nazareth. However, he rejected the charge that he had deliberately 'Christianized' his sources. On the contrary he believed that Jesus is in fact perfectly comprehensible within the parameters of Hasidic Judaism. The decisive break between Judaism and Christianity is not so much to be found in the figure of Jesus but in the Pauline and other Hellenistic communities of the early Church. The key distinction that Buber makes here is the distinction between faith as trust and faith as 'believing that', or, as he puts it using the Hebrew and Greek terms respectively, *Emunah* and *pistis*. The latter he regards as essentially alien to the faith of the Bible. Even when Jesus is portrayed as polemicizing against the Law, Buber understands this as largely akin to a fundamentally Jewish 'struggle against a withering or hardening, which knew of no other fulfilment than the carrying out of rules ...'[23] For Jesus, as for other radical movements within Judaism, 'fulfilment of the Torah means to extend the hearing of the Word to the whole dimension of human existence.'[24] Even if Jesus heightens the divine requirement to the point where we are called upon not merely to fulfil the commandments to the maximum of our ability but to strive to become perfect *as God is perfect* (an injunction that Buber regards as going beyond Pharisaic Judaism), his position is still essentially different from that of Paul who not only regarded the Torah as being unfulfillable but claimed that it was given in order to demonstrate the sinfulness of the human situation and so prepare the way for grace. However, even within a Christian tradition governed by the Pauline conception of faith, a conception that Buber regards as particularly dominant in the theology of his own age (Barth, for example), the other kind of faith can still make itself heard from time to time. 'Even

Kierkegaard, a century ago,' Buber writes, 'gave expression to the fact that there is a non-Pauline outlook...', and he goes on to cite as an example a prayer from Kierkegaard's journal that refers to 'the inwardness of speaking with one another'. This prayer, Buber says, 'is not from Paul or from John, but from Jesus'.[25]

IV

During the 1920s Buber had an especially fruitful collaboration with another Jewish scholar often counted as an existentialist writer, Franz Rosenzweig. Rosenzweig had effectively 're-converted' to Judaism when, having resolved to convert to Christianity, he attended the synagogue for the Day of Atonement services – as he thought for the last time. However, his experiences reawakened his own Judaism, and, with Buber, he became one of the leading thinkers of German-speaking Judaism until his premature death in 1929. The most significant product of their partnership was a new translation of the Hebrew scriptures into German, a translation that sought to express the resonance of the Hebrew text more immediately than the familiar translation by Luther. This translation not only represented an important aspect of their shared attempt to renew Jewish culture amongst Central European Jews, it also reflected their common interest in language and their commitment to working out a *Sprachphilosophie*, that is, a philosophy of speech, in which the living, spoken word is given its proper weight. We recall that the fundamental dichotomy between I–You and I–It is not in the first instance described as a dichotomy in Being, but as a dichotomy between the two basic words in which being is articulated. Rosenzweig's own masterpiece, *The Star of Redemption*, is also crucially concerned with the homology between linguistic and ontological structures. It was, as he put it, an exercise in 'grammatical thinking'. As well as working with Rosenzweig on their Bible translation, Buber was also involved in the adult educational work amongst the Jewish community in Frankfurt for which his friend gave up the chance of a university lectureship in Berlin.

Unlike Buber, but like a number of other existentialist thinkers, Rosenzweig had an early engagement with Hegel, writing a dissertation on *Hegel and the State*. After his re-conversion, however, he came increasingly to see that both Christianity and Judaism had come to obscure the need for revelation, offering instead a secularized faith that was in essence atheistic. In Christianity the transcendent God had been replaced by the human Jesus of history and in Judaism by the history of the community. However, he did not regard revelation as simply negating the human. As did Buber, Rosenzweig insisted on the irreducibility of the human pole of the God-relationship and on the priority of the living situation in which revelation is received. It is in this spirit that he contrasted Barthian revelationism with Kierkegaard's more existentially concerned account of the paradox of faith:

> behind each paradox of Kierkegaard one senses biographical *absurda*, and for this reason one must *credere*. While behind Barth's colossal negations one senses nothing but the wall on which they are painted, a whitewash wall, his immaculate and well-ordered life ... it is, after all, an indifferent authenticity.[26]

It is not hard to see from these comments that Rosenzweig's renunciation of the Berlin post was very much in keeping with an underlying suspicion of academic thinking.

The Star of Redemption was written during the closing months of the First World War, when Rosenzweig was serving in the German army. The early pages, originally penned on army postcards, bear the marks of this dramatic situation. The first paragraph is headed 'Concerning (or: From) Death' and opens with the declaration that 'All cognition of the All originates in death, in the fear of death' and continues by charging philosophy with the vain attempt to rob death of its sting by teaching the immortality of the soul at the expense of the mortal body. But what if this misses the true point of our fear of death?

> Let man creep like a worm into the folds of the naked earth before the fast-approaching volleys of a blind death from which there is no appeal; let him sense there, forcibly, inexorably, what he otherwise never senses: that his I would be but an It if it died; let him therefore cry his very I out with every cry that is still in his throat against Him from whom there is no appeal, from whom such unthinkable annihilation threatens – for all this dire necessity philosophy has only its vacuous smile. (*Star*, p. 3)

Where philosophy seeks to point to a 'beyond' as the 'answer' to this predicament, Rosenzweig seeks a response that is true to our earthly reality and experience. 'For', as he puts it, 'man does not really want to escape any kind of fetters; he wants to remain, he wants to – live' (*Star*, p. 3). And, famously, this book that opens with the words 'From Death' concludes, not unintentionally, with the words 'INTO LIFE'.

But if Rosenzweig's programme seems simple, *The Star* is itself a highly complex book, in which a philosophical debate with the principles of German idealism, a re-interpretation of Kabbalistic teaching and a redefining of the terms of Jewish–Christian dialogue are worked through with an extraordinary level of existential passion. Rosenzweig was himself well aware of how daunting his book might prove and wrote a shorter companion to accompany it, which he circulated on carbon copies to friends. Let us then approach *The Star* through this smaller work, called in its English translation *Understanding the Sick and the Healthy. A View of World, Man and God.*

Following two prefaces, one addressed to 'the Expert' and beginning 'Dear Sir' and one addressed 'to the Reader' and beginning 'My very dear friend', the first chapter looks at what Rosenzweig calls the paralysis induced by philosophy. Noting the Aristotelian dictum that philosophy begins with wonder, Rosenzweig asserts that wonder is naturally found in life, in the interrelationships between parents and children and men and women. Philosophical wonder is not essentially different from such natural wonder, but the philosopher 'is unwilling to accept the process of life and the passing of the numbness wonder has brought … He separates his experience of wonder from the continuous stream of life, isolating it' (*USH*, p. 28). It is not natural to ask of anything what it 'actually' or 'essentially' is – but this is precisely what philosophers ask (although even philosophers, he wryly comments, do not ask such questions when buying butter or falling in love). In contrast to the philosophical approach 'The terms of life are not "essential" but "real"; they concern not "essence" but "fact"' (*USH*, p. 30). Now (in fact!) there are relatively few philosophers, but Rosenzweig warns us that no one can safely regard themselves as entirely immune from 'this disease', a disease that reduces its victim to a 'state of utter paralysis'.

Rosenzweig goes on to mock the recommendations of the first 'doctor' to be consulted, recommendations that amount to 'a synthesis of simplified Kant and stultified Nietzsche'. These are to the effect that the patient should simply pretend. 'You wish to buy a pound of butter and discover that you have forgotten your purse – a simple matter: act as if you were paying. You'll see; the cashier will be completely satisfied. You want to marry? Just pretend you are married. It's a good deal cheaper and comes to the same thing' (*USH*, p. 32). Such advice cannot really help, however. Instead of delivering the patient from his cellar it locks him in.

In the face of philosophical paralysis there can be no universal medicine. Sometimes life itself intervenes, either in the form of 'a sudden fright, an unexpected happiness, a blow of fate beyond the ordinary' (*USH*, p. 43) or simply by the fact that it goes on, since 'one cannot exist entirely in the sublime realm of theory' (*USH*, p. 43). However, Rosenzweig does not want to be understood as suggesting the 'philistine' solution of regarding one's youthful idealism as something one grows out of. For we cannot find a lasting cure unless or until we confront the three basic realities amongst which the path of life winds its way. These are God, man and the world.

There follows an exchange of letters with the director of a sanatorium that stands at the exact geometrical centre of three mountain ranges, taken to represent these three primordial facts. The mountains are reached by a series of criss-crossing paths that, although different, share a similar pattern. In the early days of his stay the patient cannot expect a simultaneous view of all three peaks. That will come only as he becomes familiar with the paths and is able to find his way to the correct viewpoint.

The first week of the cure familiarizes the patient with the world as composed of concrete, actual entities. In response to the philosopher's question as to what the world *is* 'essentially', the answer given is: nothing. The world of essence and any God who is conceived of as the metaphysical essence of the world must be sheer nothingness. As there is therefore nothing at all to be discovered by seeking essences, the patient is counselled to turn his attention to the modest fact that 'the world is something rather than nothing, something – not I, not God, not everything' (*USH*, p. 58). Quite simply, 'There are other entities' (*USH*, p. 58). But we do not simply live in the world as subjects of experience. We live in a world that takes shape for us in and through language. This is not to be taken in the sense that the world is reducible to language, since 'Language is not the world ... It only names the things of the world ... To utter a word is to affix a seal as a witness of man's presence. The word is not part of the world; it is the seal of man' (*USH*, p. 59).

Language does not reveal the essence of the world but is a real historical process of transmission and translation in which not only a human presence but also the presence of God is stamped on the things of the world. Language does not reveal the essence of the world but in the way in which the paths of language criss-cross each other through time the world becomes the world in which God and humanity meet.

The second week of the cure sees the patient's attention directed from the world towards humanity. This is not, however, done in the spirit of the kind of cosmic egoism of some modern philosophies, to the proponents of which Rosenzweig says, 'you acted as though you headed a government of the world in exile instead of taking care of your house' (*USH*, p. 65). 'Your self', he adds, 'is of the world, a part of it – nothing more' (*USH*, p. 66). Because the self cannot be everything, though, this does not prevent it from seeking a life which is *something*, so long as the self is faithful to its situatedness, or, as Rosenzweig puts it, to 'the ancient flames burning on the stationary hearth stones' (*USH*, p. 67). Although the self has no real claim 'to the throne of the world', it is not reducible to the world any more than the world is reducible to the self.

Once more, language is taken as providing an important insight into human identity. The fact of the family name is a reminder that each of us belongs to the past, whereas the proper name is 'a declaration that this is to be a new human being; it lays claim to the present by confronting man with a future' (*USH*, p. 70).

What of the third mountain, the mountain on which the patient is to encounter God?

Rejecting interpretations of God that reduce him to nature or to mind, Rosenzweig also insists that, like humanity itself, God cannot be the 'everything' of which the world and humanity are mere aspects. Each of the three is a 'something' in its own right, not reducible to, but in relation to, each of the others. God cannot be treated as an essence to be understood but as a 'something' that cannot be defined. However, this lack of definition does not leave us speechless. Because God bears a name, a name that is not an essence or definition but a real, personal name, we are able to call upon Him in the urgency of the now, the 'today' in which God summons us, through our proper name, to action.

God, man, world: through familiarization with these three irreducible realities in their non-essential actuality, reason can be cured of its sickness. But where in life do we find them together? Where is the vantage point from which all three peaks can be seen simultaneously in their interconnection? It is, Rosenzweig says, in the holiday, the holy-day, the time of festival. The value of the holiday is not like the value of a spectacle or work of art that can be understood by contrast with life. In the holiday all the ingredients of life are present, but 'explicitly and as a whole' (*USH*, p. 84). The holiday 'knows no remote God, no isolated man, no fenced-in world. God, man and the world are for it in their constant motion; they are in transition, the three of them constantly joining and interweaving and separating' (*USH*, p. 85). Nor is the holiday itself isolated. It acquires continuity through the continuity of the whole festive years, with its cycle of festivals.[27]

We cannot, of course, spend the whole of our lives on holiday, we must, as Rosenzweig says, go back to work. Reason has been released from its paralysis, but we must also return from the experience of the eternal provided by the feast days to the reality of time in which death awaits us, a situation that no physician can prevent. We must direct our lives towards death, renouncing the futile attempt to evade it. For, in reality, Rosenzweig says, 'Health is on good terms with Death ... It knows that it will be accepted into the open arms of Death. Life's eloquent lips are put to silence and the eternally taciturn One will speak: "Do you finally recognize me? I am your brother"' (*USH*, p. 91).

Just as the book began with a double preface, one to 'the expert' and one to 'the reader', so it concludes with a double epilogue. The 'expert' is told that he will depart unrewarded. There is nothing here for expertise to get a handle on. The reader will, perhaps, be 'a little frightened'. But this is as it should be. The fear (and, dare we say, trembling) that such reflections induce reminds us that life is a serious matter and that our work, our actions and our sorrows are to be taken seriously.

The confrontation with death returns us to the beginning of *The Star*. Like *Understanding the Sick and the Healthy*, *The Star* has an essentially threefold structure, reflecting the irreducible interrelatedness of God, humanity and world. According to Rosenzweig this threefoldness is recapitulated in the threefold structure of metaphysics, metalogic and meta-ethics.

This might sound like a return to the philosophical reason that we have heard Rosenzweig describe as sick. This is not, however, the case. For metaphysics should not be understood here as involving any claims regarding what Rosenzweig calls 'cognition of the All'.

The fragile mortality of human beings makes such cognition impossible. The scope of our knowledge is ineluctably constrained by our contingency. After Kierkegaard's assault on Hegel's grand claims to knowledge of the All, philosophy decisively grasped the importance of contingency with Nietzsche. At this point 'Man in the utter singularity of his individuality ... stepped out of the world which knew itself as the conceivable world, out of the All of philosophy' (*Star*, p. 10).

The trilogy of metaphysics, metalogic and meta-ethics together constitute what Rosenzweig calls the protocosmos, the realm of primordial origins, a 'glowing tripod', as he later describes it, illuminating the 'way to the Faustian mothers' (*Star*, p. 257). This threefold structuring of the 'meta-' realm reminds us that there can be no single or simple 'first philosophy'. Since the aim of arriving at cognition of the All has been surrendered from the very beginning, the meaning and structure of the world cannot be reduced back to a single principle or essence. In their separation none of these elements can 'explain' the reality of experience and life: God is mere myth, the world an object of aesthetic admiration and man a lonely tragic figure. They can only be brought into unity within the actuality of a real world. The protocosmos must be transformed into the realm cosmos. The eternal silence of God must issue in the spoken Word of creation. The mystery, Rosenzweig says, must be transformed into the *miracle*, for it is under the figure of miracle that he sees the actual life of the cosmos, a life that is once again divided into a threefold schema: creation, revelation and redemption.[28]

Miracle here cannot, of course, mean the intrusion of a transcendent or 'wholly other' God into the regularities of an autonomous created order. Miracle means rather the revelation in and to human beings of their created splendour, seeing ourselves as God saw us in the beginning of creation, a miracle made supremely public in the miracle of love transcended in marriage: love transformed by ethical reciprocity. But if marriage reveals to us the miracle of our creaturely being, this is not the final fulfilment, for the reciprocity of love seeks a more universal expression: the Kingdom. The past of creation and the present of revelation find their meaning only in and through their relation to the future of redemption. Having begun in the protocosmos and journeyed through the manifest cosmos, Rosenzweig's vision turns towards the hyper-cosmos, the world beyond this world, the world that is to come.

Man born of woman we will see there wholly redeemed out of his every peculiarity and selfishness into the created image of God; the world, the world of flesh and blood and wood and stone, we will see wholly redeemed out of all materiality into pure soul; and God we will see redeemed from all the work of the six days' labor and from all loving distress about our miserable soul, as the Lord. (*Star*, p. 261)

As Rosenzweig now moves towards the third and last main division of his work, he introduces it by considering 'the possibility of entreating the Kingdom'. What is at stake in these reflections is precisely the role of humanity in the coming of the Kingdom and Rosenzweig, like Buber, insists that there is a genuine and irreplaceable role for human freedom in bringing the Kingdom about. We were created without our will and we were the recipients of election and revelation apart from our deserts, but the Kingdom cannot come without us. The core of this freedom is prayer – 'the possibility of entreating the Kingdom'.

Thus man must know that he is tempted from time to time for the sake of his freedom. he must learn to believe in his freedom. he must believe that his freedom, limited though it may be everywhere else, is limitless vis-à-vis God … Everything … is in God's hands except for one thing: the fear of God. (*Star*, p. 266)

Once again we find that the sphere of redemption, the hypercosmos or superworld, falls into three parts. There is the promise of eternal life, instantiated in the life of those whom Rosenzweig calls 'the eternal people', that is, the Jewish nation. But this promise must find its way through time and into history, something that Rosenzweig sees exemplified in Christian history, and finally both must be united in the eternal truth.

It is in this closing section that Rosenzweig expounds the vision implied in the title of his work, the Star of Redemption. As he sees it the eternal promise embodied in the election of the Jews is the fire burning at the heart of the star, the Christian Church, in its expansion out into the world represents the rays of the star, whilst both are united in the whole star, the figure of eternal truth. But where can we look to find this star?

In fact we need look no further than the face of our neighbour, for the star, as Rosenzweig sees it, is a perfect figure of the face. The first triangle of the star is formed by the midpoint of the centre of the forehead and the base corner points of the cheeks. This encompasses what he regards as the receptor organs, nose and ears. Over this is superimposed the second triangle of the star, whose three points are the eyes and mouth, the organs of self-expression.[29]

Throughout *The Star*, Rosenzweig's concern for language has shaped the course of his exposition. Thus the world of the proto-cosmos is also the world of the basic elements of language: metaphysics is rooted in the archetypal words of affirmation and negation, metalogic in the universality of the logos, and meta-ethics in the distinctiveness of predication. These elements remain unfulfilled in their isolation from one another, however. It is only with creation, in the reality of the cosmos, that they acquire the interconnectedness of grammar, of real language, which Rosenzweig calls 'mankind's morning gift from the Creator' (*Star*, p. 110). And he goes on to speak of language as 'the organon of revelation' and 'the thread running through everything human that steps into its miraculous splendor and into that of its ever renewed presentness of experience' (*Star*, p. 110). That thread is taken up too at the end, and only here transcended.

> The mouth is consummator and fulfiller of all expression of which the countenance is capable, both in speech as, at last, in the silence behind which speech retreats: in the kiss. It is in the eyes that the eternal countenance shines for man; it is the mouth by whose word man lives. But for our teacher Moses, who in his lifetime was privileged only to see the land of his desire, not to enter it, God sealed this completed life with a kiss of the mouth. Thus does God seal and so too does man. (*Star*, p. 423)

Rosenzweig's powerful use of the figure of the star has at its heart the image of the eternal fire blazing forth its rays of light, and fire is also a leitmotif in Buber's thought. It is striking that several of the Hasidic tales relating to the Baal Shem himself invoke fire imagery. In one story a guest is staying in the Baal Shem's house, when the Zaddik receives a message from heaven that his days of concealment are at an end, and the guest is awakened by a blazing light and at first thinks that the whole house is on fire; in another story a disciple of the Baal Shem prayed for a vision of a perfectly holy man and saw in response the Baal Shem completely transformed into fire; a circle of dancing Hasids is crowned by a ring of

blue flame; and at his death the spirit of the Baal Shem is seen rising to heaven like a blue flame. After his death his son has a vision
of his father in the form of a mountain of fire, from which innumer-
able blazing sparks showered out. He asks why his father has
appeared to him in this form. 'Because this is how I have served
God,' comes the reply. This vision clearly alludes to the cosmological myth of the divine sparks that Hasidism inherited from the
Kabbalah, but it is, fearfully, imagery that was to re-enter Jewish
history in yet another context, in the holocaust of the extermination
camps. In the face of bewildering complexity and frightful pathos
of such ambivalence, perhaps it is indeed the common testimony of
Buber's Hasidism and of Rosenzweig's *Star* that we can in truth
only be redeemed from fire by fire.[30]

NOTES

1.   However, it should be acknowledged that a number of Buber's Jewish
      critics have felt that he was too influenced by Christianity (and similar
      criticisms have been made of Rosenzweig). See Gillian Rose, *Judaism
      and Modernity* (Oxford: Basil Blackwell, 1993).
2.   Although we have, of course, already seen that the view of religious
      existentialism as being utterly individualistic is scarcely tenable in the
      light of the intense interest in social and political affairs of thinkers
      such as Tillich and Berdyaev. Buber's social concerns are particularly
      apparent in his writings about the social structures of the Jewish com-
      munity in Palestine, both before and after his own emigration. See
      especially M. Buber, *Paths in Utopia* (London: Routledge, 1949).
3.   Many have said that Buber's view of Hasidism is a tendentious and
      one-sided reading of the historical data, that says as much, perhaps,
      about what Buber wanted to see as what he found. His views were
      especially critiqued, albeit amicably, by Gershom Scholem in his own
      studies of Jewish mysticism. Here too the criticism resurfaces that
      Buber's ideal Judaism is far too Christianized, reflecting his immer-
      sion in the tradition of *Lebensphilosophie*. It is perhaps not coincidental
      that there are affinities between Buber's portrait of the Baal Shem as
      the ideal Zaddik and Dostoevsky's 'Life of Father Zossima', despite
      the great differences in cultural colouring.
4.   For the influence of the theatre on the development of the dialogical
      principle in Buber's thought, see also 'The Space Problem of the Stage',
      in M. Buber, *Pointing the Way* (New York: Harper and Row, 1957).
5.   This has sometimes been taken as implying that the young man con-
      cerned subsequently committed suicide. According to Friedman that
      is not the case: the meeting in fact occurred in 1914 and the unguessed
      questions concerned the issue of whether to enlist or not. The young

man's death was on the battlefront. In fact (like many on the left) Buber actively supported the war effort in 1914, seeing in it the entry of Austro-Hungary into the historical mainstream of European life with potentially liberative consequences for Central European Jewry. Like many others, his disillusion turned to opposition in the course of the war. See M. Friedman, *Martin Buber's Life and Work* (London: Search, 1982).

6. See M. Buber, *The Eclipse of God* (London: Gollancz, 1953), pp. 15–18.
7. As I am using Walter Kaufmann's 1970 translation, I shall follow, with some hesitation, his usage of 'I–You' for 'I–Thou'. Neither English expression is entirely satisfactory: 'I–Thou' reminds us that the relation conceived of is to a single and intimately known Other, but, outside a diminishing number of regions, 'Thou' has a literary flavour absent from the everyday German 'Du'. The 'You' here is, in other words, the form of address used naturally for friends, lovers and family: those significant others to whom we relate most easily and spontaneously. There is nothing pompous or 'stagey' about it.
8. It is somewhat ironic that one sometimes hears references to 'I-Thou experiences'.
9. On Buber's concept of dialogicality compared with that of Marcel, see E. Levinas, 'Martin Buber, Gabriel Marcel and Philosophy', in idem., *Outside the Subject* (London: Athlone, 1993).
10. On the relationship between Kierkegaard and both Buber and Rosenzweig, see S. H. Bergman, *Dialogical Philosophy from Kierkegaard to Buber* (Albany: State University of New York Press, 1991).
11. *The Eclipse of God*, p. 99.
12. Ibid., pp. 100–1.
13. For Buber's critique of Heidegger, see also J. Wahl, 'M. Buber and the Philosophies of Existence', in P. A. Schilpp and M. Friedman (eds.), *The Philosophy of Martin Buber* (La Salle, Ill.: Open Court, 1967), pp. 486ff.
14. M. Buber, *The Origin and Meaning of Hasidism* (New York: Harper, 1960), p. 172.
15. Ibid., p. 84.
16. Ibid., pp. 84–5.
17. Ibid., p. 86.
18. Ibid., p. 245.
19. Ibid., p. 244.
20. M. Buber, *For the Sake of Heaven* (New York: Meridian, 1958), p. 255.
21. Ibid., p. 256.
22. Ibid., p. 34.
23. M. Buber, *Two Kinds of Faith* (London: Routledge, 1951), p. 58.
24. Ibid.
25. Ibid., p. 167.
26. From a letter, quoted in Nahum Glatzer's 'Introduction' to *Understanding the Sick and the Healthy*, p. 21.
27. In this affirmation of the importance of the holy-day we are reminded of Rosenzweig's own re-conversion to Judaism on the occasion of attending the Yom Kippur services.

28. It may be noted that this transition is also described by Rosenzweig as the transition from the world-view of Antiquity to that of Judaeo-Christian history. The experience of the elements in their separation and tragic isolation from each other is precisely, as he sees it, the moment of need to which the Judaeo-Christian vision of the world as created, historical and destined for redemption is addressed.

29. This concluding emphasis on the face may be one source for the role of the face in the thought of another major modern Jewish writer, Emmanuel Levinas, who also has other important affinities with existentialism.

30. For a commentary on the fearful and paradoxical interweaving of fire imagery in modern Jewish history, from the fire the fire of Hasidic devotion and the fires of the concentration camps, see E. Wiesel, *Souls on Fire* and *Somewhere a Master* (Harmondsworth: Penguin, 1984). See also J. Derrida, *Of Spirit. Heidegger and the Question* (Chicago: Chicago University Press, 1989).

12

Ends and Origins

I

We have passed through the galleries of those anxious angels represented in this selection and it is time to stand back and consider the overall coherence of the exhibition and its relation to both contemporary intellectual life and the preceding tradition.

It cannot be claimed that the list of candidates for inclusion has been exhausted. As was noted in the Introduction, it would be virtually impossible to draw up a definitive list of religious existentialists, because we are not talking about a cohesive group with an agreed manifesto. There is therefore considerable scope for debating where the exact boundaries of religious existentialism should be drawn. Any conclusions reached in such a debate will, inevitably, reflect the fundamental stance towards existentialism taken by particular commentators. Those who regard it as a manifestation of decadence or as a half-way house *en route* to atheism will want to minimize any connections between their favoured thinkers and the religious existentialists. Others will, for opposite reasons, want to talk up the existential element in particular figures from the modern theological tradition.

The issue is further complicated by the fact that from the late 1920s until the early 1960s existentialism was, in more or less clearly articulated, more or less 'pure' forms, at the very epicentre of the conflicts of ideas, beliefs and values that constituted the history of European culture in that period. And not only European culture: analogous conflicts can be seen in Japan and North America, for example, although in each case shaped by the specific circumstances of time and place.

This was a period marked by constant social upheavals and a sequence of catastrophic events that included global economic collapse, world war, the Holocaust, the Atomic Bomb and the Cold War. In such times few thinkers were able to maintain a single line of thought throughout their lifetime, without subjecting it to revision, qualification and even wholesale replacement in the light of experience and of the conflicting pressures placed upon the intellectual conscience. As a result one repeatedly encounters thinkers whose careers are marked by some dramatic shift, or whose thought reflects within itself divergent and even opposing tendencies. Apart from those who were able to lock themselves into the intellectually closed systems of the Roman Catholic Church or the Communist Party, where the institution took it upon itself to answer for the conscience of the individual, and apart from those committed to an extreme form of scientific ideology that dismissed all questions of meaning and value as irrelevant, there were few who were not affected by spasms of radical self-questioning that could easily acquire an existentialist colouring. Even amongst Catholic and Communist intellectuals there were those whose intellectual doubts and questions smouldered beneath the dampening pressure of institutional orthodoxy, and who betrayed or even openly acknowledged existentialist traits.

Throughout this period, then, there were many thinkers whose centre of gravity lay outside the field of existentialism narrowly defined, but who were 'existential' in a broader and looser sense. This is no less true with regard to religious existentialism than it is in the case of secular or philosophical existentialism. Consider, for example, such influential figures as Dietrich Bonhoeffer and Simone Weil. Both have significant affinities with certain aspects of existentialism, and yet there are good reasons for regarding them as essentially non-existentialist.

Bonhoeffer's work, like that of many German theologians of his generation, reveals the influence of Kierkegaard at many points. The incognito of Christ in his incarnation, the requirement of suffering as a condition of discipleship and the need for the Church to renounce the panoply of establishment, embracing the world in its very worldliness – all such themes bring Bonhoeffer into the orbit of religious existentialism. perhaps even more telling is the story of his own trial of conscience, in which, like Kierkegaard's Abraham, he discovered that the 'universal' moral laws of obedience to the state and of non-violence had to be abrogated in the light of Christian duty. But there are also elements in Bonhoeffer that would make his inclusion in the ranks of religious existentialism questionable. An early work, *Act and Being*, illustrates the point well. Here Bonhoeffer seeks to synthesize his doctrine of the Church with a general ontology. His argument is that it is precisely in the Church, and only in the Church, that Being is decisively disclosed within the

relativity of historical time. Of course, a commitment to ontology is
not of itself conclusive as to a thinker's relation to existentialism.
As we have seen, both Tillich and Marcel regarded Being as the
ultimate focus of philosophical and theological enquiry. None the
less, in each case the question of Being is also problematized in relation to the dimensions of actual existence, and there is no *a priori*
privilege given to any particular ontic phenomenon or sphere, such
as the Church. Indeed, in their different ways both Tillich and
Marcel make it clear that the fundamental orientation of the self
towards Being challenges the epistemological and moral privilege
of the Church. On the one hand, there is no intuition, experience,
practice or institution that unambiguously expresses the truth of
Being in history and, on the other, there is no dimension of reality,
no matter how estranged or corrupted, that does not retain some
relation to Being. For neither of them would it be conceivable to
claim for the Church an exclusive relation to Being. Of course,
Bonhoeffer's view of the Church was radically transformed in the
course of his career and no one can safely guess as to where a post-
war Bonhoeffer would have been led. All the same, although there
are important distinctions between the Lutheran Bonhoeffer and
the Calvinist Barth (distinctions that, amongst other things, have
precisely to do with the role of the human subject in faith), we
can perhaps apply to Bonhoeffer the criticism that Tillich levelled
against Barth: that there is a core of dogmatic assurance that is
shielded from full exposure to the fires of critical reflection.

Of course, Christian traditionalists will retort that this is exactly
the problem with religious existentialists: that there is nothing they
are not willing to sacrifice to the critical spirit of modernity. (And the
existentialist will respond that it is only in the light of this 'nothing',
only when we have been stripped of all ontic self-assurance, that
we can even begin to talk appropriately about faith at all.)

In this disagreement, we can see a point of agreement that suggests one way of distinguishing the religious existentialist from one
kind of fellow-traveller. It does not, of course, give us a rule that we
can apply mechanically, since its application is in each case inseparable from the complex and risk-laden process of interpretation
through which alone we have access to the thinkers of the past. The
point is this: that one measure of a theologian's existential commitment is the measure with which they are prepared to surrender the
privileges and the reserve of theology in the face of the encounter
with modernity. This is not to say that religious existentialism is

straightforward modern*ism*. As has already been suggested, and as has been illustrated at many points in this study, the religious existentialists are frequently critical of modernity. The issue is not a matter of simple 'for' or 'against' but of the kind of critique of modernity that is to be made: whether it is a matter of appealing on behalf of some pre-modern form of thought or life, or whether it is by living out the destiny of modernity in such a way as to bring its inner questionableness to light.

Simone Weil is a very different case from that of Bonhoeffer. Weil's question was not so much how the Church should respond to the crises of modernity, but whether she herself, as a Jew, should accept baptism into the Church. As a spiritual 'type' she perhaps resembles no one so much as she does Kierkegaard. Both shared a telling fascination with the figure of Antigone, and, like Kierkegaard, Weil seems at times to cultivate suffering to an almost pathological degree.[1] Also like Kierkegaard, her religious writings have an intensity of focus on the singularity of the individual's religious situation that is rarely equalled. Thus, the issue of baptism is not so much a question concerning the objective truth of Christianity, but exclusively a matter of God's will for her.[2]

But if in her own person and in her spiritual writings Weil is considered as a candidate for existential sainthood, the existentialist spirit is reflected in only one aspect of her theoretical writings. She accepts the authority structure of the Catholic Church in its own terms, and although she rejects any sort of objective knowledge of God, there is none the less a kind of unqualified acceptance of the supernatural sphere and of a way of talking about the soul, that seems to be at several removes from the more typically existentialist emphasis on subjectivity. There is also a concern for discovering (or inventing) spiritual 'rules' or 'laws' that govern the sphere of the supernatural life of the soul that is profoundly non-existential. Thus, she speaks of 'affliction' as

> a marvel of divine technique. It is a simple and ingenious device which introduces into the soul of a finite creature the immensity of force, blind, brutal and cold. The infinite distance which separates God from the creature is entirely concentrated into one point to pierce the soul in its centre.[3]

The case of Simone Weil, then, highlights the point that the religious existentialists are not being regarded in terms of their 'existentialist personality', but in terms of the existential structure of their thought – although all of them would, of course, take to heart Kierkegaard's warning regarding philosophers who construct magnificent palaces in which they do not themselves live. There is no confidence in theorizing that cannot be reduplicated in life. It is precisely this orientation towards life that legitimates the kind of correlation between thought and life attempted at several points in this study. This is not reducing the history of ideas to biography, but acknowledging that the religious existentialists' commitment to self-reflection results in the actual circumstances of their lives being drawn into the structure of their thought in a manner that is rarely the case in the history of philosophy. However – and this is part of the point in considering the case of Simone Weil – we have been looking at the religious existentialists primarily as *thinkers* and not as exemplary personalities. Indeed, very little has been said about their 'personalities' at all.

These comments on Bonhoeffer and Weil are much too sketchy finally to decide the issue of their relation to religious existentialism. The point is, rather, to illustrate the lines along which we might proceed in arguing for or against the inclusion of any particular thinker in this large and loosely defined family.

Nor is it only in relation to other religious thinkers that the borders need careful, case-by-case definition. Although the gap between religious existentialism and the existentialism of Heidegger and Sartre is fairly easy to see, there are other examples where the situation is more blurred. Take, for example, Karl Jaspers. Unlike both Heidegger and Sartre, Jaspers promoted what he called a 'philosophical faith' in which the existential situation of the human subject was understood as being profoundly oriented towards Transcendence. Although Jaspers believed that what he called Transcendence was in an important sense the same as that which was intended by the symbols of the world's religions (or, as he called them 'ciphers of Transcendence'), he did not believe that any particular faith tradition had privileged access to it. Even the highest or purest images and ideas of God are ciphers, 'ever-inadequate, endlessly variable'.[4] That is why his faith is a 'philosophical' faith, because it is not committed to any one set of ciphers and, although we can never dispense with them entirely, our appropriation and use of the prevailing ciphers of any particular cultural epoch needs to be governed by the consciousness of their relativity. Clearly there is much here that recalls Bultmann's programme of demythologization, although Jaspers argued that Bultmann was still under the spell of the Judaeo-Christian image of God as a person who acts. In his own view, however, such an image is no more than one cipher amongst others.

It may be said (and especially in the light of the comments on Bonhoeffer's relation to the religious existentialists) that this is the direction in which the logic of religious existentialism inevitably leads us. None the less, if the religious existentialist typically enters more deeply than did Bonhoeffer into the modern experience of the relativity of all traditions, those we have grouped together here have still insisted on taking their place within specific religious traditions and communities and accepting the limitations of such specificity as the ineluctable basis for all compelling speech about God. Even when they have argued, often bitterly, against one or other aspect of their Church or community, they have not sought (as Jaspers seems to seek) the detachment of a position-above-all-positions.

In each case the borders dividing the religious existentialists from their fellow-travellers are porous and disputable. Yet, however endless the task of definition must inevitably prove, my contention is that such borders do exist and that, even if they themselves can rarely be fixed, the space they encompass is a very real and very substantial intellectual domain.

The prevalence of the existential mood in the middle years of the twentieth century means, as I have been saying, that there are many affinities between the anxious angels and their contemporaries. This is not only true with regard to other philosophers and theologians but also with regard to many writers and artists. We have indeed seen at a number of points how literary expression and philosophical reflection cannot always be easily separated in the work of the anxious angels themselves: Kierkegaard, Nietzsche, Unamuno and Marcel are each, in their various ways, *writers* as much as *thinkers*, and, of course, Dostoevsky is first and foremost a novelist, even if he is also regarded by interpreters such as Berdyaev as Russia's most outstanding metaphysical thinker. Mention has also been made of Bernanos and, indeed, there are any number of writers from the mid-century period who can be found in the proximity of the religious existentialist. W. H. Auden, for instance, would be one who, from the side of poetry, problematized the relationship between poetic practice and critical reflection precisely in order to articulate a highly existential understanding of Christianity, strongly influenced by Kierkegaard in its mature expression. T. S. Eliot, Vernon Watkins and R. S. Thomas would also be examples of poets whose work incorporates many of the themes discussed throughout this study. But this would be only a beginning. The literature – and for that matter the films, music and visual arts – of the high modernist era are steeped in issues that were of central concern to religious existentialists, as Tillich in particular was concerned to show.

Whilst it would be unhelpful to draw too hard and fast a line between the literary and the philosophical expressions of existentialism, however, and whilst we cannot ignore the varying functions of literature and philosophy in different cultural situations,[5] we should not rush to confound the proper distinctions between them. Novels portraying 'existential' characters, themes or motifs are one thing. The sort of experiments with literary form undertaken by Kierkegaard, Nietzsche or Unamuno are something subtly different. Here it is more a question of using literary form to extend the interpretation of questions and issues that prove resistant to the instruments of philosophical analysis and argument, and that cannot be resolved by the intervention of dogmatic authority. If the nature of existential questioning itself seems to lead to a certain 'novelization' or even 'poeticization' of philosophy and theology, this does not mean that the questions of truth or of ethical practice are lost sight of. Literary form is to serve, not to subvert critical reflection – but precisely because reason itself is being subjected to critique (since, as Shestov stated so clearly, reason is not what decides 'the truly important thing'), such reflection cannot limit itself to the traditional resources of philosophical enquiry. Literary form becomes one way of calling reason itself into question.

II

If the heyday of existentialism was reached in the decade after the end of the Second World War, the signs of its dissolution and final eclipse are discernible from the later 1950s onwards. It is, of course, an underlying assumption of this study that eclipse does not mean extinction. Not only have many of the existentialists' characteristic positions been absorbed into the ongoing stream of cultural and intellectual life, but (as the image of the 'retrospective view' is intended to suggest) there are still creative impulses and insights to be gained from revisiting the original sources themselves.

All the same, no amount of partisan enthusiasm can hide the fact that there was a decline and fall, and this too must be taken into account if we are to understand religious existentialism itself. Some of the reasons for this decline have to do with a reaction against what were taken to be existentialist doctrines. The rise of political and liberation theology (as, more recently, of feminist and green theology) are in part attempts to get away from what is widely perceived as existentialist navel-gazing. On the other hand, even these theologies owe something to the existentialist moment in theological history, since they presuppose an acceptance of the situatedness of theological questioning in the specifics of time, place, history and culture. Something similar might be said about the concern with methodology and hermeneutics that have preoccupied many theologians since the 1970s. Here too there is a reaction against and an attempt to move beyond what was seen as the excessive subjectivism of existentialism. On the other hand, the basic existentialist critique of one-sided objectivism seems to have become a basic premiss of contemporary theological method.

However, as well as such shifts of emphasis, the development of religious existentialism itself bears witness to its own undoing. We can see several symptoms of this process.

One is the thematization of existentialism itself as the object of polemical attack or apologetic appropriation. When such thematization occurred within a liberal and apologetic theological programme it was likely to see existentialist positions as being contemporary expressions of perennial Christian truths, and to seek to present them in such a way as to make them acceptable to the mainstream of the Church. An outstanding example of this was John A. T. Robinson's *Honest to God*, a work that sought to reconstruct the contemporary self-representation of Christianity on the basis of a reading of, primarily, Tillich, Bultmann and Bonhoeffer. However, there is a sense in which this pattern is already discernible in several of the earlier religious existentialists themselves. Tillich (especially) and Bultmann (sometimes) speak of existentialism almost as if it is in some sense a finished product, a well-defined set of ideas and methods available to all who choose it. Indeed, in Tillich's case, it sometimes appears as just one more phenomenon to be fitted into the grid of his method of correlation, alongside modern art, Marxism and psychoanalysis.[6]

Such an extrinsic appropriation of existentialism is, however, ambiguous. Although it gives theology a radical colouring, it is not immediately clear to what extent it allows the existentialist critique to shake the foundations of the theological edifice. As with Bonhoeffer, we sense in Robinson that there is a core of Christian truth or Christian tradition that is not thrown into the cauldron of existentialist doubt and despair. This is obviously a point that depends on a careful reading of the texts themselves and, as the comment about Tillich and Bultmann suggests, it is once again going to be extremely difficult to draw a clear-cut line of demarcation between those we might think of as 'authentic' existentialists and those who are simply appropriating their 'results' in an external way. Indeed, if we think back to Thurneysen's evocation of the experience of reading Dostoevsky as being like the encounter with a wild animal, we may be tempted to see the whole history of religious existentialism in the twentieth century as a progressive domestication of the nineteenth-century experience of Kierkegaard, Nietzsche and Dostoevsky. *Honest to God* would then be simply the penultimate stage in a development to which Robinson's own sources are already party. If this seems to belittle the stature of some of those figures we have considered here, this way of telling the tale is, I believe, much more plausible (as well as being more appreciative of the proper autonomy of religious thought) than the view that sees religious existentialism as no more than a reflection of Heideggerian or Sartrean existentialism in religious guise. But before we conclude that those who constitute the history of twentieth-century religious existentialism are mere epigones, it has to be emphasized, first, that in a process such as this it is never a matter of absolutes but of more or less, and, secondly, that even though all of those twentieth-century figures we have studied acknowledge a debt to their nineteenth-century predecessors, each of them also makes a characteristic and original contribution to the overall development of religious existentialism. They are never the mere middlemen, trading in others' original ideas. Perhaps the important point is this: that the seeds of religious existentialism's dissolution are latent in its very self-consciousness as a movement within the history of ideas, since this self-consciousness inevitably stands in tension with a commitment to the absolute seriousness of the present and individual moment of decision. Precisely as a 'movement' or a 'phenomenon' religious existentialism is always already losing the urgency of the truly *existentiell* passion and slipping into the objectivity of a *Weltanschauung* or world-view.

A further stage in this development occurs when the existentialist ontology is treated as a 'result' that can be used as the basis for theological reconstruction. One particularly striking example of this is in John Macquarrie's *Principles of Christian Theology*, where Heidegger's concept of Being is, with some qualifications, taken as a philosophical testimony to the possibility of Christian theological God-talk.[7] The implication is that Heidegger can serve modern theology as Aristotle served medieval scholasticism: as an independent philosophical corroboration of the meaningfulness of theological concepts and categories – even though such corroboration cannot predetermine the particular form that any particular doctrinal system will take. However, it is doubtful whether this procedure is justifiable in its own terms, precisely because of the differences between Heideggerian and Aristotelian approaches to the question of Being. Being in Heidegger is never disclosed unambiguously, and is never articulated in such a way as to escape a certain elusiveness. Being is always concealed, even in the moment of revelation. Being (or, as Heidegger prefers to say, the meaning of Being) is never something given, but is that towards which the thinker thinks. Indeed, Heidegger invites us to ponder whether we even know what it would mean to ask the question of Being. If this suggests a reserve that would seem to frustrate in advance any attempt at theological appropriation, even this reserve conceals an ontological ambition that goes beyond the ontical-*existentiell* self-limitation of radical religious existentialism, as we saw in discussing the relation of Heidegger to Bultmann and to Buber, as well as in Heidegger's own comments on Kierkegaard.

In its most characteristic moments, religious existentialism is profoundly indifferent to the project of ontology, and even when it allows itself to fall under the spell of the question of Being (as in Tillich and Marcel) it insists that that question must always return to the specific and unique circumstances of actual existential decision.

A second symptom of the disintegration of religious existentialism in the mid-1960s was the kind of secular Christianity, sometimes associated with Bonhoeffer, that reached its most radical expression in the so-called 'theology of the death of God'. Thomas Altizer and William Hamilton, the theologians most identified with this theology, make clear their affiliation to the line of Kierkegaard–Dostoevsky–Nietzsche. However, they are clear that the God of the Christian tradition (and not merely some more or less popular image of God) is no longer credible. It is not a question of reformulating God in terms of the 'Ground of Being' or of 'transcendence', but simply a matter of learning, with or without regrets, to do without Him.[8] A generation later something similar was undertaken in the early work of the radical English theologian Don Cupitt, who again reveals existentialist elements in his theological ancestry, although Wittgenstein and Darwin are amongst other significant early influences.[9] Although there are complex nuances and resonances amongst such death-of-God theologians, it must in general be said that they let slip the kind of paradoxical quixotic-tragic pathos that typifies religious existentialism. If faith is impossible – then it is, simply, impossible, and we must let it go.

It is not that the thought of the death of God was unknown to the religious existentialists. Even Kierkegaard could reckon with a philosophical world-view from which, despite the window-dressing of a residual theological vocabulary, all possibility of radical transcendence had been eliminated. It was none the less paradigmatic for them that in some form or other it was necessary to speak the language of transcendence – in a word: God. Not that we can find agreement amongst them as to any particular concept of God. There are those, like Kierkegaard, for whom God is still addressed as the Father to whom every detail of creation is of infinite concern, those like Tillich and Marcel for whom God is, in some sense or other, appropriately conceived in the language of ontology, and those like Unamuno whose God seems to be a suffering, emergent God. But in each case the imperative of transcendence is set up against the narrowing horizons of finitude, contingency and mortality, that seem to contain the self-denying universe of consistent modernism. Even if it is only as a gesture and not as an argument, the very existence of the religious existentialist is a wager on transcendence, and the site of religious existentialism is inconceivable except as the place where two worlds, however defined or imagined, meet.

Although primarily theological, this point has important implications for the critical stance of religious existentialism towards the culture of modernity. For it was precisely in this wager on transcendence that religious existentialism found a means of resisting absorption into the ideologies of secularism, scientific, Marxist or aesthetic. But what was staked was not merely the abstract assertion of the existence of God. For the wager was placed on behalf of the values of Christian personalism, and constituted an appeal against the belittling and even the vilification of the human person by reductionist anthropologies and by both totalitarian and conformist developments in modern mass society.

This insistence on transcendence may be judged in terms of the historical place of religious existentialism, if it is regarded as a kind of half-way house between traditional faith and whatever comes after the death of God (postmodernism perhaps?). However, as I have suggested, the thought of the death of God was not alien to our anxious angels. It is not that they failed to hear this rumour or hid their heads in the sand of tradition: it is simply that they came to a different understanding of what Tillich, in the abstract language of ontology, called 'the shock of non-being'. The death of God is not an historical fate that befalls us from outside, like some iron law of history. It is a human interpretation of the human condition and, as such, an event in relation to which we are by definition both free and responsible. If, then, the theology of the death of God seems to mark a definitive moment in the eclipse of religious existentialism, it has to be said that this should not be understood so much in terms of historical development but as a limit in relation to which we face a fundamental religious decision. Perhaps only religious existentialism both experiences that limit in its very heart of hearts *and yet* (*and maybe precisely because of this experience*) affirms, 'I believe!'

With these comments we are already broaching the question as to the continuing relevance of religious existentialism in what many regard as a postmodern culture. Before we come to this question, however, there is a further point to make with regard to the place of religious existentialism in the history of ideas.

III

Literally the place. For although I have several times touched on the periodization of religious existentialism, it is important to remember that time and place are interconnected in many and often unnoticed ways. Often existentialism is described as a phenomenon of 1940s Paris, whilst others would relocate it to 1920s Germany. However, the story we have followed suggests a much more complex picture in which the geopolitical as well as the historical dimensions are worth reflecting on. For it is clear that religious existentialism was not just the province of German-speaking theologians of the inter-war years, as if it were merely a reaction to the turbulent conditions of that time and place, or a theological response to the philosophies of existence of Heidegger and Jaspers.

Of course, Kierkegaard is usually mentioned as some kind of remote ancestor, a one-off prophet, born before his time. But in fact there is a considerable body of existential thinkers who reached intellectual maturity in the years prior to the First World War. Not only Kierkegaard, Dostoevsky and Nietzsche, but Unamuno, Shestov, Berdyaev and Buber all belonged to an older generation than Heidegger, Barth, Bultmann and Tillich, all of whom were born in the 1880s and whose defining intellectual crises coincided, more or less, with the war. But the fact that so many of our anxious angels reached their mature positions before the war is not the only striking thing about them. Taken as a group they also share the fact that they were situated at what might be called the margins of Europe: Scandinavia, Russia, Spain and Austro-Hungary (with Buber further marginalized by virtue of his Jewishness). Even Nietzsche did his best to invent a non-German identity for himself, taking pride in his supposedly Polish ancestry and celebrating what he regarded as a Mediterranean enthusiasm for life.

These observations might seem of merely anecdotal interest if they had no resonance within the works of the authors concerned, but in fact questions of national identity were of passionate concern to virtually all of them: Kierkegaard and Denmark, Dostoevsky and Berdyaev and Russia, Unamuno and Spain, Buber and Eastern European Jewry – in each case the connection is intrinsic to the shaping spirit of their work. The tension between the wild animals (Thurneysen) and those who want to domesticate them is therefore not just to be construed in terms of the Romantic and passionate nineteenth century being systematized by the twentieth century academy. It is also a matter of the relationship between the margins of Europe and those countries, chiefly France and Germany, that have come to establish themselves as the axis of modern Europe and the focus of its ongoing drive towards ever closer integration.

However, the interrelationship between religious existentialism and the question of European identity does not only concern the tensions between the nation states that make up modern Europe. It also, crucially, concerns the interplay between self and society within nations. For whereas the separation of Church and State is a fundamental datum of the American religious consciousness, such that the characterization of religious belief in individualistic terms is not generally perceived as problematic, the situation in Europe is quite different. From the time of the Constantinian settlement (and, indeed, from long before that), the European conception of religion has been shaped by the prevalence of public or state religion. Religious belief has not been a matter of my private spirituality but of the God to whom society as a whole owes allegiance. Consequently, the death or eclipse of God has a very particular set of intellectual and cultural resonances within the European situation. On the one hand, the whole question of faith acquires a tone of 'fear and trembling' and may take on a tragic aspect, as the subject struggles to formulate a faith that can be credible despite the disappearance of the traditional intellectual and social structures that gave religious belief an aura of objectivity. On the other hand, the experience and the expression of a faith that can exist only in the mode of subjectivity will quickly be challenged as to its impact on the fundamental cohesiveness of society as a whole. Even in the face of the crisis signalled by such terms as 'modernity' and 'postmodernism', the European individual cannot escape the demand of that same common culture and shared inheritance that is now experienced as fundamentally broken. In this context the religious crisis of the individual can rapidly lead to a rethinking of the fundamental contract between self and society and thereby contribute to the contemporary attempt to re-envisage the nature of community.

In the context of the present work these remarks can do no more than to indicate a dimension of the subject that has been almost entirely overlooked in the secondary literature and to suggest that the anxious angels collectively provide rich material for religious and philosophical reflection on the nature of European identity and thought.

IV

It cannot be denied that many contemporary commentators regard existentialism, religious or secular, as little more than a part of our intellectual past. Even if it is allowed a place in the process which has brought us to where we are now, it is of no more relevance than, say, the British Hegelians of the late nineteenth century. Indeed, precisely because of the connection between existentialism and modernity it would seem to be necessarily sidelined in our situation of postmodernity.

Postmodernity (or postmodernism) is, of course, a much debated and often confusing term. It is itself already acquiring something of a period flavour, evoking the intellectual and cultural climate of the 1980s and early 1990s, rather than that of the new millennium about to dawn. In any case it was rarely clear as to where exactly the line should be drawn between modernity and postmodernity. J.-F. Lyotard, a leading theorist of the postmodern condition, argued that postmodernity is in effect the accentuation and further development of a line of critical reflection already present within modernity. Similarly, the sociologist Anthony Giddens has signalled a preference for the term 'radical modernity' rather than postmodernity. This is the sort of debate that can, of course, be protracted *ad infinitum* and it would be to trivialize the issues involved to get bogged down in an argument over preferred usage. We are all at liberty to use what words we will, as long as we are prepared for critics to ask us what exactly we mean by them. However, these brief reflections suggest that it may be premature to drive too hard a wedge between modernity and postmodernity and, indeed, the very structure of the term '*post*modernity' suggests a specific affiliation rather than a blanket negation.

This is not to deny the originality or the significance of such characteristically postmodern thinkers as J. Derrida and M. Foucault, nor that there are important elements in the philosophy and culture of postmodernity that point away from existentialism. It is, for example, characteristic of postmodern theory to critique existential subjectivity no less rigorously than more objectivistic philosophies. In the postmodern perspective, the existentialist claim that the passion of the existing subject guarantees the meaning of what is asserted, constituting a kind of immediate presence that brings order to the chaotic relativities of communication, seems to contradict the nature of language itself. No more than reference to empirical objects can reference to the self call a halt to the shifting currents of linguistically encoded meaning.

This may be one point at which we can only register a fundamental difference that refuses all attempts at mediation. However, in order to be clear as to where the exact point of difference lies, it should be said that it is a misrepresentation of existentialism (in virtually all its representatives) to see it as standing for some kind of absolutization of the standpoint of the self. To be sure, the actualization of the self in subjective passion is repeatedly said to be a condition of the pursuit and expression of truth – no truth without passion – but this by no means involves any kind of ontologization of the self or its hypostatization as somehow independent of the flux of action and expression. On the contrary, the existentialists themselves (and certainly the religious existentialists) called any sort of metaphysical expansion of the subject into question. 'Subjectivity', as recommended by Kierkegaard, is not simply a substitute for 'objectivity'. Instead it points to a prioritizing of the 'how' over the 'what' of truth, something that problematizes various models of subjectivity no less than it challenges an empiricist approach to religious belief. The existentialists do not believe in the self as some kind of self-subsistent essence, but as a relation that exists only in and through the process of its self-appropriation and self-actualization in hisotry. Even when we encounter a high doctrine of personality, as in Berdyaev, personality is emphatically distinguished from all metaphysical or ontological principles of selfhood. Similarly we cannot separate Unamuno's passionate hunger for immortality from the kind of paradoxes of self, role and reality explored in his novels.

This last comment suggests a further dimension to the relationship between existentialism and postmodernity. Individually and collectively, the anxious angels are acutely aware of the problematics of communication. Nor is this meant in the idealistic sense of how a pure 'idea' can ever find transparent expression in the media of sensuous reality. The question is rather how meaning can be communicated between interdependent and free persons, who experience their common language as distorted and opaque, so that it sometimes seems, as Kierkegaard put it, that we speak only to conceal our minds. The communicative strategies of the anxious angels, strategies that include pseudonymity, dialogue, aphorism, paradox, novels, poetry, demythologization and the coining of neologisms, can all be seen as attempts to work against language within language and to awaken us from the illusion that we know what we mean. As they see it, meaning is never a mere deposit in language, something to be quarried out by the labour of interpretation. Meaning is no less at risk in every act of interpretation than it is in every act of expression.

All of this brings the religious existentialists into a certain proximity to some aspects of postmodern theories of language and communication. There is, for example, no doubt that the culture of postmodernity, with its distinctive emphases on questions of language, has generated a number of fresh (and some outstanding) approaches to Kierkegaard, which more or less bypass the existentialist aspects of his thought. Sometimes, indeed, he is hailed as a practitioner of deconstruction *avant la lettre*.

In so far as such claims and counter-claims are made in the spirit of partisan rivalry between 'modernists' and 'postmodernists', they are, of course, of no interest. In so far as they invite us to a more careful reading and a more precise mapping of the history of modern thought, however, they are invaluable. none the less, the desire to make religious existentialism topical by assimilating it to one or other current within postmodernity should not seduce us into letting go of what is distinctive in religious existentialism itself.

I have said that religious existentialism is not bound to a kind of metaphysical absolutizing of the self, nor is it committed to a naive view of language as an unambiguous and transparent medium of self-expression. Yet no matter how problematic the theorization of language and communication, the religious existentialists typically took the view that each of us undertakes a burden of commitment and responsibility by virtue of our involvement in the communicative process. Language means that we are answerable, each to other. The anxious angels therefore remind us, and required of themselves, that we put our signature to the work of reading, writing and speaking, staking our selves anew in the wager on transcendence that we make anew in every act of expression and interpretation.[10] It is in this connection striking that religious existentialism has important affinities with the dialogical philosophy of language, most obviously in the cases of Buber and Marcel. M. Bakhtin, however, is also close to religious existentialism, and it is significant that many of the ideas for which he is known were developed in his interpretation of Dostoevsky. Dialogical thought offers an approach that shares the postmodernist goal of avoiding closure, whilst securing language as a medium of ethical testimony.

V

I have been arguing that the advent of postmodernity does not justify denigrating the teaching of the anxious angels. It does not immediately follow that religious existentialism is some kind of perennial philosophy, an underground current as old as biblical faith itself, although claims like this have been made. Something like this seems to be argued by Tillich, and the point is summed up in the words of one commentator, Roger L. Shinn, who wrote that 'the existential posture is as old as human experience'.[11]

Those typically listed amongst the pre-existentialist existentialists include Augustine, Eckhart, Luther and Pascal. Sometimes Plato and the Hebrew prophets are also mentioned, whilst Shestov singles out Job as the archetypal representative of the existential protest. Such claims often exercise a certain imaginative spell, even if they involve sometimes wilful misreadings of ancient texts, as in Kierkegaard's portrayal of Abraham. Nor is it in itself incredible that religious existentialism, as part of the larger history of Jewish and Christian faith, should have significant analogies with other elements in those traditions. However, historians of ideas have become a lot more cautious in drawing too close parallels between events, persons and concepts from widely different cultural epochs and we have been made painfully aware of the absurdities that can arise when important differences are ignored.

At several points I have stressed the intimate connection between religious existentialism and the intellectual situation, typical of modernity, in which human personality seemed to be reduced to a mere spasm in an evolutionary process occurring over an unimaginably long time in an unimaginably vast space, and a social situation, no less typical of modernity, in which the doctrines and moral teaching promoted by the official organs of religion seemed increasingly impotent in the face of human needs and aspirations.

This is not to say that Paul, Augustine or Luther were unaware of important challenges to faith. However, the sheer scale of the loss of credibility suffered by religion in the early modern period, and the extent to which the generally accepted world-picture was transformed by the scientific revolution, seemed to undermine a general theistic orientation that earlier generations could plausibly appeal to as the common faith of humankind.

Nor was this merely an external crisis. Many of the most difficult questions are inseparable from the history of Western religion itself. The turn to the subject and the high value set on personal autonomy have their antecedents in the Christian cultivation of conscience and a highly personalized view of the God-relationship. Scientific progress was itself inspired at many points by a religious conviction as to the divine ordering of the universe, while the Christian claim that 'God is love' sharpened the issue of theodicy as never before. The undermining of biblical authority was in large part the result of the intense critical scrutiny of the Bible by Protestant theologians. It is not surprising therefore that Feuerbach could argue that the history of religion itself witnessed to the gradual replacement of a theological view of the world by a more humanistic vision.

The rise of a culture in which the non-existence, the absence or simply the irrelevance of God constituted a basic human assumption provided the specific context of religious existentialism. And it must be emphasized that this situation is not conceived as a crisis afflicting the Church from without. It is not simply a new form of the ancient struggle between Church and world. It is instead a crisis internal to the religious tradition itself.

The scientific revolution and a sense of internal crisis in the religious tradition divide the anxious angels from the world of Paul, Augustine and even Luther. This does not mean that there are no significant analogies to be drawn nor lines of development to be traced back through history. It is simply a warning not to underestimate the differences that colour virtually every theological statement issued from different sides of the divide separating ancient and modern. There is perhaps no major thinker earlier than Pascal who could be called existentialist in any meaningful sense, precisely because Pascal is amongst the first religious thinkers to have internalized the post-Renaissance scientific world-view.[12]

A similar caution must be recommended with regard to claims assimilating religious existentialism to mysticism. This is not only because of the general shift in world-view that separates us from the vision of someone like Meister Eckhart. It is also because experience, no less than reason, is problematized within religious existentialism under the impact of a radically historicized understanding of the human condition. Experience cannot be elevated above the process of decision, action and interpretation that provides the actual matrix of all determination of meaning. Even the mysticism of Jacob Boehme, whose influence, direct or indirect, on many of the religious existentialists has been noted at several points in this study, is divided from that of earlier mystical writers precisely by virtue of a dynamic conception of the relationship between God and the world. This is not to say that there is no value in reading Eckhart or *The Cloud of Unknowing* alongside the anxious angels. It is simply to emphasize that such reading will require us to set one text against the other – to complement and to correct, but not to conflate.[13]

The anxious angels, then: a phenomenon of modernity, from whom we can still learn and by whom we can still be provoked into rethinking the interrelated questions of God, faith and the value of the human person. Just because they asked such questions without imposing on them the deadening hand of theological closure, they can serve the contemporary development of an open and dialogical faith, that, qualified by uncertainty on every side, requires us to stake not only all that we have but all that we are.

NOTES

1. See, e.g., A. Loades, 'Simone Weil and Antigone: Innocence and Affliction', in Richard H. Bell (ed.), *Simone Weil's Philosophy of Culture. Readings Toward a Divine Humanity* (Cambridge: Cambridge University Press, 1993).
2. See S. Weil, 'Hesitations Concerning Baptism' in idem., *Waiting on God* (London: Routledge and Kegan Paul, 1951).
3. *Waiting on God*, p. 77.
4. K. Jaspers, *Philosophical Faith and Revelation* (London: Collins, 1967).
5. In Dostoevsky's Russia, for instance, as in later totalitarian situations, literature was often a vehicle for ideas that, elsewhere, would have been regarded as the province of philosophers.
6. This impression, though understandable, is, I believe, misplaced. Existentialism is not one partner-in-dialogue amongst others: it is the all-inclusive category to which Marxism, psychoanalysis and modern art are subordinate.
7. See J. Macquarrie, *Principles of Christian Theology* (London: SCM, 1966), especially Chapter 5, 'Being and God'.
8. See T. J. J. Altizer and W. Hamilton, *Radical Theology and the Death of God* (Harmondsworth: Penguin, 1968).
9. See, e.g., D. Cupitt, *Taking Leave of God* (London: SCM, 1980).
10. This does not imply that I accept the view that postmodernity, as represented by, for example, Derrida, is ethically *ir*responsible in its use of language. None the less, responsibility is differently accentuated in existentialism and in postmodernity.
11. Roger L. Shinn, *The Existentialist Posture* (New York, Association Press, 1970 [revised edition]), p. 29.
12. For a more detailed study of the continuities and discontinuities between the figures discussed here, see my *Agnosis: Theology in the Void* (Macmillan: Basingstoke, 1996).
13. It is my own view that religious existentialism does in fact need the corrective offered by a more exeprience-oriented approach to religion, although this in turn requires the discipline of existential critique not to sink into naivety. Important work has been done here by a number of recent Japanese philosophers. See *Agnosis* (1996), especially Chapters 3–5. It should, however, be noticed that some contemporary theological interpretations of mystical literature claim that it is a misunderstanding to think of mystical theology as an attempt to express or to describe an ineffable experience. See, for example, D. Turner, *The Darkness of God. Negativity in Christian Mysticism* (Cambridge: Cambridge University Press, 1995).

Selective Bibliography

As this bibliography is intended primarily to assist the student who wishes to make a closer study of the primary sources and of the important secondary literature, I have divided it according to the sequence of topics in the book. In each case the primary sources are listed first, followed by secondary reading in aphabetic order. I have prioritized English-language literature.

SCHELLING

F. W. J. Schelling, *Philosophische Untersuchungen über das Wesen der menschlichen Freiheit und die damit zusammenhängenden Gegenstände* (Frankfurt: a.M.: Suhrkamp, 1975). English translation: *Of Human Freedom* (Chicago: Chicago University Press, 1936).
——*The Ages of the World* (New York: Columbia University Press, 1942).
A. Bowie, *Schelling and Modern European Philosophy* (London: Routledge, 1993).
F. Engels, 'Schelling on Hegel', 'Schelling and Revelation' and 'Schelling, Philosopher in Christ', in Karl Marx and Frederick Engels, *Collected Works* (Moscow: Progress, 1975).
S. Kierkegaard, 'Notes on Schelling's Berlin Lectures', in *The Concept of Irony together with Notes on Schelling's Berlin Lectures* (Princeton: Princeton University Press, 1989).
P. Tillich, *Mysticism and Guilt-Consciousness* (Lewisburg, PA: Bucknell University Press, 1974).

FEUERBACH

L. Feuerbach, *The Essence of Christianity* (New York: Harper and Row, 1957).
——*Principles of the Philosophy of the Future* (Indianapolis: Hackett, 1986).

K. Barth, 'An Introductory Essay', in Feuerbach (1957).

Van A. Harvey, *Feuerbach and the Interpretation of Religion* (Cambridge: Cambridge University Press, 1995).

M. W. Wartofsky, *Feuerbach* (Cambridge: Cambridge University Press, 1977).

KIERKEGAARD

Princeton University Press are in the process of issuing the first complete English translation of Kierkegaard's published works under the editorship of Howard V. and Edna H. Hong. The following volumes are the most directly relevant to Kierkegaard *qua* existentialist:

S. Kierkegaard, *The Concept of Anxiety* (Princeton, NJ: Princeton University Press, 1980).

————*Concluding Unscientific Postscript* (Princeton, NJ: Princeton University Press, 1989).

————*Either/Or* (Princeton, NJ: Princeton University Press, 1987).

————*Fear and Trembling* and *Repetition* (Princeton, NJ: Princeton University Press, 1983).

————*Søren Kierkegaard's Journals and Papers*, trans. and ed. H. V. and E. H. Hong (Bloomington and London: Indiana University Press; Vol. 1, 1967; Vol. 2, 1970; Vols. 3 and 4, 1975; Vols. 5–7, 1978).

————*Kierkegaard's Attack upon 'Christendom'*, trans. W. Lowrie (Princeton, NJ: Princeton University Press, 1944).

————*Stages on Life's Way* (Princeton, NJ: Princeton University Press, 1988).

————*The Sickness Unto Death* (Princeton: Princeton University Press, 1980).

————*Two Ages: the Age of Revolution and the Present Age. A Literary Review* (Princeton: Princeton University Press, 1978).

J. Heywood Thomas, *Philosophy of Religion in Kierkegaard's Writings* (reprint of: *Subjectivity and Paradox*: Lampeter: Edwin Mellen Press, 1994).

M. Matustík and M. Westphal (eds.), *Kierkegaard in Post/Modernity* (Bloomington and Indianapolis: Indiana University Press, 1995).

G. Pattison, *Kierkegaard and the Crisis of Faith: an Introduction to his Thought* (London: SPCK, 1997).

J.-P. Sartre, 'The Universal Singular', in idem., *Between Existentialism and Marxism* (London: Verso, 1983).

M. Weston, *Kierkegaard and Modern Continental Philosophy* (London: Routledge, 1994).

DOSTOEVSKY

I have used Constance Garnett's classic translation, except where otherwise indicated. Many other adequate translations of all the major works are readily available.

F. M. Dostoevsky, *The Brothers Karamazov* (London: Heinemann, 1912).
———*Dostoievsky: The Diary of a Writer*, trans. B. Brasol (Haslemere: Ianmead, 1984).
———*Crime and Punishment* (London: Heinemann, 1914).
———*The Idiot* (London: Heinemann, 1913).
———*The Possessed* (London: Heinemann, 1914 [also translated as *The Devils*]).
———*A Raw Youth* (London: Heinemann, 1916 [also translated as *The Adolescent* and *An Accidental Family*]).
———*White Nights and Other Stories* (London: Heinemann, 1918).
M. Bakhtin, *Problems of Dostoevsky's Poetics* (Minneapolis: Minnesota University Press, 1984).
A. Boyce Gibson, *The Religion of Dostoevsky* (Philadelphia: Westminster Press, 1973).
A. Gide, *Dostoevsky* (Norfolk, CT: New Directions, 1961).
J. Frank, *Dostoevsky* (London: Robson; 5 vols., 1976–continuing).
G. Steiner, *Tolstoy or Dostoevsky* (London: Faber and Faber, 1960).
(See also under Thurneysen, Berdyaev and Shestov.)

NIETZSCHE

As with Dostoevsky, various translations are available of the major works, especially in the series by Cambridge University Press, Foulis (out of print), Penguin Classics and Vintage.

F. Nietzsche, *The Birth of Tragedy* and *The Genealogy of Morals* (New York: Doubleday Anchor, 1956).
———*The Joyful Wisdom* (London: Foulis, 1910 [also translated as *The Gay Science*]).
———*Thus Spoke Zarathustra* (Harmondsworth: Penguin, 1969).
———*Twilight of the Idols* and *The Anti-Christ* (Harmondsworth: Penguin, 1968).

————*The Will to Power* (New York: Vintage Books, 1968).

M. Heidegger, *Nietzsche* (San Francisco: Harper, 4 vols. in two, 1991).

W. Kaufmann, *Nietzsche: Philosopher, Psychologist, Antichrist* (Princeton: Princeton University Press, 1968).

J. P. Stern, *Nietzsche* (London: Fontana [Modern Masters], 1978).

DIALECTICAL THEOLOGY

K. Barth, *The Epistle to the Romans* (London: Oxford University Press, 1933).

J. Robinson (ed.), *The Beginnings of Dialectic [sic] Theology* (Richmond VA: John Knox Press, 1968).

J. D. Smart, *Revolutionary Theology in the Making. Barth–Thurneysen Correspondence 1914–25* (London: The Epworth Press, 1964).

E. Thurneysen, *Dostoevsky* (London: The Epworth Press, 1961).

BULTMANN

H. W. Bartsch (ed.), *Kerygma and Myth. A Theological Debate* (London: SPCK, 1972).

R. Bultmann, *Existence and Faith* (London: Collins, 1964).

————*Faith and Understanding* (London: SCM, 1969).

————*History and Eschatology* (Edinburgh: The University Press, 1975).

————*Jesus and the Word* (London: Fontana, 1958).

F. Gogarten, *Demythologizing and History* (London: SCM, 1955).

G. Jones, *Bultmann. Towards a Critical Theology* (Cambridge: Polity Press, 1991).

J. F. Kay, *Christus Praesens. A Reconsideration of Rudolf Bultmann's Christology* (Grand Rapids: Eerdmans, 1994).

J. Macquarrie, *An Existentialist Theology* (London: SCM, 1955).

————*The Scope of Demythologizing* (London: SCM, 1960).

TILLICH

P. Tillich, *On Art and Architecture* (New York: Corssroad, 1987).

————*The Boundaries of Being* (London: Fontana, [containing *The New Being*, *The Eternal Now* and *On the Boundary*]).

————*The Courage to Be* (London: Fontana, 1962).

————*The Interpretation of History* (New York: Charles Scribner, 1936).

————*The Religious Situation* (New York: Meridian, 1956).

————*The Shaking of the Foundations* (Harmondsworth: Penguin, 1962).

————*Systematic Theology* (Welwyn Garden City: J. Nisbet, 1968 [3 vols in one]).

————*Theology of Culture* (New York and London: Oxford University Press, 1959).

BERDYAEV AND SHESTOV

N. Berdyaev, *The Beginning and the End* (London: G. Bles, 1952).

————*Dostoievsky* (London: Sheed and Ward, 1934).

————*Dream and Reality* (London: G. Bles, 1950).

————*Freedom and the Spirit* (London: G. Bles, 1935).

————*The Meaning of the Creative Act* (London: V. Gollancz, 1955).

————*The Realm of Spirit and the Realm of Caesar* (London: V. Gollancz, 1952).

————*The Russian Idea* (London: G. Bles, 1947).

————*Slavery and Freedom* (London: G. Bles, 1943).

————*Spirit and Reality* (London: G. Bles, 1939).

————*Towards a New Epoch* (London: G. Bles, 1949).

L. Shestov, *Athens and Jerusalem* (Athens: Ohio University Press, 1966).

————*Dostoievsky, Tolstoy and Nietzsche* (Athens: Ohio University Press, 1966).

————(spelt 'Chestov'), *In Job's Balances* (London: J. M. Dent, 1932).

————*Kierkegaard and the Existential Philosophy* (Athens: Ohio University Press, 1969).

————*Anton Tchekov and Other Essays* (Dublin and London: Maunsel and Co., 1916).

C. S. Callan, *The Significance of Eschatology in the Thoughts of Nicolas Berdyaev* (Leiden: E. J. Brill, 1965).

F. C. Copleston, *Philosophy in Russia from Herzen to Lenin and Berdyaev* (Tunbridge Wells: Search Press, 1986).

E. Lampert, *Nicholas Berdyaev and the New Middle Ages* (London: James Clarke, n.d.).

D. Lowrie, *Rebellious Prophet* (London: V. Gollancz, 1960).

J. M. McLachlan, 'Shestov's Reading and Misreading of Kierkegaard', in *Canadian Slavonic Papers*, Vol. XVIII, No. 2, pp. 174–86.

B. G. Rosenthal and M. Bohachevsky-Comiak (eds.), *A Revolution of the Spirit: Crisis of Value in Russia 1980–1924* (New York: Fordham University Press, 1924).

B. Shragin and A. Todd (eds.), *Landmarks: a Collection of Essays on the Russian Intelligentsia* (New York: Karz Howard, 1977).

A. Valevicias, *Lev Shestov and his Times* (New York: Peter Lang, 1993).

J. C. S. Wernham, *Two Russian Thinkers* (Toronto: University of Toronto Press, 1968).

UNAMUNO AND MARCEL

G. Marcel, *Being and Having* (London: Fontana, 1965).

———*Coleridge et Schelling* (Paris: Aubier-Montaigne, 1971).

———*Creative Fidelity* (New York: Crossroad, 1982).

———*Homo Viator* (London: V. Gollancz, 1951).

———*A Metaphysical Journal* (London: Rockcliff, 1952).

———*Men Against Humanity* (London: Harvill, 1952).

———*The Mystery of Being* (London: Harvill, 2 vols., 1950, 1951).

———*The Philosophy of Existence* (London: Harvill, 1948).

———*Tragic Wisdom and Beyond* (Evanston, Ill.: Northwestern University Press).

M. de Unamuno, *The Agony of Christianity and Essays on Faith* (Princeton: Bollingen Series, Princeton University Press, n.d.).

———*The Life of Don Quixote and Sancho according to Miguel de Cervantes Saavedra* (London: A. Knopf, 1927).

———*Novela/Nivola* (London: Bollingen Series, Routledge and Kegan Paul, 1976).

———*Tragic Sense of Life* (New York: Dover, 1954).

J. Chenu, *Le Théatre de Garbiel Marcel et sa Signification Métaphysique* (Paris: Aubier Montaigne, 1948).

———R. R. Ellis, *The Tragic Pursuit of Being. Unamuno and Sartre* (Tuscaloosa: University of Alabama Press, 1988).

N. Gillman, *Gabriel Marcel on Religious Knowledge* (Washington: University Press of America, 1980).

E. Gilson (ed.), *Existentialisme Chrétien* (Paris: Plon, 1947).

P. Ilie, *Unamuno: An Existential View of Self and Society* (Madison, Milwaukee and London: Wisconsin University Press, 1967).

F. Wyers, *Miguel de Unamuno: The Contrary Self* (London: Tamesis, 1976).

BUBER AND ROSENZWEIG

M. Buber, *Between Man and Man* (London: Fontana, 1961).
———*Daniel. Dialogues on Realization* (New York: McGraw-Hill, 1965).
———*Eclipse of God* (London: V. Gollancz, 1953).
———*Die Erzählungen der Chassidim* (Zürich: Manesse, 1949).
———*For the Sake of Heaven* (New York, Meridian, 1958).
———*I and Thou*, trans. Kaufmann (Edinburgh: T. & T. Clark, 1970).
———*On the Origin and Meaning of Hasidism* (New York: Harper and Row, 1960).
———*Pointing the Way* (New York: Harper and Row, 1957).
———*Two Kinds of Faith* (London: Routledge, 1951).
F. Rosenzweig, *The Star of Redemption* (Notre Dame, IN: Notre Dame Press, 1985).
———*Understanding the Sick and the Healthy. A View of the World, Man and God* (New York: Noonday, 1954).
S. H. Bergman, *Dialogical Philosophy from Kierkegaard to Buber* (Albany: State University of New York Press, 1991).
M. Friedman, *Martin Buber's Life and Work* (New York: Dutton, 3 vols., 1981, 1983, 1983).
Y. K. Greenberg, *Better than Wine. Love, Poetry and Prayer in the Thought of Franz Rosenzweig* (Atlanta GA: Scholars Press, 1996).
P. A. Schilpp and M. Friedman (eds.), *The Philosophy of Martin Buber* (La Salle, Ill.: Open Court, 1967).

GENERAL

T. J. J. Altizer and W. Hamilton, *Radical Theology and the Death of God* (Harmondsworth: Penguin, 1968).
D. Anderson, *The Tragic Protest* (London: SCM, 1969).
K. Jaspers, *Philosophical Faith and Revelation* (London: Collins, 1967).
H. Hawton, *The Feast of Unreason* (London: Watts, 1952).
W. Hubben, *Dostoevsky, Kierkegaard, Nietzsche and Kafka* (New York: Touchstone, 1997).
W. Kaufmann, *Existentialism, Religion and Death* (New York: Meridian, 1976).

A. Kee, *The Way of Transcendence. Christian Faith without Belief in God* (Harmondsworth: Penguin, 1971).

H. Kuhn, *Encounter with Nothingness* (London: Methuen, 1951).

J. Macquarrie, *Existentialism* (Harmondsworth: Pelican, 1973).

――*Principles of Christian Theology* (London: SCM, 1966).

G. Pattison, *Agnosis: Theology in the Void* (Basingstoke: Macmillan, 1996).

D. E. Roberts, *Existentialism and Religious Belief* (New York: Oxford University Press, 1959).

R. L. Shinn, *The Existentialist Posture* (New York: Associated Books, 1970).

C. Wilson, *Religion and the Rebel* (London: V. Gollancz, 1957).

Index